TRIBALS, BATTLES
AND DARINGS

TRIBALS, BATTLES AND DARINGS

The Genesis of the Modern Destroyer

ALEXANDER CLARKE

Foreword by Andrew Lambert FKC

This book is dedicated to the three guiding lights of my childhood, my grandfather who taught me to think, my father who taught me to question and my mum who taught me to speak out about what I believe to be right.

First published in Great Britain in 2022 by
Seaforth Publishing,
A division of Pen & Sword Books Ltd,
47 Church Street,
Barnsley S70 2AS
www.seaforthpublishing.com

British Library Cataloguing in Publication Data
A catalogue record for this book is available from the British Library

ISBN 978 1 5267 7290 9 (HARDBACK)
ISBN 978 1 5267 7291 6 (EPUB)
ISBN 978 1 5267 7292 3 (KINDLE)

Pen & Sword Books Limited incorporates the imprints of Atlas, Archaeology, Aviation, Discovery, Family History, Fiction, History, Maritime, Military, Military Classics, Politics, Select, Transport, True Crime, Air World, Frontline Publishing, Leo Cooper, Remember When, Seaforth Publishing, The Praetorian Press, Wharncliffe Local History, Wharncliffe Transport, Wharncliffe True Crime and White Owl

Typeset and designed by Neil Sayer

Printed and bound in India by Replika Press Pvt Ltd

CONTENTS

FOREWORD

This is a book about options and choices in defence policy-making, about individuals who made a difference, how decisions are tested in war, and how far it is possible to anticipate future trends. These issues retain their relevance today, long after these large mid-century destroyers have passed into history. As I write this foreword a new HMS *Defender* has just conducted a hugely significant Freedom of Navigation Operation off the coast of the Crimea, an operation that was made credible by the impressive capabilities of the ship. Such diplomatic missions provide an alternative highlight of this book, emphasising how destroyers were brought into the full spectrum of peacetime maritime operations at a time when the overall size of the fleet was restricted by international agreements, as well as budgetary pressures. In a world dominated by images, their presence was enhanced by aesthetic design, the architectural languages of power and speed emphasising national strength.

Alex Clarke demonstrates that the 'Tribal' class were always intended to be something more than simply larger destroyers, taking up specific roles in fleet and aircraft carrier operations, as well as fulfilling detached missions as cruiser substitutes. They had achieved an esprit de corps befitting these enhanced roles before the outbreak of war in 1939, in part through their constant presence in the combat zone, their capabilities, and the outstanding personnel who manned and commanded them. The cost was high, three-quarters of the Royal Navy 'Tribals' were sunk in action, the others survived serious damage and continued in front-line service across six years. Their success had already prompted thinking about a follow-on class that would become the 'Battles', a design that evolved as the experience of war emphasised new threats from the air, threats that demanded new weapons and sensors, and ultimately evolved into the *Daring* class, the last gun-armed destroyers, which left a powerful legacy of names and battle honours for the new Type 45s.

Andrew Lambert FKC
Laughton Professor of Naval History, King's College London.

PREFACE

This book describes the conception and evolution, through inter-war tensions, global war and the later post-war years of Cold War hostility, of the Royal Navy's large fleet destroyers, their 'back pocket cruisers'. The 'Tribal', 'Battle' and *Daring* classes provided the Royal Navy with a significant portion of both their naval fighting and naval diplomatic capability sets for one of the most critical periods in its, and the nation's, history. They did this not only by design and construction, but also by culture, not just by image, but also by service. They were very much ships of their era, but they also provided the roots for the capabilities and capacities which are looked for in current and future destroyer construction.

CHAPTER 1

THE ROYAL NAVY OF THE 1930s

The desperate hunt for *Bismarck* was over, and the Atlantic had swallowed the physical remnants of the anger, fear and vengeance which the episode had created. The 'Tribal' destroyers *Tartar* and *Mashona* were making their way home at the most economical speed, trying to eke out their precious remaining fuel. It was at this precarious time the ships were discovered, southwest of Ireland, by a roaming Focke-Wulf 200 Condor.[1] Soon after this sighting, Heinkel He 111 bombers appeared and started attacking; waves of aircraft tried and failed to hit the already exhausted ships, but sometimes it can take just one lucky, or in this case unlucky, bomb.

> Perhaps the Middle Bomb in one stick [of bombs] had a bent fin. It seemed to wobble a bit as it fell. That one did not miss. It struck *Mashona*'s port side abreast the fore funnel, penetrated No. 1 boiler room and exploded there, blowing a huge hole in the side. No. 2 boiler room bulkhead held and shoring up began, but nothing could be done with the forward bulkhead – it looked like a lace curtain.[2]

This was not the end of the attacks. Despite valiant efforts to keep the ship fighting and, most importantly, afloat, after 45 minutes their captain, Commander Selby, was forced to concede defeat.[3] They abandoned ship and transferred to *Tartar*, luckily for the ship's company this tricky operation coincided with an hour-long lull in the bombing.[4] The ordeal was not yet over, however. Demonstrating the toughness of design and construction that was a 'Tribal' trait, *Mashona* remained doggedly afloat. In fact, after *Tartar* had missed her with a torpedo, it was left to two more destroyers (*Sherwood*, a 'Clemson/Town' class Lend-Lease destroyer, and HMCS *St Claire*, a 'Wickes/Town' class Lend-Lease destroyer) which had joined them, to sink *Mashona* with gunfire.[5]

Such an end was not unusual for this class. *Mashona* was the fourth of thirteen 'Tribal' destroyers that would be lost in the Second World War. This was out of the twenty-three of the class completed in time to serve in the conflict.[6] Notably, the twelve Royal Navy 'Tribals' sunk were all lost in the war's most desperate days, between 1940 and 1942.[7] They were hard-fighting ships and, in a strange way, the losses were due to them being such good ships. As a well-balanced, capable design, manned by personnel who considered themselves an

Afridi, first of the class, looking resplendent in a Mediterranean Fleet white inter-war paint scheme. White was chosen because it was felt to have an impressive and positive impact (from the British Government's perspective) on viewers of the ship, especially if kept pristine; it was also considered beneficial for the crew as in hot climates it reflected the heat. (Drachinifel Collection)

Somali on 24 August 1937, the day of her launch, showing how much work is left to be done. *(Drachinifel Collection)*

elite coterie (in the traditions of the Royal Navy, destroyer crews considered themselves far more select than those of the battleships), they were regularly chosen for difficult operations; and even more so when there was a shortage of ships. The 'Tribals' were risked again and again.[8] Eventually, their luck had to run out. This, though, was their wartime fate; the 'Tribals', and the role they were intended for, were conceived in peacetime.[9] Different factors hold sway in war and peace and peace tends to bring with it far closer scrutiny of value for money than wartime fighting capability.

As they proved themselves in service and their luck started to run out, their image gave birth to the first of their successors, the 'Battle' class. Conceived at the

Aisne, one of the 1943 Batch of 'Battle' class destroyers. This 1947 picture illustrates the lines that exemplified the 'Battle' class's shape and purpose. *(Maritime Quest)*

height of the war, but completed too late to be of much use in it, they would provide the Navy with much needed 'muscle' in the financially stringent post-war era. This class was most definitely a transitional class. It was the *Daring* class, the post-war successors, that would really take on and exemplify the lessons of the 'Tribal' class in their construction. All this was far in the future at the time 'Tribals' were first mooted as a concept, let alone designed or ordered.

By the mid-1930s the Admiralty, and other departments of the British Government such as the Foreign and Cabinet Offices, were having to confront the fact that they had fewer warships to meet the same, arguably greater, level of commitment than before the First World War. After the war the Navy had evaluated its operational needs, assessing a requirement for seventy cruisers in order to fulfil its peacetime duties.[10] However, due to international treaties, financial constraints and the requirements of maintenance, it never really had more than fifty-five available during the period.[11] A shortage made much more difficult by the fact that by 1936 only twenty-three of these could be called

'modern'.[12] As part of the solution to this problem the Navy designed and built the 'Tribal' class destroyers, a class specifically intended as general-purpose ships able to undertake both cruiser and destroyer duties. Although not as good as purpose-built vessels for specialist roles, they were designed to be 'good enough' and as such provide much of the required capability where and when needed.[13] The coming of the Second World War would prove the worth of this concept and, as has been said already, the class were to become heavily relied upon. The beginning, however, was less certain.

The London Naval Treaty of 1930 – Origin of the 'Super-Destroyer'

When the 'Tribals' were conceived in the mid-1930s, naval construction was limited by a series of naval armament treaties, agreements that were negotiated between the major powers to prevent another naval arms race such as that which had preceded and, arguably, contributed to the First World War. Starting with the Washington Treaty of 1922, and followed by the 1930 and 1936 London Naval Treaties, limits were set for both the total tonnage of each category of ship and the size of each vessel within that tonnage. Under the Washington Treaty the Navy had accepted theoretical parity with the United States Navy (USN), although it was only qualitative parity in terms of cruisers and destroyers. With Articles 15, 16 and 17 of the First London Treaty this was extended to quantitative limitations as well, the USN being allowed to put more tonnage towards heavy cruisers, while the Royal Navy allotted more to light cruisers, a compromise which might seem strange, but for which the Navy had good reasons.[14]

Article 16 of the 1930 London Naval Treaty

1. The completed tonnage in the cruiser, destroyer and submarine categories which is not to be exceeded on the 31st December, 1936, is given in the following table.

2. Vessels which cause the total tonnage in any category to exceed the figures given in the foregoing table shall be disposed of gradually during the period ending on the 31st December, 1936.

3. The maximum number of cruisers of subcategory (a) shall be as follows: for the United States, eighteen; for the British Commonwealth of Nations, fifteen; for Japan, twelve.

4. In the destroyer category not more than sixteen per cent of the allowed total tonnage shall be employed in vessels over 1,500 tons (1,524 metric tons) standard displacement. Destroyers completed or under construction on the 1st April, 1930, in excess of this percentage may be retained, but no other destroyers exceeding 1,500 tons (1,524 metric tons) standard displacement shall be constructed or acquired until a reduction to such sixteen per cent. has been effected.

5. Not more than twenty-five per cent of the allowed total tonnage in the cruiser category may be fitted with a landing-on platform or deck for aircraft.

6. It is understood that the submarines referred to in paragraphs 2 and 3 of Article 7 will be counted as part of the total submarine tonnage of the High Contracting Party concerned.

7. The tonnage off any vessels retained under Article 13 or disposed of in accordance with Annex II to Part II of the present Treaty shall not be included in the tonnage subject to limitation.

The reason the Navy wanted more light cruisers, and had been willing to sacrifice heavy cruisers for them, was to try to build enough ships to secure the stability of the British Empire in peacetime, let alone in the face of war. Cruisers were cornerstones of imperial presence, both in terms of policing and security, fulfilling the duties of everything from local crisis response force to heavyweight diplomatic intervention. They could, in the passage of a week, let alone a month, conduct

Categories	United States	British Commonwealth of Nations	Japan
Cruisers			
(a) With guns of more than 6.1 in (155mm) calibre	180,000 tons (182,880 metric tons)	146,800 tons (149,149 metric tons)	108,400 tons (110,134 metric tons)
(b) With guns of 6.1 in (155mm) calibre or less	143,500 tons (145,796 metric tons)	192,200 tons (195,275 metric tons)	100,450 tons (102,057 metric tons)
Destroyers	150,000 tons (152,400 metric tons)	150,000 tons (152,400 metric tons)	105,500 tons (107,188 metric tons)
Submarines	52,700 tons (53,543 metric tons)	52,700 tons (53,543 metric tons)	52,700 tons (53,543 metric tons)

counter piracy operations, find a lost merchant ship, exchange words with the cruiser of another imperial power and host an event for indigenous and colonial leaders. All this had to be catered for within any design as well as fighting requirements.

Working with a £10,000 per ton, or less, budget per ship was no easy task, particularly as the American and Japanese navies did not have these pressures and could, unlike the Admiralty, afford to focus their ships solely on fighting a Pacific war. The Navy might fight in the Pacific, Atlantic and Indian Oceans, or the Mediterranean Sea, anywhere or everywhere else, and they had to serve and protect a global empire; and all this with ships that could displace no more than those of their potential opponents, and were to be limited in number. Politically, perhaps even strategically, it can be argued the naval treaties made good sense. If they had not it is doubtful that Britain would have hosted two of the three conferences that mediated them. Practically though, for the Navy, they were a constant source of frustration. This frustration had a name, the 'cruiser gap', and was the difference between the seventy ships that the Navy defined as necessary for peacetime missions and the fifty-five they could actually call upon. However, the 1930 treaty, specifically Article 16.4, also provided an opportunity, with the newly defined category of 'Destroyer Leader'.[15]

Whilst other destroyers were limited to 1,500 tons, each signatory was permitted to use 16 per cent of their total allowed destroyer tonnage for vessels of up to 1,850 tons. Theoretically, these larger ships were to act as the flag vessel, the 'Leader', for each destroyer flotilla; at least that is what had been stated at the conferences which produced the treaties. Destroyers had proved an essential offensive weapon in the First World War, and at the Battle of Jutland and in countless other engagements in which they had been involved; evidence of their potential impact had grown. The definition 'destroyer leader' presented a potential opportunity, but the problem was that by using this destroyer tonnage for a cruiser role, if done badly, it could decisively weaken one of the fleet's most capable offensive weapons.

The conundrum was how to strike a balance between the roles. Cruisers were the general-purpose ships, capable of carrying out all missions, and primarily relying upon guns for fighting. In contrast destroyers, the offensive tools, were built around their array of torpedoes. This did not mean that their guns were not important. They were also expected to 'act defensively' against their counterparts, so carried quick-firing guns for that role, but these guns were very much the secondary system of the traditional destroyer. So much so that the guns fitted were often single mounts, and in some designs even without shields to protect the crews who served them.

The 'Tribal' class design was to be a balance, a compromise, between these two roles. Their guns would be, by necessity, the core of their armament and their fighting capability, unlike any other destroyer then in British service. More than this, however, their design would have to be that of a cruiser in shrunken form, meaning they would cost more than an ordinary destroyer, but

Dainty as built. Like the 'Battle' and 'Tribal' class, if viewed from ahead at a distance she could well be confused for a cruiser, with the imposing height and shaping of the superstructure. (*Drachinifel Collection*)

less than a cruiser (especially in terms of 'tonnage'), if they were to maintain enough of the destroyer capabilities to enable them to operate alongside their more conventional counterparts. And it was understood from the beginning that the crews of these ships would need to live up to this hybrid nature. As a result the 'Tribal' class were, right from the start, treated as an elite group. This was a conscious attempt to retain their offensive nature in the face of their less traditionally offensive destroyer form, through the encouragement and generation of 'spirit'. This aim was helped by the fact that their design, despite not being traditional destroyer, was very striking. They had a presence which resonates even in photographs today, but which mattered even more at the time. Nothing illustrates this better than the impression of the then Sub-Lieutenant Ludovic Kennedy on seeing *Tartar* for the first time, during the Second World War.

> When T— returned to harbour I packed my few belongings, said good-bye to my hosts and to Able Seaman Kelly, whom I happened to pass on the quarterdeck, and climbed down the gangway to the boat. I saw my ship for the first time alongside an oiler. She was a fine-looking vessel, with sloping bows and gracious lines. Her main armament of 4.7-inch guns stood out boldly against the evening sky; the White Ensign fluttered at her mainmast. I thanked God then that I had not been appointed to a drifter or a trawler as many of my messmates at King Alfred and Portsmouth had been. Here was a ship built to attack. Here were power and majesty and beauty; sleek, sharp lines and wicked-looking guns; bows which could cut through the water like scissors through paper; a streamlined bridge from which to command, and to control the power of forty-four thousand horse. Amidships were the tubes housing the 'tin fish,' those sinister weapons which speed through the water at forty knots and approach their target unseen, and often unheard.[16]

Conception, Design and Construction

The actual design study which led to the development of the 'Tribals' was initiated in 1933 by the then Third Sea Lord and Controller, Admiral Sir Charles M Forbes, looking for a new light cruiser.[17] However, it did not get far and it was under his successor, Vice Admiral Sir Reginald G H Henderson, that the study bore fruit, first with the 'Tribal' class 'super-destroyers' (referred to as 'V' class Leader in the study) and then the *Dido* class cruisers.[18] Possibly this was because Henderson took less notice of the responses of the Com-

mander-in-Chief Mediterranean, Admiral Sir William Wordsworth Fisher, than the C-in-C Home Admiral Sir William Boyle, 12th Earl of Corke and Orrery, or the C-in-C China Station, Admiral Sir Fredric Dreyer.[19] The Mediterranean Staff may have had their case partially undermined by the fact they complained a lot about the potential sea-keeping of the vessels, yet the Home Fleet and the China Station which were, and would be, the operational commands with rougher seas did not.[20]

Admiral Fisher and his staff were most definitely not supportive of the concept of a general-purpose destroyer. They were more concerned with size in their analysis of what was needed for the cruiser role in general, and a Rear Admiral, Destroyers, flagship in particular.[21] The response did not stop there, it went much further, for it provided a wide-ranging overview of his opinions on both Admiralty and Government policy. This was further supplemented by attached supporting documents from his Vice Admiral and the Rear Admiral, Destroyers, of the Mediterranean Fleet. The latter post was held, at the time, by Andrew Cunningham, or ABC as he was known, who would command the Mediterranean Fleet for many of its successes during the war. Their view could best be summarised as destroyers were to be destroyers, cruisers were to be cruisers, and that the Navy needed to match design and construction with others of the types and not deviate.[22] The major criticism was that the proposed ship would not be as good for either air defence or as a pure air defence ship, as good at destroyer work as a regular destroyer, or as good in a cruiser role as a conventional cruiser; they would not be as good as three specialist vessels.

This was an interesting response considering that the study had arisen because the Navy was already bucking the trend established in other navies by the treaties. Their preference for light cruisers over heavy cruisers, their negotiations and the reworking of the treaties to allow the shifting of tonnage from one category to the other, are all testimony to how far the Navy was prepared to go. The response from the Admiralty to Fisher is therefore unsurprising. They latched on to his words, using them to define more clearly what they were looking for. Furthermore, their discussion of roles shows that the priority of the Admiralty was very different to that of Fisher's almost First World War style analysis.[23] Curiously, Henderson did not write a long riposte to the points of Fisher as the assistant Chief of the Naval Staff and others had done.

Henderson did not even discuss the proposed 4,500-ton design option which would have required precious cruiser tonnage. Instead he gives, in his words, 'some notes on certain material questions arising out of these papers,' and writes one word, 'Noted', plus his signature, which he ascribes to all his points, and in other papers that is his only response when no more is needed.[24] The reason for the 'noted' this time, was more to highlight to other, subsequent, readers of the file that he, Henderson, had seen and read this – but it does not have a bearing on his opinion. His more detailed responses are exemplified by that discussing anti-aircraft fire control: 'A form of H.A. control suitable for small vessels is to be tested in a sloop of the 1934 programme, but its use when there is considerable motion on the ship will be very limited until some form of stabilisation is in sight'.[25]

In effect, he was pointing out where the Mediterranean Fleet officers had put forward excellent ideas, but also showing how disconnected they were from current technological developments, and subtly emphasising that their less suitable ideas were not practicable. Henderson could afford to employ a minimalist response because he had won. As the whole of the ADM 1/8828 file illustrates, Henderson had won because he and his staff in the Controller's office had amassed a huge amount of detail and information. In 1934 he was estimating the cost of the 'V' class Leader at £480,000, an estimate that was within 7 per cent of the final revised and modified design.[26]

More than this, however, Henderson won because whilst Fisher had read, and even quoted from statements and publications of the Lords of the Admiralty, he had not understood that their interpretation of their meaning, and their strategic perspective, might be different from his own. This lack of comprehension of the direction of the Navy might also explain why Fisher, when stepping down in 1936, unusually after performing so well in the premier role of C-in-C Mediterranean, did not go on to the Admiralty. As a result, Admiral Ernle Chatfield, who had become First Sea Lord in 1933 at the age of 60, stayed in post. He was succeeded in 1938 by Admiral Sir Roger Blackhouse, former C-in-C Home Fleet, and in 1939 by Admiral Sir Dudley Pound, following his three years as the C-in-C Mediterranean. Fisher was instead given command of Portsmouth and died aged 62 in 1937 after a year in post.

Through all this Henderson was supported by Sir Stanley Vernon Goodall, the Director of Naval Construction and the Navy's most senior architect. Goodall's responses were often far more verbose than Henderson's and they certainly did not always see eye to eye (they had very strong written disputes on car-

rier design) but on destroyer design they were in accord. Henderson supplied the vision and political manoeuvres, while Goodall provided the detail and engineering ingenuity, and both were equally committed to the personal responsibility and investment in their designs. Goodall was a critical voice when Henderson was fighting the Whitehall battles, often providing the key data and technical know-how to offset some of the more particular comments on manning, layout and displacement. In the late 1930s their partnership dominated naval ship design and would define the debates on it for next two decades. They were, in large part, responsible for the decisions which shaped the Navy not just at the beginning of the war but, because of their part in creating its foundations, for the whole of its duration and even afterwards into the post-war years.

The Navy was not necessarily aiming to build up to the limit of the treaties for individual ships. Instead, it was aiming to build up to the limit of the total tonnage. This was because the Navy was more focussed on the role, rather than the competition, especially when it came to wartime reconnaissance and peacetime presence. In fact, it is arguable the decision had more to do with peace and its preservation, through deterrence rather than war. Fisher and the Mediterranean Staff would appear to have ascribed to the philosophy of the Italian fleet of the time: that what mattered were numbers and strength on paper, not what was actually built. The Admiralty favoured a peace through presence approach, believing it was necessary to build the best ships they could, in order to project 'real' capability. This meant fewer ships could be built on the allowances, as 'real' capability required 'real' tonnage. Put another way, in peacetime the Admiralty wanted to be spread across the world, so they could prevent or shape a potential conflict by presence; in wartime they wanted to find and destroy the enemy as quickly as possible. Both goals required quality every bit as much as quantity. It is no surprise, therefore, that in 1936 the Tactical School, an advanced training unit based at Greenwich Naval Academy which was used almost as in-house think tank, summed up the intended combat roles of the 'Tribal' class as:

used to supplement cruisers in reconnaissance and screening duties, including screening aircraft-carriers, and as support for the destroyers in opening the way for torpedo attack: they may also be used for shadowing at night and to supplement the anti-aircraft fire of battleships, one 'Tribal' forming astern of each battleship when air attack is anticipated.[27]

They would be not only a light cruiser substitute, they would also be the spiritual successors of the First World War Harwich Force, which had made its name in the bitter fights between the light forces that had contested the North Sea.[28] The institutional memory of this force, and the near-mythological status it had achieved, combined with very detailed post-war analysis, was influential at every step of the design process that aimed to fulfil the uniquely British need for which the 'Tribals' were designed..

Traditionally, British ship design developed in response to ship design of other countries, and this was the case with 'super destroyers', designed for the traditional destroyer roles. In contrast, 'Tribals' were seen as 'force multipliers' to enable the Navy not only to secure Britain's global trade, but also to provide the primary defence of the British Empire. There were constant difficulties finding enough ships to cover all areas and, when comparing numbers to stated requirements, resulted in shortages in nearly every classification, for example the fifty-five rather than seventy cruisers being just one of many such examples.

Not only a shortage of cruisers worried the Navy, but the viability of their destroyers in fleet actions was also a concern. Designed to attack enemy surface ships by mass attack with torpedoes, they would be of little use if a lack of gun support from accompanying cruisers resulted in their elimination before they could launch those torpedoes, or if they were split up to provide air defence pickets on 'no fly days' and so were unable to mass for an attack.[31] The reconnaissance role/picket duty of the 'Tribals' allowed the flotilla destroyers to be kept together. Furthermore, with their gun armament they would provide the necessary cover for any attack those destroyers mounted. They were in effect the 'meat' of the Destroyer Leader role, without in theory their broader command duties, although as will be seen they also took on those tasks.[32]

First put forward as part of the 1935 proposals, there were two batches of 'Tribal' class which, whilst sharing a basic design and layout, differed in armament and crew.[33] Although there was still some opposition, Vice Admiral Henderson navigated the class through all the necessary procedures in good time and the first flotilla was ordered in 1936. The sixteen originals were the Navy's own two flotillas, which was the maximum under treaty allowances, though the treaty system was unravelling as they were being built. These were not the only members of the class. Eleven modified 'Tribal' vessels were ordered in 1940, eight for the Royal Canadian Navy (RCN) and three for the Royal Australian Navy (RAN). As well as having the desired capability,

it transpired the 'Tribal' class was also cost efficient, a crucial factor in ship procurement due to the Treasury's peacetime pre-eminence.[34]

The cost efficiency is highlighted by the fact that, despite changes in design introduced by war and the differing batches, the twenty-seven 'Tribal' class vessels were procured for an average unit price of £513,412 (based on a cumulative class cost of £13,862,133).[35] Whilst costly in comparison with other contemporary destroyer classes of the time (the 1939 'K' class destroyer averaged around £500,000), they were in fact exceptional value for money given that they were in effect acting as substitutes for light cruisers. The contemporary Dido class light cruisers cost £1,480,000 each.[36] It becomes an even clearer bargain when considering the cost of Sikh, the twelfth 'Tribal' class destroyer to be built, and the cheapest at £510,046. She was procured as part of the 1936 programme, and ordered from Alexander Stephen and Sons on the Clyde in Glasgow.[37] Built within fifteen months and commissioned within twenty-five, she was astonishing value for money considering her career would include facing down an Italian battleship, the Littorio, as well as taking a leading role in the sinking of two Italian cruisers in 1941 at the Battle of Cape Bon, all many times her size and cost.

Displacement was in line with the treaty maximum (1,850 tons), but eventually varied between 1,959 tons (standard) and 2,519 tons (deep).[38] As such they exceeded by a margin the treaty regulations which had helped create them, although by the time of their launch those treaties were hardly worth the paper they were written on. They were a good size for a destroyer hull, with a length of 377ft, a beam of 36ft 6in, and a draft of 11ft 3in. The hull was powered by three Admiralty 3-drum boilers driving, via turbines, two geared shafts. This arrangement developed 44,000 HP and enabled the class to reach 36 knots whilst also having a range of 5,700 nautical miles at 15 knots.[39] This turn of speed beat the top speed of Arethusa and Dido class light cruisers by at least four knots.[40] Their top speed was in line for destroyers, while their endurance, the defining quality of cruisers, was satisfactory.[41] The 'Tribal' endurance was slightly better than other destroyer classes and proportionally comparable to the Arethusa (6,500 nautical miles at 16 knots) and the Dido (5,500 nautical miles at 16 knots).[42] Nonetheless, the 'Tribal' class was still felt to be underpowered by some officers and certainly suffered from strain because of the constant high speed operations that wartime imposed on them.[43]

In line with the requirement to provide gun support to the flotilla destroyers the original design as built included eight twin QF (Quick Firing) 4.7in Mk XII guns in four CP twin Mk XIX mountings; the volume of fire provided by eight 4.7in guns was considered preferable when engaging other light forces to fewer slower firing, heavier weapons. To supplement these weapons for anti-aircraft defence they were initially fitted with a single quadruple QF 2pdr on a Mk VII★ (P) mounting and two quadruple QF 0.5in on 'M' Mk III mountings; but an almost uniform wartime modification was the replacement of the 'X' mount 4.7in guns by a double 4in AA weapon to increase AA capability.[44] The standard armament was completed with a single quadruple 21in torpedo mount and twenty depth charges split between a single rack and two throwers.[45] The modified designs of the RAN and RCN 'Tribals' were slightly less regular. They were of early wartime construction and fitting was often dependent upon the availability of equipment.

The 'Tribal' design proved both an advantage and a limitation. Its space meant that when it was realised that there had been a navy-wide miscalculation of the nature of the air threat it was fixable. The Mk XII mount, the class's primary weapon system, had been designed to elevate to a maximum of 40°. This was fine for combating low-level bombers, not high enough to deal with dive bomber attacks.

Providentially, for their supporters, the 'Tribal' class proved more adaptable than most, so after *Afridi* and *Gurkha* were lost during the Norway Campaign, the high angle 4.7in twin Mk XIX mounting in 'X' position was replaced with the high angle 4in gun mounting for the rest of the class with no appreciable loss of capability.[46] It is interesting that this change had to be made, because no less an advocate than the C-in-C Home Fleet in 1934, Admiral Sir William Boyle, made his only major comment on the theoretical design.

Whilst there is the necessity that the 'V' Leaders under consideration should have a powerful long range anti-aircraft armament which is clearly recognised, I strongly urge that every consideration should be given to improving the short-range armament as well. This is particularly necessary to assist in repelling aircraft torpedo and dive-bombing attacks.[47]

It had not been fitted before, because the Navy felt it was deploying enough AA armament with the pom-pom and the heavy machine guns. Interestingly, it was also noted at the time that the change was potentially beneficial for more than just an anti-aircraft role. Whilst it represented a reduced ability against bigger ships, the rapid fire nature of the 4in gave it an advantage when engaging S-boats and Italian MAS torpedo boats. As destroyers, and especially smaller craft, were still often conned from open bridges, even a well-aimed 4in gun could cause significant damage to the fighting ability of an enemy ship. This easy transition was in contrast to other pre-war destroyer classes, which often lost their second torpedo mount to provide room for the increased AA armament, which meant a 50 per cent reduction in what was their primary weapon system. However, it was not only weapons that were different for the 'Tribal' class.

In line with their multi-role design, the class was fitted with ASDIC (early sonar) to take part in anti-submarine (AS) operation as well as operating as directors for surface and AA operations. The 'Tribal' class were the first destroyers to be fitted with the 'Fuze Keeping Clock Mk II' analogue fire-control computer to enable its AA capabilities.[48] This system was the product of a long gestation, with much debate about its form and capabilities.[49] In simple terms the 'clock' was a modified, arguably more accurate, variant of the simplified version of the High Angle Control System which had been fitted to the 'C' and 'D' class destroyers.[50]

The system was designed to improve the quality of the gunnery in both air and surface roles.[51] The system consisted of a director control tower (DCT), containing the control officer, his team and the director sight, that would feed data to a transmitting station containing the 'clock' and range finder.[52] The purpose of the 'clock' was to calculate the deflection due to movements of ship, enemy and wind, then to apply other factors such as the rate of change, before transmitting all the required data to the guns to provide them with the best possible chance of hitting the target.[53] This provided the 'Tribal' class with arguably the best targeting solution of any destroyer at the time, not only in the Navy, but possibly in the world.

Vice Admiral Henderson

Henderson was a born leader of men, owing nothing to tradition or rank for his ascendancy over them; it was a matter of personality with him. He was never bound by routine or convention if he saw advantage to the Service in departure from them; he had an original mind, great ability and quickness of grasp, but was impatient of any suggestion of formalism or red tape, so that his methods were often unorthodox; but they always justified themselves.[54]

So went the obituary issued by the Institution of Naval Architects, and it must be wondered if the Vice Presi-

Admiral R G H Henderson as pictured in his Obituary from the 1939 *Transactions of the Institution of Naval Architects* (p.348). He was in many ways the architect of not just the Fighting Destroyer/Cruiser Destroyer or 'back pocket cruiser' concept, but also the wider Royal Navy which would fight the Second World War, having served as Third Sea Lord & Controller from 1933–9, the crucial seven years when the 'war fleet' was conceived and commenced. *(Author's collection)*

mirals, Sir Reginald Friend Hannam Henderson and Sir William Hannam Henderson. Thus there were three admirals in two generations, all of whom would have an impact on the Navy. With both a father and uncles in the service it is only really surprising that Henderson's older brother, Henry May Henderson, had not preceded him when he joined *Britannia* as a naval cadet in 1895.

Seven years later, in 1902 Henderson was appointed sub-lieutenant and posted to the *Myrmidon* class destroyer *Syren*. In 1911, at the age of 30, he married the 28-year-old Islay Campbell, with whom he had two sons. In an age when officers often found the requirements of service at odds with family life, this sets him apart. In 1913 he took part in the naval mission to Greece, following which he was made a commander and second-in-command of the battleship *Erin* (ordered by, but never delivered to, Turkey), and in which he served aboard at the Battle of Jutland. Following Jutland, Henderson was posted to the Admiralty, and took part in the Battle of the Atlantic, during which he carried out a critical analysis to make the case for the adoption of convoys, which would be so crucial in winning that contest.

After the war he was posted as chief of staff to the Commander of the China Station, Admiral Alexander Duff, where he remained until taking up a post at the Greenwich Naval Academy in 1923. This was in many ways another excellent post for an officer on the rise. In 1926 he received his first real brush with naval aviation, commanding the carrier HMS *Furious* before, in 1928, acceding to that most political of postings, Aide-de-Camp to King George V. In 1931 he was promoted Rear Admiral, becoming the first Rear Admiral Aircraft Carriers, and lauded by both the Navy and the Royal Air Force for his work.[55] By 1934 he had had experience in destroyers, battleships, cruisers (the main component of the China Station) and naval aviation. He also had Admiralty as well as political experience, and he had encountered Britain's many friends and foes around the world. Whilst this was not a particularly unusual career for an officer of the period, it had prepared him exceptionally well for the post in which he was to be installed.

As Third Sea Lord, Henderson actively thought about how best to sell politically what he needed. This meant ships would often be promoted as different things to different audiences, or rather would have different capabilities emphasised, of which the aircraft repair ship *Unicorn* is perhaps the most obvious example. For reasons already discussed, in the 1920s and 1930s the Navy put a lot of effort into planning how to sup-

dent of the time, the serving DNC and Henderson's colleague and friend, Stanley Goodall, had a hand in the writing of it. It was written at the end of his career of course; it had been very different in the beginning. Then he had the makings of being all about tradition, routine and convention. Reginald Guy Hannam Henderson was born the son of Commander John Hannam Henderson and his wife Betsy Ann May in Falmouth, Cornwall. Henderson's family connections with the Navy did not stop there, He was a nephew to two adport operations a long way from home bases. Operating, especially on the other side of the world, far from the home manufacturing base, meant a lengthy, and therefore dangerous, chain of supply. Anything which reduced the pressure on, or the danger to, the chain would be beneficial, and *Unicorn* did both.

She could carry a large quantity of stores, and she could operate aircraft herself. Yet despite being the forerunner and template for the light fleet carriers with which the Navy fought the war, she was marketed as an 'FAA support ship'. Everyone outside the Navy was largely sold on her being neither another aircraft carrier nor an offensive ship, but a support ship. Within the Navy she was certainly sold to some key groups as an aircraft carrier, as a ship which either *in extremis* or through necessity could fulfil the roles of trade protec-

Mohawk from bow-on as she makes her way down the slipway during launch on 15 October 1937. This photograph highlights the hull and especially the bow shaping which had been carefully calibrated to enable both high operational speed and a stable platform for the firing of the guns. *(Maritime Quest)*

tion or secondary carrier in operations. In fact, she would serve in both the carrier role and support role during the war, achieving honours in both. Henderson, however, did not limit his creativity to naval aviation. The 'Tribal' class was, as has already been discussed, another prime example of his marketing. There were other classes too, but just getting ships built was not his only contribution.

Henderson was a fact-based thinker, who had real practical experience, and he had achieved high office in the Admiralty without abandoning his opinions. Ships built during his tenure all show a focus on rate of fire over range and an understanding of what was useful and what was theoretical. For example, there is no point having the extra reach if it cannot be used, and it becomes a hindrance if it slows down rate of fire at the ranges for which it will be used. This showed an intuitive understanding of something which we are still grappling with today and which has only been growing in magnitude since even before the First World War: what to do when weapon range exceeds information range, ie target confirmation. What is the point of having something which can shoot 50 miles if information is only available about the first 10 miles? This was especially a factor in the days before radar, and also in relation to the Navy's preferred hours of daylight operation.

Henderson, along with Admiral Chatfield and Admiral Cunningham, had been part of a group of officers who focused the Navy on night fighting. On realising that the odds were such that, wherever or whenever war started, the Fleet would be outnumbered locally, a way had to be found either to win battles or at least to not to lose them so badly that the war would also be lost. The Navy turned to the experience of Jutland, but it was not the 'good parts' which interested them. Instead, they focussed on the bad: the fact that the Germans had escaped at night. To the British officers this did not seem a particularly intelligent move, and it was felt the German's had squandered an opportunity because the Navy was just as bad as the Germans at fighting at night; and the British had more reason to be careful when firing as there were more of their own ships to be accidentally hit. Any Royal Navy admiral in the same position would have attacked. This was the philosophy which started guiding British ship design, especially during Henderson's tenure: that ships, aircraft, and the naval service as whole, would be the best at fighting in the dark.

This was accomplished, and in the Second World War the Royal Navy would dominate the night. In fact, even the US Navy would not achieve equivalent parity (ie, that all components were equally capable of fighting at night as during the day) until after the war. This was a unique selling point, along with the armoured carriers, the versatile cruisers and aggressively handled destroyers. It was a whole force approach, the components of which were good and able to act independently if necessary; but in combination were really formidable, exactly as Henderson had intended. As a result he was promoted to Vice Admiral and retained in post. Unfortunately, he never commanded the force which he created because in May 1939 he died while still in post. Many at the time attributed his death to overwork, to the sixteen or more hours a day he spent to prepare the nation, and the Navy he loved, for the coming war.

His loss was a shame for several reasons. An officer of his calibre would have no doubt become a theatre commander, as did his successor Admiral Sir Bruce Fraser. Henderson could possibly have even taken over the Mediterranean from Cunningham or succeeded Noble in the China Station, and who knows how different actions at sea might have concluded with an officer of equal drive, but arguably greater technological savvy and understanding, at the helm? More importantly he was a leader, a proven ship officer, a fleet officer and a Whitehall Warrior; it would be not beyond the realms of possibility to envisage a timeline where he became First Sea Lord. When the impact of his time as Third Sea Lord is considered, a more senior post might have enabled him to have had an even more profound influence on the Navy.

Construction

Built at seven different yards around Britain, the 'Tribals' represented a true national project, involving Vickers-Armstrong, Denny, Fairfield, Thornycroft, Scott's, Alexander Stephen and Swan Hunter, names which have today mostly slipped from national consciousness, but which then rang out as bells of national pride. This policy had many benefits. It kept multiple yards experienced in building the very best of destroyer designs, and by spreading work it helped keep multiple yards in business. Furthermore, in a period just waking up to the repercussions of universal suffrage, it increased the number of MPs whose constituencies would have significant numbers of workers involved, and the Admiralty, which had long faced the necessity of a pragmatic approach to politics, needed voices to fight its case in the House of Commons; the Admiralty had to garner support in whatever ways it could. However, to build in so many yards presented not insignificant challenges, which perhaps explains why top builders were chosen. It was not unusual for destroyer classes, or even large vessel type classes, to be built at multiple yards, but the 'Tribals' were a class which had to obey the letter of the treaty to which Britain was trying to hold others, whilst enticing more to join; any deviation would be problematic.

Another complication was the selection of names. The class name was chosen both with an eye to history, to the politics of empire and the potential for future conflict. The story of *Ashanti* and her name will be discussed later in this chapter, and most of the class will be covered as the individual ships come to prominence in events. But the naming stories of *Afridi*, *Mashona*, *Matabele* and *Tartar* can be examined here.

Afridi was to be leader of the 1st 'Tribal' Flotilla, which eventually became 4th Destroyer Flotilla. Her name did have one precedent. That vessel, built in 1907, had been built by Armstrong-Whitworth, a previous incarnation of the builders of the 1938 *Afridi*. Her name was that of a tribe of Pashtun, in Northern British India and territory which is still in India, but also split with Pakistan, Afghanistan and potentially China. The Afridi were known as fierce warriors, who dominated key strategic areas such as the Khyber Pass. Historically they had fought both for and against the British, especially during the Anglo-Afghan wars, gained a reputation that earned them the descriptor 'martial race'. Some even served with the Khyber Rifles.

The Afridi were and are a long way away from the sea, but if it is remembered that one of the possible scenarios at the start of the war was a Soviet descent through central Asia on India, good links start to take on a greater significance. Considered in terms of a broader strategy, this was a 'fine warrior race', and any war that ensued, especially a Far Eastern conflict, would depend upon the Indian Army's ability to grow and sustain its increased size for the duration of the conflict. The Afridi and the wider Pashtun community would be key recruiting grounds, essential to achieving the aim not only of numbers in service, but also stability whilst troops were needed elsewhere. Finally, any positive feelings generated, either amongst British people for empire or amongst the subjects for British rule, would help in lessening the risk of complications caused by disunity of purpose.

It was not just India though, which was the focus of these efforts to make friends and influence people. The next two vessels, *Mashona* and *Matabele* were both named after Zimbabwean tribes. Neither name had ever been used before, nor indeed since. *Mashona* was named after the populous Shona tribe, whilst *Matabele* is an Anglicisation of the less populous, Zulu related,

The 'Tribal' Class

Name	Constructor	Laying Down	Commission	Normal Displacement (tons)	History of Name when bestowed	Initial Flotilla
Afridi (Capt. D)	Vickers-Armstrong (Newcastle)	9 June 1936	3 May 1938	2,244	Only one predecessor a member of the 1907 class of 'Tribal' destroyers	1st TF/ 4th DF
Cossack	Vickers-Armstrong	9 June 1936	7 June 1938	2,030	A traditional small ship name, five predecessors had born it with pride, including a member of the previous 'Tribal' class	1st TF/ 4th DF
Gurkha	Fairfield Shipbuilding & Engineering Company (Govan, Glasgow)	6 July 1936	21 October 1938	1,999	A name with precedent, two previous ships, a torpedo boat in the Royal Indian Marine and a member of the previous 'Tribal' class	1st TF/ 4th DF
Maori	Fairfield	6 July 1936	2 January 1939	2,006	Again only one predecessor a member of the 1907 class of 'Tribal' destroyers	1st TF/ 4th DF
Mohawk	John I. Thornycroft & Company (Southampton)	16 July 1936	7 September 1938	2,017	A very traditional small ship name, thirteen predecessors had born it, including a member of the previous 'Tribal' class and a 16-gun 'Snow' type	1st TF/ 4th DF
Eskimo*	Vickers-Armstrong	5 August 1936	30 December 1938	1,987	A new name in 1936	2nd TF/ 6th DF
Mashona	Vickers-Armstrong	5 August 1936	28 March 1939	1,990	A new name in 1936	2nd TF/ 6th DF
Zulu	Alexander Stephen and Sons (Glasgow)	10 August 1936	7 September 1939	2,050	One predecessor, unsurprisingly a member of the 1907 class of 'Tribal' destroyers	1st TF/ 4th DF
Somali (Capt. D)	Swan Hunter & Wigham Richardson (Wallsend, Tyne & Wear)	26 August 1936	12 December 1938	2,014	A new name in 1936	2nd TF/ 6th DF
Tartar*	Swan Hunter	26 August 1936	10 March 1939	2,025	A traditional small ship name, seven predecessors had born it, including a member of the previous 'Tribal' class	2nd TF/ 6th DF
Sikh	Stephen's	24 September 1936	12 October 1938	2,015	Just two predecessors, a torpedo boat in the Royal Indian Marine and an 'S' class destroyer which had only been sold in 1927	1st TF/ 4th DF
Matabele	Scotts Shipbuilding and Engineering Company (Greenock)	1 October 1936	25 January 1939	1,964	A new name in 1936	2nd TF/ 6th DF
Punjabi	Scott's	1 October 1936	29 March 1939	1,990	A new name in 1936	2nd TF/ 6th DF
Ashanti*	William Denny & Brothers (Dumbarton)	23 November 1936	21 December 1938	2,020	A new name in 1936	2nd TF/ 6th DF
Bedouin	Denny	1 January 1937	15 March 1939	2,035	A new name in 1937	2nd TF/ 6th DF

*= survived WWII   Capt D = Flotilla Leader

Shipyards and launch dates compiled by author from various records including those held at the UK National Archives and the work of Martin Brice (1957)

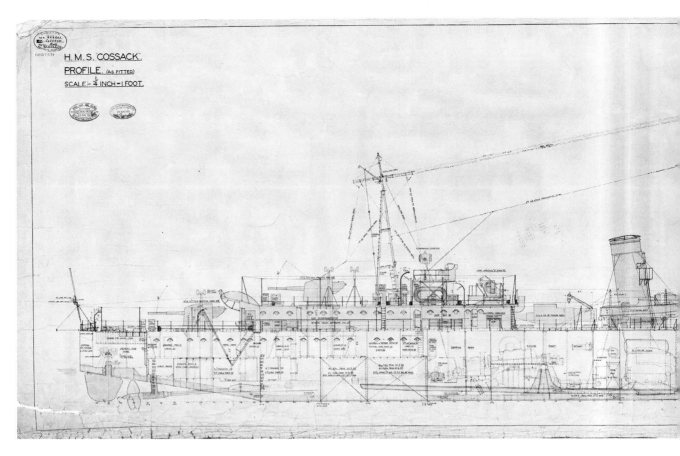

Builders profile of *Cossack*, as fitted, 1935. (© National Maritime Museum, Greenwich, London)

Ndebele. Zimbabwe (then the colony of Southern Rhodesia) was important in this period for its agriculture and mining; especially the cash crop tobacco and the metal chrome. Furthermore, whilst there was no vast African army ready to be called upon as necessary, the country did represent a potentially fertile recruiting ground, especially if indigenous African regiments needed to be found to take the place of regiments called away to fight in a European war. Furthermore, both tribes were respected for their military prowess and heritage, the Mashona, for having run quite sizeable kingdoms, the Matabele for being connected with the Zulus and having taken down one of the Mashona kingdoms. The establishment of the self-governing British Crown Colony of Southern Rhodesia in 1923, incorporating the lands of the Mashona and Matabele, brought these new names to the fore and demonstrate the changing perspectives on the Empire.

Whilst the others vessels were predominantly named after important tribes within the British Empire, *Tartar*

was one of the two that definitely was not. Illogical as this name might seem for a class of destroyers, designed in some ways to bind the Empire together, there was sense it. She was the eighth vessel to bear the name. The first had been a 28-gun Sixth Rate frigate, built in 1756 which served during the Seven Years War. She subsequently carried the fourth Harrison time-keeper on a trial to Barbados. *Tartar* (1756) served in both the American and French Revolutionary Wars, capturing eleven ships during her service, which ended in 1797 when she was wrecked off Saint-Domingue.[56] The second was a 32-gun Fifth Rate, which also earned renown, and it is only today that the Royal Navy finds itself in the longest period since 1756 that there has been no *Tartar* in commission; and that is only since 1984 when the 1960-built frigate *Tartar* was sold to Indonesia.

What attracted the Navy to *Tartar* as a name in 1756? At the time the only plausible answer was the image the name inspired. Tartars were known to be fierce warriors, fleet of movement, who had fought alongside Genghis Khan and the Mongol hordes, and gone on to establish their own vast semi-nomadic empires. Despite so many forebears, there was one 'Tribal' destroyer with more, which was *Mohawk* with eleven.

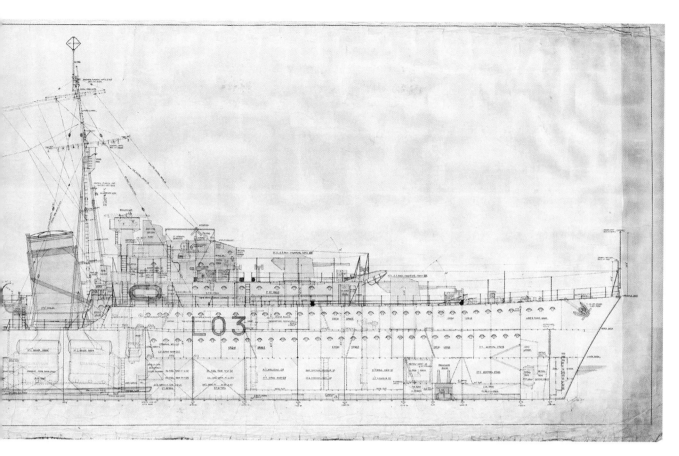

Despite this distinguished pedigree the name was perhaps a somewhat odd choice and might have better been bestowed on one of the Canadian 'Tribals'.

What proved the most complicated factor in the build was something no one had really anticipated – an advanced targeting aid coupled with relative conventional guns and mounts. They knew it was complicated but thought they had already ironed out the potential issues with extensive testing prior to inclusion in the design. Furthermore, within the gunnery system as a whole, the mounts and the barrels which were fairly conventional, and the innovative fire-control system (which was really more of an advanced targeting aid but still very useful), it was always presumed that if any problems were found it would be with the latter. After all, the guns and mounts were practically off-the-shelf purchases. However, during trials the most consistent problems came from the mounts, not the new targeting aid. The actual gun sights, which were part of the mounts, were shown during testing to be frequently off target when being fired together, and even on individual mounts not only were they not aligned with the barrel, but the layer's telescope would diverge from the trainer's telescope.[57] The entire class had issues with the

sighting and aiming of what was their 'primary' weapon system in the first tests.[58]

The reality was that most of the errors were small. Despite this, the Director of Naval Ordnance was called in, full studies carried out, and it was clear that the problem was the result of the design being a scaled up single-barrel system that had been designed for destroyers without the fire-control equipment that the 'Tribals' were given. For most of the ships the solution was found by the fitting of needle roller bearings on the deflection picot. Some vessels also required a redesign of the mountings to accommodate the evolved 4.7in weapon system (as each manufacturer, whilst building to the same specifications, had constructed them a little differently); in a couple of cases the work had to go further, with the rebuilding of the firing gear and push rods in order to make things work as they should.[59] Crucially, there was nothing that could not be solved. All the problems had been seen in slightly different contexts in other classes. The DNO and Director of Naval Construction, the shipyards and the naval officers tasked with the testing were all well versed in the weapon systems. Despite therefore some significant rebuilding of the primary weapon systems for some

Mohawk in profile after the tugs have moved into help the newly-christened ship to a fitting-out berth where she would acquire her guns, masts and other equipment. *(Maritime Quest)*

vessels, the class were barely held up and most of the ships kept to their original delivery schedules.

How had this happened? Though the double mount had been developed earlier in the 1930s, it was really the 'Tribals' and the more conventional 'J' class destroyers, built shortly afterwards, that were the first classes in which it was deployed.[60] In reality these were teething troubles, The problems were caused mainly by the design of the primary bearing under the mount, which had to be light enough to be used aboard a destroyer, but strong enough to take the force of the double recoil, especially when the gun was angled away from the centreline or the horizontal, which in both cases added substantial stress. It was largely therefore fixed as described above by adding in the rigidity and support which had been lost in the drive to save weight.

Entering Service

'...commanding a Tribal was like owning a Rolls-Royce. No other ship would be quite the same.'[61] This quotation comes from perhaps the only really good book about the 'Tribal' class, written by Martin Brice. So what makes a class of relatively small warships inspire so much emotion?

The 'Tribals' only just came into service before the Second World War began, the 1935 batch mostly commissioning in 1938, and the 1936 batch commissioning before the end of March 1939. However, even as they were commissioning and finding their feet, they were already making a name for themselves in various pre-war operations.

These were mostly in the Mediterranean Fleet's area of operations, and as a consequence of the Spanish Civil War; and a Mussolini-led Italy also required attention from the Navy.[62] It was therefore unsurprising, considering the Mediterranean Fleet's shortage of cruisers, that the first 'Tribal' flotilla was deployed there. It was originally named, appropriately, the 1st 'Tribal' Destroyer Flotilla, but by May 1939 this formation had become the 4th Destroyer Flotilla.[63] *Afridi*, the Flotilla Leader, having passed her acceptance trials on 29 April 1938, was commissioned on 3 May and arrived in Malta on 3 June to take up her duties, exactly five weeks after commissioning.[64]

On 4 July 1938 she left Malta on her first patrol of the Spanish Mediterranean Coast. Her 'B' mount was painted with broad red, white and blue bands that would identify her as British, and therefore neutral.[65] During this trip *Afridi* visited Palma, Barcelona, Marseilles, Gandia and Alperello (modern-day El Perelló), carrying out a solo cruise of what was an extensive, and at times, problematic area due to the ongoing Spanish Civil War. The patrols had been established to deter 'pirates' from attacking British and French shipping in Spanish waters, pirates strongly suspected to be Italian submarines, but even though the Regia Marina would join with Royal Navy and French Navy in the patrols, and the attacks ceased, the patrols did not.

After this singular solitary patrol *Afridi* returned to Malta for a short visit in the second week in August and

was immediately thrust to the fore of Mediterranean fleet duties, with Rear Admiral Tovey (Rear Admiral Destroyers, Mediterranean 1938) embarking on her for the trip to the Ionian Sea where destroyer exercises were scheduled for August 1938; she returned to Malta on the 25th. Doubtless he took the opportunity to familiarise himself with his newest ship.[66] This was also an opportunity for the Navy to show off to the Italians, in their backyard, the quality and capability of the Navy's destroyer force. Such high-profile exercises were, as today, often used as a form of deterrent, and it was thought beneficial to include the newest ships along with capital units – battleships and carriers – to give the exercise greater impact. This might also garner more press attention, which was useful in the domestic political funding battles.

Staying at Malta until 14 September, *Afridi* then met up with her newly commissioned sister ship *Cossack* and the eleven-year-old *County* class heavy cruiser *Devonshire* off Delos on 18 September, with the intention

Another perspective of a 'Tribal' being launched at Thornycroft's yard. The photo is captioned *Mohawk* but it could be her sister *Nubian*.

Sikh in 1938, the year she was commissioned, but also the year she made her contribution to the 'Tribal' class's royal connection, being sent to Boulogne to collect King Carol and Crown Prince Michael of Romania and then taking them to Dover. *(Drachinifel Collection)*

of embarking on a Black Sea cruise.[67] The selection of the two 'Tribals' probably had the added foreign policy dimension of sending the message to Russia of Britain's resolve in the Middle East. They arrived in Istanbul on 19 September, but remained for only two days before being recalled to Alexandra due to the Czechoslovakian Crisis and the Navy's preparations for war.[68] This crisis passed and the two 'Tribals' returned to Malta where *Afridi* was dry-docked.[69] Despite having been in commission for just seven months, *Afridi* had sailed the length and breadth of the Mediterranean, entered the Black Sea, taken part in major fleet exercises and visited dozens of ports. She had, by any measure, accomplished a great deal in a very short period of time.[70]

Cossack, the second of the class and arguably (due to her later wartime exploits under Phillip Vian) the most famous 'Tribal' class destroyer, had accompanied her for some of the time.[71] Then, when serving as division leader with three even newer members of the Tribal flotilla, *Maori*, *Zulu* and *Nubian*, she escorted Admiral Cunningham travelling aboard *Warspite* for his goodwill visit to Istanbul in early August 1939, *Cossack*'s second visit to the city.[72] This was a key part of the 'Tribal' class's utility; their size, their armament, their sweeping design, all served to make them impressive, and alongside the refitted and updated *Warspite*, this was a daunting force. Its intention was to impress

on the Turks not to mirror the Ottoman Empire should any conflict occur. After the experience of Gallipoli the British were certainly hoping to avoid such a conflict again, and proactive engagement, diplomacy and, to use a modern phrase, 'smart power' deployment – visible hard power in the form of potent warships, coupled with soft power in the person of a senior admiral hosting, listening and talking – were seen as crucial tools.

There were lighter times, touches of soft power, when for example *Cossack* acted as an ambulance in August 1938. She had been sent to collect the British consul from Barcelona, but he slipped while boarding her whaler, so he was rushed to hospital in Marseilles at 30 knots.[73] Such halcyon days, however, were not to last.

It was not just the Mediterranean 'Tribal' Flotilla which had been active. The Home Fleet's Flotilla (originally called the 2nd 'Tribal' Destroyer Flotilla, but becoming the 6th Destroyer Flotilla) was also working up under the leadership of *Somali* as the flotilla leader.[74]

Ashanti's Durbar

'Captains of warships, my dear Woodie, are not only naval officers. What we do or don't do is being constantly interpreted one way or another by friends and enemies... or neutrals.' Despite being a line from the film *The Battle of the River Plate*, these lines which were put into the mouth of Commodore Harwood by the script writers could not be a more accurate representation of a captain's position. Whether in peace or war, they need to constantly anticipate not just the first order effects, but also the second and third, of any action they take. With this in mind, *Ashanti* is a prime example of 'Tribal' class pre-war activity; of how, despite being a destroyer, she became involved with peacetime cruiser missions. *Ashanti*'s story begins not so much with her commissioning, as with her visit to the tribe she was named after.[75] She was the only 'Tribal' to accomplish this.

Ashanti was named for the Ashanti (also called the Asante) tribe which even today makes up the largest population proportion of modern Ghana, and which in the late 1930s, as the British colony The Gold Coast, was hugely important. The Gold Coast was not just a colony, but a vital one. As its name suggests, there were not only large deposits of gold, but also wood and other vital war materials. So going to the effort of honouring and winning over such a tribe was worthwhile. A visit which served to remind them of the power of Britain, and which also bound them to the Empire, represented the very essence of imperial power play, and *Ashanti*'s 2,020 tons of steel embodied, despite treaty limitations and Britain's law-abiding image, demonstrable and overwhelming power.[76] With this in mind, it puts an interesting slant on what actually happened during the visit.

Ashanti arrived in Takoradi (Ghana's deep water seaport) on 27 February 1939, the site of the first harbour which the British had built on the Gold Coast and begun during the tenure of Frederick Gordon Guggisberg (Gold Coast Governor 1921–7), and completed after he had left in 1928.[77] The harbour was of major economic and political significance, and a visit by a warship named after the local tribe, a little over a decade after its completion, was a big event.

After docking, a party of officers and men travelled to Kumasi, where the then Governor of the Gold Coast, Sir Arnold Hodson, held a Durbar (a sort of Imperial era civil-military party) in the Prince of Wales Park.[78] That it was held in Kumasi was important. The Gold Coast was originally made up of three regions, with the coast being the original colony, followed by the Ashanti region and above that the Northern Territories. The gold was mostly found in the Ashanti region. Kumasi was previously the capital, when it was known as the Ashanti Confederacy. British colonial power changed

this, but after a 30-year exile the King of the Ashanti was allowed to return in 1926. With his return and the administrative changes that came along with it, by 1935 most of the regional power had been returned to that city; although not to the king, or Asanthene as is the more correct title. He was allowed considerable influence as it was felt participation would reduce likelihood of repetition of past rebellious endeavours. It was therefore considered good politics, good for 'hearts and minds' to use the modern phrase, for the eighty naval personnel to make the journey inland to Kumasi.

As part of this effort at the Durbar, it was not the governor who took centre stage; it was the Asanthene, Chief Prempeh II, who greeted the sailors and presented the gifts; and, of course, as has been said, this was the man who had returned from exile just 13 years previously.[79] He too was playing the political game, after all if he couldn't beat the British then the best option for his people was to try to get the best deal he could out of them as their friend. The gifts, a silver bell and a golden shield, illustrate the wealth of the colony.[80] The shield was made by local smiths, and featured crossed weapons which symbolised protection as well as the emblem and motto of the *Ashanti*. Prempeh was most emphatic that, whatever happened to or befell the destroyer, these items had to stay with her throughout her career both at war and peace. Not only did these gifts highlight the mineral wealth of the region, but their martial nature, along with Prempeh's utterances, were taken as positive signs of overall support for Britain. It was a very public commitment, which built significant bridges in the minds of the British.

As befitted the occasion, there was a parade followed by a party, full of pomp and protocol, but this event was not the end of the ceremonies. When the party returned to *Ashanti*, she was opened to visitors in Takoradi for about a week. On the first day Ashanti Obayifo's (High Priests of the tribe) arrived, presenting further emblems of good fortune, before reciting prayers of valour and survival.[81] Thousands came to look and visit, and she was taken to the heart of the Ashanti people, a success that augured well for her career, as well as suggesting that the Navy's naming policy for the class had not perhaps been without some merit.

After this happy period, *Ashanti* returned to 6th DF, the Home Fleet 'Tribal' Destroyer Flotilla, and once again was immediately thrust into the fore of diplomatic efforts. This time it was closer to home, Cherbourg, for a goodwill visit with the French fleet. Again, offered a premium moment for diplomacy she rose to the occasion. This time she was part of a whole division of 'Tribals', comprising *Somali*, *Matabele* and *Eskimo*. In

Ashanti's Durbar

Above: Priests and warriors of the Assante gathered by the Asanthene to take part in the ceremony. (TNA-ADM 1.10160, Author's collection)

Above: *Ashanti* in Freetown, where senior tribal representatives and important local figures gather to view and bless the ship.

Right: Processing past the Governor of the Gold Coast, Sir Arnold Hodson at the Prince of Wales Park, Kumasi.

Below: The front cover of the Durbar's official programme.

Ashanti alongside at Freetown, showing the efforts the crew have gone to get her ready for her special visitors.

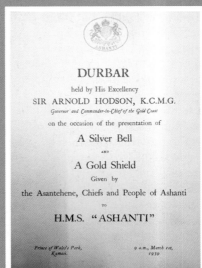

DURBAR
held by His Excellency
SIR ARNOLD HODSON, K.C.M.G.
Governor and Commander-in-Chief of the Gold Coast
on the occasion of the presentation of
A Silver Bell
AND
A Gold Shield
Given by
the Asantehene, Chiefs and People of Ashanti
TO
H.M.S. "ASHANTI"

Prince of Wales's Park, Kumasi.   9 a.m., March 1st, 1939

The gifts themselves, the bell and the shield, which were presented to the ship and which would protect her throughout the course of the Second World War.

Above: The naval party from *Ashanti* marching through the Prince of Wales Park.

Right: *Ashanti* in profile from the roof of the one of harbour buildings in Freetown.

Below: The Governor, Sir Arnold Hodson.

Above: The 'Asanthene' Chief Prempeh II, making his speech on the platform set up for the presentation.

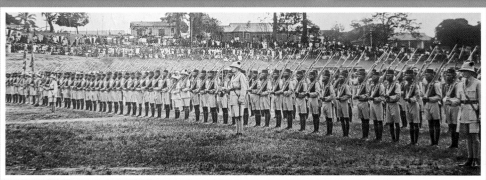

A detachment of the Gold Coast Regiment at the Prince of Wales Park.(TNA-ADM 1.10160, Author's Own Picture)

May 1939, war was looming and the visit was important. It was presumed that allied destroyers would have to operate closely together, making it crucial they were not only allies but friends.[82] With this in mind, everything that could be done was done to build such a relationship. Parties and dances of all kinds, excursions and sports events, along with as many 'professional' meetings as possible were crammed in, and the ships even found time for some harbour exercises.[83]

Ashanti really did fight her way through the war, the 6th DF being heavily involved with the Home Fleet's myriad duties, providing protection for fleet movements and convoys, anti-submarine sweeps and commando raids. An incident near Trondheim during the Norway campaign set the tone for much of the war. On 26 April 1940, her sisters *Sikh* and *Mohawk* patrolled the mouth of Trondheimsfjorden, while *Ashanti* and *Nubian* went up the fiord, and on to Kraakvaagsfjord looking for German destroyers. The Luftwaffe were none too happy having the Navy quite so close to their newly acquired airfield, but the hundred bombs they dropped did not stop the destroyers escaping, although one near miss blew *Ashanti*'s main turbo-generator off its bedplate. Despite losing electricity she got away, and after a moderately eventful trip home, and then some repairs, she was back in service.

This set the tone for much of her service. She was to take part in many high risk operations, including Claymore, Anklet, Pedestal and Torch to name just four. She avoided being sunk, though she sustained enough damage to require considerable time undergoing repairs on occasion, for instance after running into another destroyer, *Fame* (which had run aground due to a navigational error) off Whitburn Rifle Range. This collision required her to remain with Swan Hunter & Wigham Richardson at Wallsend (the firm that had built her sisters, *Somali* and *Tartar*) from November 1940 to August 1941.

Ashanti was one of just four 'Tribals' to survive the war, remaining in commission, but not really in service, until 1949.[84] Perhaps the tokens and prayers of the Ashanti helped her survive when others did not.[85] Arguably, her war service was not quite as significant as the service she had rendered the empire before the war in 1939. From that visit to the Gold Coast flowed tangible diplomatic and practical benefits for the Royal Navy and for Britain at a very dangerous time.[86] For the duration of the war Britain could rely upon its west African colony for treasure, for materials and for men, men who would fight in the Far East with distinction. *Ashanti* had played a big part in making all that a reality.

The *Thetis* Incident

Before the years of peace came to an end, the 'Tribals' of the recently named 6th DF of the Home Fleet found themselves involved in one of the saddest losses which the Royal Navy had ever sustained, and which resulted in the greatest peacetime loss of life for the service. Whilst still on trials in Liverpool Bay off the Welsh coast, the submarine *Thetis*, due to a combination of design faults, the quality of build and human error, sank bow first to the bottom of the Irish Sea. The event caused a chain reaction which saw the 4th DF dashing to the rescue at full speed, before being called upon to act as taxis, salvage ships, and flagships for admirals. It saw them put to good use not only their critical asset, the space built into their design, but also, when the British weather during the course of the incident prevented other ships holding station, their manoeuvrability and powerful engines which enabled them to stay on station.

Thetis had failed to surface by her appointed time of 1600hrs (she had been diving at 1400hrs so this was supposed to provide plenty of time for the checks to be carried out) in the approximate position 53° 33'N; 04° 00'W,[87] and at 1745hrs on Thursday 1 June 1939 Rear Admiral (Submarines) (or 'S') Bertram Watson (who would go on to become a Vice Admiral and Flag Officer Iceland during the war) decided to take emergency action. Ships were dispatched to begin the search, including two special formations, the 1st Minesweeping Flotilla (MF) from Brixham, and the 6th DF from Portland. In addition, *Brazen*, a 1930-built 'B' class destroyer, which had been crossing the Irish Sea at the time, was also diverted.

Winchelsea, a First World War vintage 'W' class destroyer raced from Portsmouth with the Rear Admiral's Chief Staff Officer aboard in charge of operations. Watson himself was sick.[88] The warships were in addition to specialist vessels such as the deep diving tender *Tedworth*, and a little later, after *Thetis* had been discovered by *Brazen*, ships came from Liverpool to support the submarine in the precarious position she had been found. This included *Vigilant*, a type of salvage ship sometimes referred to as a camel, which attempted to pass a wire around the *Thetis*'s stern whilst it was still visible. However, with the forward compartments flooded she proved immovable and as the tide not only began to rise but drew her under, the wire parted and she disappeared underwater.

The 6th DF arrived at 1030hrs on 2 June when Captain Randolph Nicholson of *Somali* assumed command, until the arrival of Watson, well after *Thetis* had dipped below the waves, who was brought from Liverpool by another 'Tribal', *Bedouin*.[89] Watson set up his staff aboard *Somali*, quickly deciding it was the most suitable ship for the mission. During an early meeting, chaired by Nicholson, as Watson felt he was still getting up to speed, it was decided that every effort was to be made to release those still trapped (three crew and one Cammell Laird employee had escaped before being overcome by the carbon monoxide poisoning) in the submarine by cutting a hole in the stern and, if necessary, into the after tank and through its bulkhead.[90] This was a risky operation, as the report states.

It was realised that in such a decision, grave risk of total flooding was being accepted, but judged by conditions of survivors at the time of their escape nine hours earlier, it was obvious that desperate measures were essential to meet a desperate situation.[91]

Unfortunately, as the hours ticked by the operation turned from recovery to salvage. At 0630hrs on 3 June two divers went down to tap near the control room but there was no response. Nevertheless, they carried on with their plan to try to connect an air supply. By 1300hrs, despite the wires between the camel and the submarine having slipped and no fresh wires connected because of the strong tide, they were still working on the air supply.[92] But at 1700hrs orders arrived from the Admiralty to cease life-saving operations, as there was now no hope of survival, the crew having been trapped

for 48 hours.[93] However, it was not until 0300hrs on the following morning, and after another meeting aboard *Somali*, which this time included the recently-arrived Commander-in-Chief Plymouth, Admiral Sir Martin Dunbar-Nasmith, that the rescue mission was called off.[94] Ninety-nine people died on board, including twenty-six employees of Cammell Laird, and one diver died later during the salvage operation. She was salvaged in good enough order and she was then commissioned as *Thunderbolt* and went on to have a successful career until sunk in the Mediterranean in 1943.

The 'Tribals' and the large destroyer concept impressed many observers, notably the new Controller, Vice Admiral Bruce Fraser (brought out aboard *Ashanti* from Liverpool), and Rear Admiral (Submarines) Bertram Watson. What particularly attracted attention was their speed of 30 knots, a speed that was not just achieved for a short sprint, but which was maintained for most of the journey. In a number of cases their engine rooms had been under the command of the most senior rating, rather than officers, because so many of their crew had been ashore when the ships were ordered to sea, though *Ashanti* had been left behind to bring out stragglers.[95] The 'Tribal' Taxi Service, which was set up between the stricken submarine and the Liverpool, and which facilitated an almost constant flow of people and equipment, had clearly demonstrated their capabilities.

CHAPTER 2

FORGED BY WAR 1939–40

The 'Tribal' class were conceived and designed, in part, for the Fleet cruiser role, which was confirmed and outlined in their initial operations document: 'Tribal Class and I Class Destroyers – Disposition of on Completion with Regard to Organisation of the Fleet and Destroyer Flotillas'. The phraseology was from the proposals of the Tactical School but went further than those had dared, stating: '…(a) By Day – Reconnaissance and counter action against enemy flotillas. (b) By Night – Shadowing and/or Screening. (c) In General – as a counter to the large Leader type of other countries. …Their duties are thus more in the nature of those of cruisers than of destroyers.'[96]

This clearly indicates their intended duties were to include those of a 'cruiser' but the vessels were nonetheless destroyers, and when war came the 'Tribal' class were expected to perform both duties often, as in peacetime, carrying out both roles simultaneously.[97] Their deployment to the Home Fleet and Mediterranean Fleet meant it eased the strain on the available cruisers that were to be spread thinly in these areas, especially the Mediterranean where, despite their im-

Afridi in her role as the leader of the then 1st 'Tribal' Flotilla (later to become 4th Destroyer Flotilla). In this role she would set the standards for all that would come after her. This picture highlights how her weaponry has been laid to provide coverage against attacks on all quarters. (Drachinifel Collection)

mediate predecessor Admiral Fisher's professed reservations, both Admiral Sir Dudley Pound and then Admiral Andrew Cunningham embraced them enthusiastically. Selecting the 4th DF for critical operations, and exercising them extensively, they were the vessels of choice for these officers when faced with complicated and critical assignments.

This favour perhaps could have been considered natural for a destroyer officer such as Cunningham who was a ready advocate for such ships, though he had, as Rear Admiral (Destroyers) under Fisher, written in opposition to them. Why the change of heart? Perhaps it was due to their obvious qualities, or the fact the battleship officer, Pound, who held the role of C-in-C Mediterranean in between Fisher and Cunningham, had been impressed by them. It may, of course, simply have been necessity that led to their being such coveted tools of naval power. Whatever the case, by the time war came they were already critical assets, used in the roles of their concept and deployment, to free up cruisers and regular destroyers for other duties, by providing the functional proximity of both.

Such duties were hard, and required more from their crews than destroyers or cruisers due to the need to maintain the standards of spit and polish to achieve the poise of the latter, whilst also throwing themselves into training and every situation with absolute commitment to embody the aggression of the former. They did this with such aplomb, that even if they had not already felt

Afridi from the stern profiling her pre-war weapons and mast fit. *(Maritime Quest)*

themselves elite crews, the rest of the Fleet's reaction to them soon would have told them. As a result, when war came it was an opportunity for them to build upon a reputation, rather than providing the opportunity to prove their capabilities.

With the Home Fleet

The 6th DF began the war off Iceland with a force of British and French battlecruisers. Two hours after war was declared Captain Nicholson captured the first German merchant ship of the conflict, the 2,377-ton *Hannah Böge*. When *Somali* first sighted a strange vessel on the horizon, she seemed to be flying South American flags; as they got closer they could see men painting out her name. *Somali* ordered the merchant vessel to stop and prepare to be boarded, which she was with one officer accompanied by eight sailors. They took her with a prize crew to Kirkwall, in the Orkneys, arriving there on 5 September. It was an auspicious start to the war.

It was not long before the rest of the 6th DF were back in Scapa Flow, deployed with many of the Home Fleet's heavy ships, but most importantly with the 18th Cruiser Squadron (CS), the squadron made up of the

'Town' class, the fast, large, light cruisers which were the pride and, arguably, the elite of the Navy's cruiser force. This squadron, which was combined with the Tribals of 6th DF and five 'F' class destroyers of 8th DF under the command of the Home Fleet's Rear Admiral Destroyers was, by itself, a potent striking force. Yet, the Navy did not settle for this alone. Anchored in Scapa, alongside this powerful force, were the fleet carriers *Ark Royal* and *Furious*, the seaplane carrier *Pegasus*, the battlecruisers *Hood*, *Repulse* and *Renown*, and the battleships *Nelson* and *Rodney*, forming an overwhelming force, particularly for any potential Kriegsmarine task group.

This, however, proved unnecessary. The feared German mass break-out into the North Atlantic and any fleet action for which this force was amassed never materialised, and it was instead broken up to cover convoys, patrol the Faroes/Norway gap and start the waging of an even greater global maritime conflict than had been experienced in the First World War. Convoy duty proved wearing on what were fleet/scout vessels, with hulls unsuited to the constant hum of convoy duty. However, they threw themselves into the role. The convoy that brought the damaged submarine *Spearfish* back home safely to Rosyth in September 1939 was notable for *Somali* along with her sisters, *Mashona* and

Eskimo, getting their first taste of enemy bombing, as well as the royal gratitude of King George VI when he visited the Home Fleet Destroyers in October.[98]

Convoys were the day-to-day life of the 6th DF. For example, on 12 December 1939 it was the 6th DF that was stationed at the front of other destroyers and capital ships to secure SS *Aquitania*, SS *Empress of Britain*, SS *Empress of Australia*, SS *Duchess of Richmond* and SS *Monarch of Bermuda*, otherwise known as Convoy HX1, and which was carrying a third of the 1st Canadian Infantry Division.[99] This was a critical mission both in terms of numbers of personnel it carried, and the fact that it was in many ways more a product of domestic Canadian politics than a response to a British Government request; it was, in that sense, a significant development in terms of politics and the Empire.

It was the case with the 'Tribals' and the subsequent general-purpose destroyers, that they were often where it was 'important' to be, not always where it was 'critical'. The critical incidents required the cruisers, the destroyers, the full fleet of ships needed, or at least those which could be spared. Important incidents had to make do with whatever ships might be available; which meant that it was often the assignment that best fitted the ships which could multi-role. Coastal convoys were important, in fact arguably critical. The transatlantic convoys, the anti-surface raider groups were critical at the beginning of the war. 'Tribals' were often called upon for all of them, sometimes in the same mission. That is why, even though coastal convoys were important, the Northern Barrier was critical and thus would have first call on the 6th DF if needed. It is because of this that they were so often stationed at Scapa Flow and why they were present during the infamous sinking of *Royal Oak*.

A *Revenge*-class class battleship, with eight 15in guns, *Royal Oak* was a powerful unit. Having undergone two extensive modernisation refits in 1922–4 and 1934–6, she was one of the better vessels of the class. The unmodernised battleships would be a constant problem throughout the war. On paper they mattered, but in reality they were not the vessels the Navy wanted to find in a fleet battle, and not even in a duel with a significant surface raider; this was especially true for Admiral Somerville in charge of the Eastern Fleet. Although *Royal Oak* lacked the speed necessary for a fast battle fleet, as a convoy protection vessel or for amphibious bombardments she would have been very useful. Besides which, a war is fought with what is available, not necessarily with what might be wished for.

Royal Oak was available, worked up and serving as the flagship of 2nd Battle Squadron (2nd BS). In fact, in similar circumstance she had proved crucial during the Spanish Civil War, fulfilling many duties and earning herself the honour of being the most attacked British ship involved in that conflict.[100] She was anchored in Scapa Flow when she was torpedoed and sunk in the early hours of 14 October 1939 by *U-47*, which had threaded through the defences the Admiralty had thought impregnable. This attack caused uproar, not just the loss of life (835 died either that night or of their injuries, including Rear Admiral Henry Blagrove, the newly appointed commander of 2nd BS), but the shock that the northern fleet fortress, the bulwark for the Northern Patrol, had been violated. Immediately after the attack, *Somali*, *Mashona*, *Ashanti* and *Eskimo* swung into action. Their Asdic picked up an echo in the middle of the Flow itself. Shortly afterwards it was lost, then recovered and subsequently depth charged, and the contact was still being investigated (plans were in place for a diver to go down) on 17 October when an air attack came in. This time the Germans were targeting *Iron Duke*, the former flagship of the Grand Fleet, but now a gunnery training ship. Whilst the 'Tribals' accounted for two of the attacking aircraft, two near misses had damaged the older ship and she ended up being beached with *Eskimo* providing emergency power till her own systems could be repaired. The war was already proving eventful not only for 6th DF, but also for their sister ships of 4th DF.

On Mediterranean Service

At the same time, *Afridi* and *Cossack*, together with the rest of the 4th DF, were deployed in the Red Sea.[101] 4th DF was under the command of Captain George Creswell, aboard *Afridi*.[102] Although at times command of the flotilla would be transferred to *Cossack*.[103] Creswell was a 34-year-old veteran, who had been the first commander of the original 1st 'Tribal' Flotilla, and stayed in command when it became the 4th DF. This posting was arguably the zenith of what he had worked for in his career as a destroyer officer (although he would go on to become Rear Admiral, before retiring and being recalled to service), having first achieved command of a destroyer as a Lieutenant-in-Command of the 'C' class destroyer *Dove* in May 1915.[104] She was the first of seven destroyers he would command, with *Afridi* being the last. In many ways it was Creswell, the dedicated but unconventional officer (he had found time in the inter-war years to design a very useful anti-aircraft sight), who set the mould for subsequent commanders of the 'Tribal' class and, as such, defined the image that commanders of the 'Battle' and *Daring* classes would aspire to.[105]

Zulu and the battlecruiser *Hood* at Malta in 1938 during the Spanish Civil War deployments, a partnership which often was repeated during the remainder of *Hood*'s career. The visual impact of the 'Tribal' class's design and lines were key to their peacetime mission role, as well as underpinning their wartime function. *(Maritime Quest)*

4th DF had been deployed to the Red Sea for commerce protection, principally against submarines. In this largely forgotten campaign of the war, the flotilla did outstandingly well. They were also deployed there in case any German raiders should choose that rich hunting ground for their operations.[106] In fact, those ships were considered the more likely foe. Because logistics and infrastructure were limited for the Axis powers, the longer range and greater sustainability of surface raiders made them the likelier threat in this theatre. They included those surface raiders disguised as merchant ships, but potentially also the heavy cruisers, the 'pocket battleships' of the *Deutschland* class, which had slipped out before the declaration of war. It would be the *Graf Spee*, one of that class, which would visit the Indian Ocean in November 1939, although she did not stray far enough north to receive 'Tribal' attention.

Gurkha was the first of the class to be sunk in the war, partly due to the limitations of the 'Tribal' class's primary gun systems, the 4.7in mount. Despite being built as a general-purpose destroyer they simply did not have the range of elevation necessary for the air battles they found themselves fighting. *(Drachinifel Collection)*

Bedouin in 1937, quite soon after her commissioning. This photo shows her in her mid-grey scheme which was favoured by the destroyers of the Home Fleet to which the 2nd 'Tribal' Flotilla/6th Destroyer Flotilla belonged. *(Drachinifel Collection)*

However, it was the Italian submarines operating from their African colonies that were the publically discussed threat and which had justified the deployment, principally to try and deter others from entering the fray.

The 4th DF was also well positioned to act as a forward force in case either a surge to the Far East was needed or a reserve for the eastern Mediterranean required. In simple terms, if Japan or Italy suddenly decided to join the war, the flotilla was well positioned to move rapidly to any theatre in which it might be needed. The ships could provide this critical capability whilst also still fulfilling another very important mission which was that of multi-role and force multiplier. To put it another way, the 4th DF was, in effect, covering for the Navy's lack of cruisers and destroyers by acting as both in their principal assumed cruiser role of trade protection, and simultaneously in a destroyer role of anti-submarine warfare.

Together with escorting/scouting for the Fleet, these were roles for which they were used extensively before and during the Norway Campaign.[107] Creswell was awarded a Distinguished Service Order for the flotilla's anti-submarine work during the first three months of the war.[108] And those anti-submarine duties, along with the salvage of the *Thetis*, the various convoy skirmishes, their activity around the sinking of *Royal Oak*, awards for services in the Indian Ocean and Mediterranean, it is easy to understand why the 'Tribals' were acquiring a reputation as submarine hunters; and this made them even more in demand for operations, a circumstance that came with consequences.

Returning to the 4th DF at this time, when war began neither Italy nor Japan entered the fray and, consequently, the expected attacks failed to materialise in the Red Sea or the Mediterranean, but in the North Sea and Atlantic the threats were clearer and the 4th DF was needed at home.[109] Between 10 and 12 October the ships of the flotilla departed from Gibraltar, leaving the Mediterranean in ones and twos,[11] in part to move the force more quickly, in part to disguise the move from observers; but more importantly the staggered departures were intended to avoid creating a large target for the voyage north.

The 4th DF gathered again at Scapa Flow, the home of their sister flotilla the 6th DF, where they refitted for northern waters.[111] The journey itself had not been without its incidents, including one which would lead to the highest award granted to a 'Tribal' class officer during the war.[112] On 16 October, *Cossack*'s division, comprising *Maori*, *Zulu* and *Mohawk* (replacing *Sikh*, which had engine trouble), entered the Firth of Forth swept channels.[113] Before this they had been escorting a convoy, but after an Asdic contact the merchant ships had been diverted to Methil on the north coast of the Firth of Forth for safety and the division was proceeding unencumbered. At 1100hrs the first air attack by the Luftwaffe on Britain began, aimed at shipping in the Firth of Forth and at Edinburgh.[114]

The 'Tribals' were caught at the worse possible moment, inside the cleared channels where the narrow passages between the defensive minefields offered no opportunity to manoeuvre, a situation made worse by delay in identification which was caused mainly by the knowledge that RAF aircraft were operating in the area.[115] The enemy aircraft were not identified as thought hostile until they were almost upon them. The Ju 88 released two bombs which straddled *Mohawk* on the diagonal, one detonating to starboard of the bridge,

the other to port of the torpedo launcher. The aircraft was also firing its guns as it passed and the bullets, combined with splinters from the bombs, decimated the exposed crew members.[116] The mooring party and the bridge crew suffered the most, with fifteen killed instantly and thirty injured, most experienced officers and petty officers.[117]

Among those injured was *Mohawk*'s commanding officer, Commander Richard Jolly, who was shot through the stomach. Yet with so many other injured there was no relief available and his ship had a busy and difficult passage to navigate. Whilst the remaining officers organised engine room personnel into first-aid parties, with the wounded taken to emergency quarters and the dead wrapped up in their sea coats, he stayed on the bridge, denying himself medical attention in order to get his vessel and ship's company.[118] For thirty-five miles and eighty minutes, as his strength slowly ebbed and his voice was reduced to a hoarse whisper, he conned his ship with the aid of his navigating officer, who himself had a chest wound and was not in a much

Cossack during her time on the neutrality patrol for the Spanish Civil War. The red, white and blue stripes stand out clearly on 'B' mount was intended to protect her from miss-identification. *(Drachinifel Collection)*

better condition than his captain. At the Forth Bridge, *Mohawk* met the 'Town' class cruisers of the 2nd CS, *Edinburgh* and *Southampton*, which had also been attacked.

The customary salute was sounded and as Commander Jolly turned in his chair to salute the flagship, he collapsed. He survived for another five hours whilst tugs took his ship under the bridge and into the dockyard, from where he was rushed to hospital at South Queensferry, where he died.[119] Creswell recommended

Cossack as newly completed, sporting a similar Mediterranean Fleet white paint scheme as *Afridi* did in the photo on page 31. Here she is, shown at speed, surging through the water with awning suspended from the director level protecting the bridge crew from the sun. *(Maritime Quest)*

Cossack returns home to Rosyth (Scotland) from the *Altmark* Incident 17 December 1939, laden with 200 rescued sailors and as many stories from the crew who, along with their ship, became national, even international, stars. *(Maritime Quest)*

at Rosyth, primarily to escort East Coast convoys.[123] This allowed them to also serve as a forward-based re-action force, rather like the battlecruiser force had been when it was based there during the First World War. In theory they were co-located with cruisers but in prac-tice they were the permanent force as the cruisers were always needed elsewhere urgently.[124] As the forward-based force their key role was scouting for the Fleet (often manning what was termed the A-K line, the scouting line which was postulated to operate far in front of the main force), a role for which they were used extensively up to, and particularly during, the Norwe-gian campaign.[125]

Admiral of the Fleet Philip Vian, the Intuitive Officer

Publically, professionally and even posthumously, Philip Vian could never be accused of being timid or diffident. Internally he might have felt fear, or a second of doubt, but he would never let it show nor ever want anyone to know about it. To understand this one has only to read Oliver Warner's introduction to Vian's au-tobiography *Action this Day* in which he wrote: 'When

Jolly for a medal. No one thought it would be the Empire Gallantry Medal which was announced a week later, particularly as it was the first time it had been awarded to someone who had died.[120] Later on, after the institution of the George Cross as the second high-est medal in the British order of precedence after the Victoria Cross, it was declared that all those who had received the Empire Gallantry Medal posthumously during the war would have it replaced by a George Cross.[121] After the bombing raid, *Cossack*, *Maori* and *Zulu* were judged capable of the voyage, so were quickly despatched to Scapa Flow; which although not considered safe from submarines at that point, was con-sidered reasonably safe from air attack.

They were not to remain in Scapa Flow; despite the 4th DF often operating alongside as part of the Home Fleet, after a short period *Afridi*'s band were moved on between March and April.[122] Instead of calling Scapa Flow home, the ships were mainly based further south

Captain Philip Vian aboard *Cossack*. The photo illustrates the exposed position that was required to command a destroyer. Vian had the virtue of being 'ranked among the handful of officers of the armed forces who were trained, equipped, and of appropriate seniority and experience' to influence the outcome of the war. Authority and energy would be the hallmarks of his time with the 'Tribals', and during his subsequent career. *(Maritime Quest)*

Zulu in 1939, making her contribution to the Spanish Civil War neutrality patrol. while it was certainly not a successful international effort, due to a combination of half-heartedness and flagrant violation, it demonstrated to many within the British Government the need to rapidly rearm due to the changing global dynamic. *(Maritime Quest)*

war broke out in 1939, Captain Vian, as he then was, ranked among the handful of officers of the armed forces who were trained, equipped, and of appropriate seniority and experience to make it obvious that, if the struggle were to be protracted, it would be upon them that tactical success would depend.'[126]

If any naval officer of the era could be written about in such a way it was Vian. He was a perfectionist who expected perfectionism in others; a taskmaster who should by any normal standards have provoked another *Bounty* mutiny. Unlike Captain Bligh, however, Vian was also inspirational, successful and lucky. He made every unit he commanded feel they were the elite. When put in command of a 'Tribal' destroyer flotilla he not only found his niche; the Navy created a perfect fit. He may have been tough, but he expected nothing more of the men under his command than he expected from himself.

His luck began early in his career. Whilst at Osborne Naval College, he made friends with Prince Edward (the then Prince of Wales's heir) which afforded him an opportunity to meet Lord Fisher, the First Sea Lord, and earn a favour from him by taking a photograph. Only Vian had brought a camera, and Fisher promised that if he were to send the picture with a note, he would try to help. This Vian did, and it secured him a transfer during 1915 from an old cruiser, *Argonaut*, patrolling off the African coast in search of a surface raider, to the latest and fastest destroyer in Grand Fleet, the Yarrow-built 'M' class *Morning Star*.[127] It was from this vessel that he witnessed the Battle of Jutland and it was this vessel which launched his destroyer career. After serv-

Zulu with flag signals hoisted. Flags were still a key part of naval communication. With their experience from the First World War in mind, the Navy were always worried about unnecessary radio transmissions. *(Drachinifel Collection)*

A regular ally of the 'Tribal' class in their wartime operations were the Free Polish destroyers. ORP *Piorun*, pictured here, was often present, and her name is often found alongside 'Tribal' names in operational lists. *(Roger Litwiller Collection)*

ing as First Lieutenant in two other destroyers, he went on his gunnery course, again finding luck and connections, being on the same course as George, Marquess of Milford-Haven, brother of Earl Mountbatten.[128] Following this course he served as a gunnery officer on the flagship of the Royal Australian Navy, HMAS *Australia*, under the squadron gunnery officer, Harold Burroughs, who was later famous for running convoys to Malta. When, in his own words, economy and Admiralty interfered in his career, *Australia* was paid off, but instead of taking the post as ADC to the Governor-General, Vian was called home to the Cadet Training Battleship, *Thunderer*.[129]

Vian's career continued on its charmed trajectory. Despite much hard work on his part, he nevertheless managed to fit in a three-month honeymoon, a busy Admiralty posting and still manage to lead a destroyer division of the Mediterranean 3rd Flotilla in 1932, something even he admitted was unusual for a specialist officer such as he had become.[130] Even more remarkably, whilst in command of his destroyer *Active* within the division of the 3rd Flotilla, he damaged her badly enough whilst docking with the depot ship to require a dockyard trip; yet despite this he was appointed to the rank of captain in 1934, at the comparatively young age of 40, after just twenty-two years in the Navy.[131]

At this point in their careers, Royal Navy officers would commonly become held up on their career path. They would face time ashore which would delay them acquiring either the sea time, the command experience or the opportunity to distinguish themselves afloat needed for promotion. However, Mussolini and the Abyssinian crisis of October 1935 intervened, compelling the Navy to practise a mass mobilisation. Admiral William Wordsworth Fisher, C-in-C Mediterranean, asked for Vian to command the additional destroyer flotilla commissioned from reserve to support him.[132]

Then, with the advent of the Spanish Civil War, instead of demobilising, the flotilla was kept in the Mediterranean, which included Vian himself. Instead of attending Staff College he was granted a flag captaincy and command of the cruiser *Arethusa*, and consistently given opportunities to hone his skills and impress his superiors, in a way that other officers might not have come by; they might, on the other hand, not have been as confident in promoting themselves and pushing their cases.[133]

When his time on *Arethusa* came to an end, and aided by the threat of imminent war, Vian continued to dodge Staff College. At the beginning of the conflict he returned to command another reserve flotilla, but it was not long before Vian was given command of the 4th DF of 'Tribal' class destroyers in January 1940. From then on his career would be woven closely with the 'Tribals'.[134] All that had gone before had built the man he had become at the time of this command; the Vian who stepped on to the bridge of the *Afridi* and assumed command of his new flotilla; the man who could project, even if he did not always feel it, absolute confidence in his judgement and his role; a leader who, because of this confidence, could, and just as importantly would, take risks, risks which, on balance, paid off more than their cost. While he never aspired to it, Vian would achieve personal fame through his time with the 4th DF, not aboard his flagship *Afridi*, but in *Cossack*, in an operation which not only highlights the 'Tribal' class's duality of role, but also became the cornerstone of the case made for their successor classes. The February 1940 *Altmark* incident, for which Vian was awarded the DSO, also closed the *Graf Spee* saga, and heralded the beginning of the Norway phase of the 'Tribals' service.

Altmark Incident

In the 1930s, after the failure of the Hague convention to reach any agreement on territorial waters, most countries still observed a three-mile limit as the extent of 'national waters'. This distance was defined in the eighteenth century by a Dutch judge, Cornelius van Bynkershoek, because it was at that time the maximum range of a cannon. Whatever the questionable logic behind it, this was the distance that still mattered in February 1940. Furthermore, considering that the pertinent events of the *Altmark* incident largely took place inside Jossingfiord, it could be argued that they actually took place in Norway, let alone within its territorial waters. That though did not matter to the Navy or Churchill, who was first Lord of the Admiralty at the time; this was a battle at the start of a long war in which merchant seaman would be the lifeblood of the

FORGED BY WAR 1939–40

Battle of the Atlantic, and here were a number of experienced sailors who could be rescued and who could prove critical; and successful intervention would halt the German government claiming any more victories from the cruise of the *Graf Spee*, and play well for domestic political consumption, for which the Battle of the River Plate had already proved critical to morale. Most importantly, it would be a statement of intent and confidence from the most powerful navy in the world at the time, that it would do whatever was necessary to win the war that was to come. However, this did not mean that the 1908 Hague convention was either irrelevant or unimportant.

Article 1.

Belligerents are bound to respect the sovereign rights of neutral Powers and to abstain, in neutral territory or neutral waters, from any act which would, if knowingly permitted by any Power, constitute a violation of neutrality.

Article 2.

Any act of hostility, including capture and the exercise of the right of search, committed by belligerent war-ships in the territorial waters of a neutral Power, constitutes a violation of neutrality and is strictly forbidden.

Article 3.

When a ship has been captured in the territorial waters of a neutral Power, this Power must employ, if the prize is still within its jurisdiction, the means at its disposal to release the prize with its officers and crew, and to intern the prize crew.

If the prize is not in the jurisdiction of the neutral Power, the captor Government, on the demand of that Power, must liberate the prize with its officers

The first three articles of Treaty XIII of the 1907 Hague Convention are as explicit as diplomatic language ever gets. A total of thirty-three articles provided the basis for the security of merchant shipping, then and now. In 1940 it was the mantra which not only the Royal Navy, but everyone was supposed to follow. The taking of *Altmark* would violate Article 1, although that was only proved by the operation – an operation which would violate Article 2; although the Navy would be very good about not violating Article 3, as tempting as the capture of a merchant ship might have been.

It was from *Cossack* that Captain Vian's commanded operations during February 1940, a command which would propel *Cossack* and the 'Tribals' into the public eye. On 14 February 1940 she put to sea with her sisters *Maori*, *Sikh*, *Nubian*, two 1936/37 completed 'I' class destroyers *Intrepid* and *Ivanhoe* (both of which were fitted as minelayers), and *Arethusa*, a 1934 completed light cruiser of the class bearing her name.[135] This force was officially at sea to intercept German iron ore ships in the Skagerrak; it was a capable and well-armed force for such a mission.[136] Its strength had been further supplemented by having its influenza-affected crewmen replaced with crew from *Arethusa*'s sister *Aurora*. These were then organised into boarding parties.[137] The force was thus substantial enough and well-provisioned enough to take on normally lightly crewed, and lightly or unarmed merchant ships.

Whatever the true mission (and despite the number of educated guesses, we are unlikely ever to know), it was on 15 February the force learnt that the Kriegsmarine supply vessel *Altmark*, with an estimated 300 British merchant seamen prisoners captured by *Graf Spee* during its raiding, was near Trondheim.[138] *Altmark* was

Another Spanish Neutrality Patrol photo, this time of *Gurkha* at Malta. *(Drachinifel Collection)*

F20

Eskimo as built, prior to the Second World War. *(Maritime Quest)*

HMS *Eskimo* after the Battle of Narvik where she lost her bow to a German torpedo. Everything forward of 'B' mount was destroyed. 'A' mount was dangling down on the bent deck plating which had be cut off, and 'B' mount removed, just prior to this photo being taken, as part of the process to make her safe to take back across the North Sea. (Maritime Quest)

within Norwegian waters, posing as a merchant ship. This was illegal under international law because she was carrying prisoners so was technically a combatant. What the Navy was about to do would also be a violation of the law.[139]

With these issues in mind, after much fruitless discussion with the Norwegian navy and at the urging of the First Lord of the Admiralty, Winston Churchill, on 16 February *Cossack* alone entered into Jossingfjord to 'verify' *Altmark*'s merchant status.[140] As she approached, *Altmark* turned on her searchlights to try to dazzle the bridge crew, whilst at the same time manoeuvred in an attempt to crush *Cossack*. It was here that the manoeuvrability of the destroyer-sized cruiser, combined with the Navy's well established ship handling skills, saved the day.[141] The result was not what *Altmark* had intended as, while it did bring the ships together, *Cossack* escaped serious damage and the opportunity arose, in the tradition of Drake and Nelson, for some of the boarding party to leap across the gap between the ships.[142] The first members of the boarding party were soon joined by others, including *Cossack*'s First Lieutenant who 'forcibly dispossessed' the *Altmark*'s captain of his ship.[143] It was an action in which four Germans were killed, five wounded and 299 prisoners rescued. *Cossack* left the fjord, leaving the *Altmark* aground with her crew.[144]

This story of heroism and success (features of 'Tribal' destroyer actions throughout their service), at a time when there was little to buoy the public mood, would

have been enough on its own to secure a place for *Cossack* in the public consciousness but her war was really only just beginning;[145] and her involvement, with others of her class, in Norway would be the next chapter.

Norway

Gurkha was named to fight and, as a 'Tribal' class destroyer, she was built to do so; and in the concentrated German air attack off Norway on 9 April, under sustained bombing, she fought to the death.[146] The sixth of her class to commission, she was the first to be sunk.[147] 1940 had started well for *Gurkha*. Together with *Nubian* she had been repeatedly engaged in hunting U-boats, without loss, but without any confirmed sinkings. However, she was eventually found success when partnered with *Le Fantasque*, the lead ship of the French *Le Fantasque* destroyer class, sinking *U-53* on 21 February.[148] Less than seven weeks later, whilst escorting the Home Fleet in tempestuous weather, she would meet her fate. At 1400hrs on 9 April the force came under attack by German Junker Ju 88 and He 111 bombers. The weather made adequate AA defence difficult, so *Ghurkha* made the courageous move to alter course in order to bring her guns to bear on the attacking aircraft. However, the new course took her away from the rest of the screen.[149] Easily singled out, she came under concentrated attack and was hit by a single bomb.[150]

The bomb struck home aft, ripping a 40ft wide hole in the starboard side, causing the aft magazine to flood and fire to break out. This led to a 45° list to starboard and the stern became awash. At 1900hrs she sank, firing into the sky almost to the very end; and it was fortunate she did so because *Aurora*, the *Arethusa* class light cruiser, alerted by the firing of high explosive shells, arrived to rescue her crew, of which 190 survived.[152]

At the beginning of the war such a response to an air attack was not unusual. There had been a continuing debate, which to some extent still exists today, about how individual ships, and groups of ships, should best respond to air attacks. The idea behind the aggressive response was that by moving into the most advantageous position for their guns to bear on targets, for example with a surface combatant fight, they would have the greatest chance of shooting down enemy aircraft. Such manoeuvring was clearly predicated on the belief that the most effective method for stopping an enemy air attack was to destroy the aircraft, but it inevitably splits up a task force, and ships can find themselves beyond the range from which they can provide mutual support. The alternative was for ships to stay together, presenting a joint wall of 'fire' which sought to drive enemy aircraft away as much as destroy them; this was the more defensive approach and became standard thinking, but the experience of *Gurkha* and other ships lost filtered into the debate.

Gurkha's loss was the subject of discussion, and responsibility for her loss sought. In his autobiography, the then Admiral Philip Vian who had commanded wrote:

> One destroyer of the Flotilla, *Gurkha*, was commanded by a noted gunnery officer, Commander Sir Anthony Buzzard. After years of training, presented at last with live targets, he was excessively annoyed by his inability to hit them, and turned his ship away from the wind and sea, to better the conditions for the control and fire of the guns.
>
> This involved leaving the cruiser screen, and I should have recalled him at once; but in those very early days of air attack on ships, the tactics to be pursued by surface forces were still being worked out, and there was no set policy. Buzzard's manoeuvre

cost him his ship, and very nearly the lives of his crew. [153]

From an officer whose writing and service suggest candour, this was an unusually equivocal summing up. Perhaps the reason is that until the Second World War no one really knew, despite the many exercises and the quantity of ink expounded upon it, what an air attack would be like. Just as with every previous war officers were quickly learning that the theory, the exercises and the training they had all completed, were only based on the best possible assumptions at the time. In war, as opposed to in naval exercises, the wrong decision could lead to much graver consequences. It is worth noting that, in the immediate aftermath, Rear Admiral Destroyers, Ronald Hamilton Curzon Hallifax, who had overall authority over destroyers in the Home Fleet at the time, wrote:

> 8. Captain (D) IV in paragraph 1 of minute II has generously accepted the responsibility for allowing GURKHA to become detached, but his minute was written on the 22nd April by which time all or most of us had realised that to remain concentrated was the best defence against air attack, whereas on the 9th April, when the attack took place this was not generally realised. Destroyers escorting Norwegian convoys when under air attack had often been out of supporting distance from each other and no harm had come to them. I knew this and had issued no instructions on the matter. I do not, therefore, consider that Captain (D) IV, is any more to blame than I am, except for the omission to notice that the GURKHA had detached herself completely as opposed to taking independent avoiding action.[154]

In his own report, Commander Buzzard cited the maximum angle of elevation of the 4.7in guns as the reason for his manoeuvre. 4in guns with a far higher angle of elevation would replace 'X' mount later in the war. However, he also claimed he was targeting a four-engined bomber type aircraft, something which is disputed as the only German aircraft of that type, the Fw 200 Condor, did not arrive in Norway for another week.[155] Buzzard's decision made at the time was, thanks to this and other experiences, not something that would be repeated. Vian recalled in his memoirs that, 'Returning from this meeting ... I observed to Captain Mountbatten ... how I viewed the Admiral's opinions about bombing with foreboding; it amounted, if hit, to losing one's reputation in addition to one's ship and, possibly, life."[156]

This was after the previously mentioned RA(D), Hallifax, following his experience of the air attacks which resulted in the loss of *Gurkha*, insisted that whether a ship was hit by a bomb or not depended upon the actions of the captain.[157] This did not sit well with either Mountbatten or Vian, both of whom seemed to grasp early on that it was an educated guess which way to dodge when the bombs dropped, and no one's honour should hang on the whim of fate such a guess.

Eskimo with her final pennant number clearly visible. Partly as a way to confuse enemies and partly as a way of reshaping the fleet, *Eskimo* changed designator letter for her pennant twice in her career. She entered serves as L75, then became F75 and finally served out the remainder of her career as G75. *(Drachinifel Collection)*

Eskimo photographed taken from the carrier *Furious* during Operation Pedestal, sporting her new bow and engaging the enemy as furiously as she could, acting as 'goalkeeper' or 'preferred last line of defence' for aircraft carriers. *(Maritime Quest)*

When discussing Norway and destroyers, however, there is one place which almost always demands most attention – Narvik. There were three battles. In one the Norwegians were overwhelmed; another ended in a draw with the Navy losing good ships; and one ended in annihilation of the enemy with the Kriegsmarine beaching destroyers so that their crews might escape. The 'Tribals' were involved in the third, but as the Navy only count the last two, it has become the Second Battle of Narvik.[158]

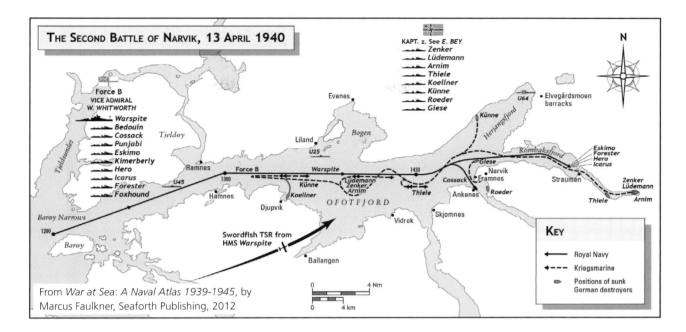

THE SECOND BATTLE OF NARVIK, 13 APRIL 1940

From *War at Sea: A Naval Atlas 1939-1945*, by Marcus Faulkner, Seaforth Publishing, 2012

The Second Battle of Narvik

It was almost exactly a month after the *Altmark* incident, when *Cossack* was back under the command of Commander Sherbrooke (who would go on to become a rear admiral and earn a Victoria Cross whilst in command of the destroyer *Onslow*), that she would achieve her next battle honour at the Second Battle of Narvik.[159] This battle would demonstrate the value of having an armament of a larger number of faster-firing guns, rather than fewer heavier guns. The First Battle of Narvik, on 10 April 1940, had been a wild affair. German ships had been badly damaged during the battle, but they had retained control of the water, while the British lost the majority of what had been a fairly effective flotilla. The Second Battle, on 13 April 1940, would correct the result. This battle had three significant differences to the first: there was a battleship in support, *Warspite*; her Swordfish airplane was able to scout ahead; and the Navy sent in its 'fighting destroyers', the 'Tribal' class.[161]

The force deployed under Admiral Whitworth contained, in addition to *Warspite*, nine destroyers: four 'Tribals', *Cossack*, *Bedouin*, *Eskimo*, and *Punjabi*; the 1935 constructed 'H' class *Hero*, whose sisters had fought in the First Battle of Narvik; the 1936 'I' class *Icarus*; the 1939 'K' class *Kimberley*; and the two 1934 'F' class vessels, *Forester* and *Foxhound*.[162] These last five ships were very much Treaty destroyers, built to the letter of the agreements, and designed for torpedo attack. Although good ships, they were at a disadvantage compared to 'Tribal' vessels in the fast-flowing skir-

mishes which followed. It was a significant force, designed to finish off any remaining German naval forces in the Narvik area, and capable of dealing with any defences that the Germans had managed to erect after the First Battle.

The effect of the aerial reconnaissance was felt almost immediately. One German destroyer, *Erich Koellner*, had been so badly damaged during the First Battle of Narvik that she was judged fit for an ambush only. However, she never made it to her ambush point of Taastadt. Instead, upon sighting the British force making their way in, she and her escort (*Hermann Kunne*) split up, with *Koellner* retreating to Djupvik Bay, from where she still hoped to launch an ambush at an opportune moment. It was not to be. They were spotted by the Swordfish crew, and when the starboard column of destroyers – the three 'Tribals' *Bedouin*, *Punjabi* and *Eskimo* – rounded the entrance to Djupvik, British guns and torpedoes had already been sighted. This resulted in a very quick, almost one-sided exchange. A torpedo and the destroyers' shells were fired in the initial salvo. These were quickly followed by shells from *Warspite* as she too rounded the southern point. Unsurprisingly, under such a weight of firepower, *Koellner* rolled over and sank.[163]

Hermann Künne had used this time to raise the alarm and had formed up with *Hans Lüdemann*, *Wolfgang Zenker* and *Bernd von Arnim* to make a run at the British force together.[164] This resulted in a melee, similar to the First Battle of Narvik, but this time the Germans were forced back up the fjord by the Navy's 'solid front line' of destroyers constantly 'altering courses and speeds as necessary to avoid the enemy fall of shot, while maintaining a steady and continuous pressure'.[165] It is here that the qualities of the 'Tribals' firepower came to the fore. However, it was not only their strength of firepower, but also their strength of design which was tested. *Punjabi* attracted particularly heavy fire, suffering much damage and casualties, but after retiring for an hour to repair herself, she re-joined the force fully combat capable, highlighting once again the resilience enshrined in the 'Tribal' class design.[166] The *Hermann Künne* split from the other three and made for Herjangsfjord, but was pursued and torpedoed by *Eskimo*, forcing her captain to beach her.[167]

At this point the British destroyers divided into two groups, one heading into Narvik harbour, led by *Cossack*, and the remainder, led by *Eskimo*, following the German destroyers as they made for Rombaksfjord.[168] *Cossack* discovered Narvik harbour still held a German destroyer, the *Diether von Roeder*.[169] This vessel had been largely immobilised in the First Battle, but still put up such fierce fire that Whitworth, looking on from *Warspite* thought it was a shore battery.[170] Despite this heavy fire and grounding on a wreck while manoeuvring and firing, *Cossack* silenced her opponent.[171] She had sustained damage, including one shell that penetrated her transmitting station[172] which housed the clock for her fire-control system, whilst another shell severed the main steam pipe, and yet another damaged a boiler room.[173] Despite this, she kept firing on local control, with the gunnery crews demonstrating their training by doing all the fire-control work manually. Targets included a troublesome German mortar on the shore, but the job mainly comprised of methodically working through any other German craft in the harbour.[174] The damage suffered by *Cossack* and *Punjabi* paled in comparison to that which *Eskimo* survived, however.

Eskimo, twice bowless but unbowed

Some people are described as being 'born under a lucky star', and if viewed in that way *Eskimo* must have been launched under an unusually lucky star. She had a long war. She had joined 6th DF, the Home Fleet 'Tribal' destroyer flotilla, just in time for the 1939 combined fleet exercises at Gibraltar where, by highlighting the strength of the Fleet,[175] the Navy tried to buy time for diplomacy. After Easter leave, she was, with her sisters *Ashanti* and *Matabele*, on a goodwill visit to Cherbourg. Once again naval diplomacy was at work, but on this occasion it was more about soft power and building of relationships, than about the open display of naval strength which took place at Gibraltar.[176] Following this her high level of activity continued unabated.

Eskimo was involved in the *Thetis* disaster, and almost fought a battle with *Faulknor*, *Foxhound* and *Firedrake* during a night passage to Scapa Flow in September 1939 when both groups were at high alert and failed to recognise each other. With her draw towards action, it is unsurprising she was in the Fourth Estuary when the first air raid took place on 17 October.[177] Her activities did not stop there, and after a winter of patrols, convoys and maintenance she was refitted just in time for the Norway campaign.

All the three Narvik battles were dirty, fast and hard; they were close-range destroyer fights, and the difficulty for the Germans was that these were the fights for which the 'Tribal' class had been built. They were the fighting cover, the suppressing fire that would allow their more conventional destroyer sisters to get close enough to launch a massed torpedo attack which, according to contemporary theory, would decide a battle. For the ships of this class, with their all-round fields of fire, the swirling mixture of smoke, metal and fire was their metier. *Eskimo* was to the fore, and exposed as she was lost her whole bow forward of 'B' mount; nonetheless she kept on fighting.[178]

Eskimo had been the last to join the force as it was being amassed, and almost immediately upon arrival took up station in the starboard line (relative to *Warspite*), with her sisters *Punjabi* and *Bedouin*. *Cossack* was in the port line, with *Kimberley* and *Foxhound*).[179] During transit these lines remained stationed close to *Warspite*, but once Ototfiord was reached they were thrown forward for optimum offensive impact. First blood went to *Eskimo* and her sisters in the starboard line, due in large part to *Warspite*'s Swordfish aircraft, which had spotted the *Erich Koellner* loitering with intent just inside the entrance to Ballengenfiord, leading to Djupvik.[180] This turned a potential ambush into a one-sided rout. The guns of the three 'Tribals' enveloped the *Erich Koellner* in such fire that she had no chance to avoid the torpedo fired by *Bedouin* which disabled her, let alone mount a proper defence.

The fight continued all the way up Ototfiord, where German vessels joined the fray, only to be forced back under weight of fire. This was something more conventionally designed British destroyers could not have achieved, but for which the design of the 'Tribals' made them more than capable. *Eskimo* and the *Hermann Künne* veered off from the main fight, the German vessel probably seeking to work around the British destroyers and either make a run for the *Warspite* or the open sea, or engage in a one-on-one duel.[181] Steaming

at speed while firing with everything they had, the engagement ended suddenly with *Eskimo* emerging victorious and the *Hermann Künne* sunk by a torpedo in Herjangsfiord. Her men had certainly acquitted themselves with honour.[182]

It was after this action that the fight reached the harbour of Narvik. It was there that the British destroyers, divided into two groups. One led by *Cossack* forced its way into Narvik while the other, led by *Eskimo*, continued to chase the retreating Germans.[183] The battle was now in its final phase. Surging up Rombaksfiord after the remaining German destroyers, *Eskimo*, *Bedouin*, *Hero*, *Icarus* and *Forester* reached the point, two thirds of the way up, where it suddenly narrows; the British destroyers knew it would be a perfect trap.

Eskimo went first; *Forrester* and *Hero* followed close behind. *Eskimo* was fulfilling the role for which her class had been built, providing cover to allow the conventional torpedo destroyers to get closer to the enemy. This she succeeded in doing, shepherding her small force through the narrows and towards the denouement of the battle. The British destroyers pushed the Germans on under a remorseless hail of fire, the Germans responding as best they could; one of their number, *Georg Thiele*, had become a blazing wreck, but in a last act of defiance, as she rolled over and sank, launched her torpedoes.[184] As *Eskimo*, along with her charges, avoided other torpedoes launched by the *Hans Lüdemann*, and tried herself to fire her last torpedo, one of the *Thiele*'s struck her forward.

The torpedo struck like Thor's hammer Mjölnir, taking off with one blow *Eskimo's* bow section up to the 'B' mount, and obliterating both 'A' mount along with seventeen crew. The strength of the design is revealed in the subsequent events. *Eskimo* did not stop. She completed her turn, fired her torpedo and the 'B' mounting

continued firing until the ammunition ran out.[185] The crew went to work lightening the upper works and shoring up the bulkheads so that she could get home.

The battle was over. Any German ships not sunk by this point had been beached by their crews, and the British destroyers were busy making sure they were properly wrecked and that no other useful shipping could be salvaged from the fiords. *Eskimo* meanwhile managed to reverse out of the fiord and was escorted back to the UK by her sister *Bedouin*, together with the two destroyers, *Hostile* and *Ivanhoe*.[186] Thus ended Narvik, one of the most notable destroyer actions of the early part of the war.

The battle demonstrated again how tough and versatile the 'Tribal' destroyers were. Even discounting Operational Irregular, *Eskimo* dodged potential destruction on a regular basis, and though she suffered more than enough severe damage, she never completely succumbed like so many of her colleagues.[187] Not only did she lose her bow at Narvik, but she lost it for a second time later in the war in a collision with *Javelin*, took part in Lofoten raid and the *Bismarck* chase, and received major bomb damage in 1943.[188] *Eskimo* played a significant part in many actions including, together with *Ashanti* and *Tartar*, Operation Torch, Operation Husky and Operation Neptune.[189] Her use in such an array of missions is proof of the 'Tribal' class design's versatility. She epitomised the fighting spirit associated with the 'Tribals', so clearly demonstrated by *Cossack* when called upon to engage the *Altmark*, or by *Sikh* at Sirte in 1942. This was a spirit of resilience, persistence and leadership, over and above what duty expected; it was a spirit which was the hallmark of the class's service, and which was a constant theme of *Eskimo*'s career.

Namsos: The Central Norwegian Campaign

With the disposal of the enemy destroyers the Navy had secured the control of the sea which had eluded them after the First Battle of Narvik. This was exploited throughout the remainder of the Norway campaign, and the 'Tribal' flotillas were significant participants. *Afridi*, as flotilla leader, was at the head of the amphibious operations conducted around Namsos as part of the Central Norway campaign, and playing a vital role supporting the land forces. During the preliminary reconnaissance, for instance, it was the 4th DF which investigated the possible landing sites and were key to the selection of Namsos.[190]

For the insertion of the troops, *Somali* was left behind to help establish a base at Namsos, after which the 'Tribals' escorted the converted liner/troop ships to Namsos, and ferried the troops to Lillesjona.[191] For operational command, both *Afridi* and *Somali* were used as general headquarters by Major General Carton De Wiart.[192] For both assignments, the increased size of the 'Tribal' design and the space it provided in comparison to other destroyers was crucial. At the same time their size in comparison to larger cruisers meant they could operate with greater nimbleness further up the narrow fiords. Later, after the withdrawal, in an operation that had foreshadowed the evacuation from Dunkirk a few weeks later, the Navy earned high praise from Carton De Wiart. 'In the course of that last endless day I got a message from the Navy to say that they would evacuate the whole of my force that night. I thought it was impossible, but learned a few hours later that the Navy do not know the word.'[193]

Such involvement could not be without cost. On 3 May 1940, exactly two years after her commission, during the transit home following the successful withdrawal, *Afridi*'s luck ran out.[194] As the convoy of transports and escorts reached the main fleet, a large force of Stukas attacked. *Afridi* was bracketed by two attacking dive bombers. Already turning to starboard, Captain Vian decided to continue the turn, but despite this attempted evasion *Afridi* was hit, the first bomb landing in the foremost boiler room causing massive damage and starting a fire; the second taking out much of the hull portside just forward of the bridge.[195] This proved too much damage even for a 'Tribal' destroyer to take although, judging from *Eskimo*'s experience, she might well have coped with either one or the other, but not both. Captain Vian and most of the ship's company were rescued before she rolled over and sank. From this point on *Cossack* became the 4th DF's main leader, a role that raised her to even greater prominence in their next major operation. *Afridi* and the 4th DF had succeeded in their mission; the troops had been withdrawn and not a single transport lost. As at Dunkirk, so at Namsos, the Navy had covered the Army's back.

Even before the Norwegian campaign was over, the use of the 'Tribals' in the destroyer flotilla formations was reduced. Subsequently this accelerated, due in part to their losses and in part to the shrinking of flotillas for strategic reasons, but mostly it was due to the operational need for these capable vessels elsewhere; their fighting power and the morale they could lend to other destroyers had been recognised. It now became more common for the class to operate in pairs. For example, by 17 May 1940, *Mohawk* and *Nubian* had been transferred from the 4th DF to the 14th DF and returned to the Mediterranean.[196] However, there were still occasions when four or more 'Tribals' would be grouped together in future battles, some of which will be discussed in later chapters.

A DIFFERENT AND NOT SO DIFFERENT KIND OF WAR 1941–2

By 1941 the war was well into its second year, a year which was marked by the entry of America, Japan and the Soviet Union, thereby turning it into a global conflict. But at the start of the year, however, this was not foreseen and the Admiralty were really expecting more of the same: Axis superiority on land in Europe offset by Britain, its Dominions and the Empire and their strength and resiliency at sea. A hard year was anticipated, but it was not expected by many to be a decisive one; it was going to take time for Britain to gather the resources to launch a counter attack, although after the successful 1940 North African Campaign the confidence for it was there.

This confidence for offensive action would fortify not only the land forces but also those at sea, and it coincided with the unleashing of a new and potent force, a force which would often collaborate with the 'Tribals' in this phase of war: the commando units. During 1941–2 the commandos and the 'Tribals' increasingly operated together. This not only influenced warship design and development during the war, but still applies in the present as modern escorts are increasingly designed to allow for the deployment of land forces, either for maritime or littoral missions. The Royal Navy were to lose ten 'Tribals' during this period, and *Somali*, torpedoed by *U-703* in September 1942, had the dubious honour to be the last 'Tribal' to be lost during the war.

The Battle of Matapan

Matapan is perhaps a less well-known battle than it should be, particularly in Britain. It was the largest fleet action the Royal Navy fought during the Second World War, and was unusual for turning out almost exactly as theorised by the one of the participants pre-war. The traditional maxim is that no plan survives first contact with the enemy, but on this occasion, from the 27 to 29 March 1941, the first, second, third and fourth contacts

Mohawk was the command of Commander Richard Jolly when war began, but after his fatal wounding on 16 October 1939, command was take up by Commander John Eaton who would command her till she was lost in 1941. *(Drachinifel Collection)*

Mashona, like most of her sisters. has relatively few photos of her taken of her as her service life was so relatively short. Here she is in 1940. *(Drachinifel Collection)*

almost went to the plan which the Navy had carried out in many pre-war exercises.

The Navy had planned for a chasing battle, one in which a fleet seeks either to disengage or at the least avoid a confrontation, whilst the other fleet 'chases' it. Rather like the development of the strike carrier *Ark Royal*, intended to carry as many strike aircraft as possible and to be able attack the enemy both at sea and in harbour and which emerged from the research done for the Harbour Attack Committee, a sub-committee of the Parliamentary Committee for Imperial Defence, this battle plan was a product of experience in the First World War, of post-Jutland frustration. However, the

Matabele started the war with the newest propellers. After the *Thetis* incident she had been dry-docked and had them replaced. She would be perfectly placed to go to the help of HMS *Spearfish*, another submarine in trouble, in September 1939, which had a happier resolution than the *Thetis* incident. *(Drachinifel Collection)*

plan was not without its difficulties, especially if it was to be implemented at night. The biggest impediment to success was communication. How would ships keep their communications discreet in order not to reveal their position, yet exchange enough information for an Admiral to co-ordinate a tricky series of manoeuvres to achieve the desired consequence? What was this plan?

It was a plan which involved ranges and rates of interception. The longest range and the highest rate of interception belonged to the carrier-borne aircraft, which would be used to slow down the enemy fleet's progress by launching attacks on their ships. Torpedo bombers were ideally suited to this role. A torpedo would either hit and damage a ship, or the manoeuvring of ships trying to avoid torpedo attack would break up the cohesion and formation of the fleet. With multiple aircraft striking from as many points on the compass as could be achieved, this type of battle becomes a defending admiral's nightmare. The enemy fleet would be located either by scouting cruisers or aircraft, and if not already there at the point when the enemy fleet is smarting from air attack, cruisers would move in to maintain contact if weather made air shadowing impossible; they

would also provide a better guide point for subsequent air attacks rather than bearings estimates based on sightings. It was in this role that the involvement of the 'Tribals' came into being, making up for the lack of cruiser numbers and filling gaps in the scouting line.

However, this was neither the end of their involvement, nor the end of the plan. It would be the battleships and any other available cruisers closing in, as attacks by aircraft continued, possibly supplemented by 'Tribal' torpedo attacks, that would further impede enemy progress. The ideal culmination of such a battle would be the launching of devastating fire from massed heavy artillery, combined with air attack and a massed destroyer attack, spearheaded by the 'Tribals'.[197] This was a well thought-through battle plan and it was adaptable to circumstances.

More importantly, however, especially in the light of the events of the battle, this was something which had been practised live as well as war gamed, sometimes even through extensive exercises which combined both mediums, and most often in the Mediterranean. For such a decisively offensive plan, the circumstances of its implementation were defensive, in that they were about maintaining dominance in the Mediterranean, not achieving control. So, despite the propaganda, it

Bedouin in Iceland after Narvik, preparing to escort *Southern Prince* across the Atlantic with equipment for the battleship *Rodney*'s refit. (*Maritime Quest*)

was no Trafalgar, but also no Jutland; if any battle was its forerunner, in terms of impact and damage at least, then it would be the First Battle of Heligoland Bight. For the 'Tribal' class the battle was important because two of their number, *Mohawk* and *Nubian*, of the 14th DF, were selected by Admiral Cunningham for a critical role in an act of subterfuge. It was not a role for which they had been particularly planned or conceived, but it was a role which was critical if Cunningham was to not only overcome the major problem, locating the enemy, but to actually succeed in carrying the battle plan out.

It was, because of the difficulty of finding the enemy and their co-operating by being in the right place for a battle, unlikely that the plan would come to fruition. Cunningham and the Mediterranean Fleet therefore went to a lot of trouble to increase its likelihood, to encourage the Regia Marina to come out to sea and to encourage it as far towards the eastern Mediterranean as they could. This included staging their own 'maskirovka', which although a term drawn from Russian operational theory denoting a combined political, strategic and tactical military deception, describes well the level of operational subterfuge which Cunningham conceived and enacted. However, even with all that work, intelligence suggested that battle was still not thought a likely outcome. The Navy were relying on signals traffic analysis – the increase in frequency and length of transmissions, along with some intercepts – which suggested the Italians were heading to sea from Naples to attack

Maori had not had quite the same experience and blessing as her sister *Ashanti*, but she did receive two 'tiki' (Maori Totem Poles) from New Zealand and instructions for how to perform a Hakka. (*Drachinifel Collection*)

the Greek convoy running between Greece and Egypt.

The movement of the Italian cruisers in the Ionian Sea, confirmed by a sighting from a Sunderland flying boat, finally provided Cunningham and his officers with the opportunity to enact their plan. On 27 March Cunningham went ashore in Alexandria with an empty suitcase, in order to look as if he was going to stay the night in order to play golf at the same club as the Japanese Ambassador. The ships issued dinner invitations and put up awnings to provide outside entertaining space. In simple terms, the Navy looked as if it had little intention of going to sea. The 'Tribals' played a part in this; if any ships were likely to be deployed to reinforce the convoys it would be them, but they were in harbour and just as stately adorned as if they had been cruisers.

With all this in place, and with the Italian Air Force being less than attentive the plan worked and, other than picking up the cruiser squadron, the Regia Marina did not realise the extent of the Navy's deployment. The RAF maximised air reconnaissance over the southern Ionian and Aegean seas, which complemented that being carried out by the fleet. When Cunningham arrived back onboard *Warspite* in the early evening the flags were hoisted and the Battle Squadron made for sea.

This fleet was a formidable force, with Cunningham's direct command, Force A alone containing, alongside *Warspite*, two of her *Queen Elizabeth* class sisters, *Barham* and *Valiant*, along with the *Illustrious* class aircraft carrier *Formidable*, nine destroyers, including the two 'Tribals' *Mohawk* and *Nubian*, grouped into

the 14th DF with the 'J' class vessels *Janus* and *Jervis*. At sea already was Force B under the command of Vice Admiral Light Forces, Henry Daniel Pridham-Wippell, which comprised of four light cruisers, *Ajax*, *Gloucester*, *Orion* and the Australian *Sydney*, as well as three destroyers. Cunningham could also call upon the escorts of two convoys, three more light cruisers, including the *Dido* class *Bonaventure* and five destroyers. Whilst the abandoning convoys would be unusual, as later events involving 'Tribal' class vessels during the hunting of the *Bismarck* will illustrate, it was not unknown if the situation required it.

Thanks to the air reconnaissance the Navy quickly found the Italian forces, but Cunningham's flagship, *Warspite*, had trouble getting up speed, while Vice Admiral Pridham-Wippell, who had sailed from Piraeus, was engaging the Italian cruisers away to the northwest. *Warspite*'s sister ship, *Valiant*, along with *Mohawk* and *Nubian* were therefore ordered to surge ahead of the main fleet to support them.

Hardly had the order been sent than it was cancelled because the Italians had broken off the engagement and were attempting to withdraw. During the afternoon, after the carrier *Formidable* had launched her first strike at the Italian force, the Regia Marina continued to withdraw, albeit at a slower pace. Cunningham grew worried about the security of his communications. Using radio would in all probability have alerted the Italians to the presence of Force A, and thereby reveal the scale of the operation. Cunningham therefore deployed the 'Tribal' sisters forward to provide a visual signal link using flags and signal lamps between *Warspite* and Pridham-Wippell.

This was critical. Cunningham was attempting to manoeuvre in preparation for a decisive battle, which, if successful, could deliver permanent superiority in the Mediterranean, consolidating the strategic security which the airstrike on the Italian fleet at Taranto had provided all too briefly. A successful battle could, in theory, have destroyed not only the Regia Marina flagship, *Vittorio Veneto*, but also a large number of their vital heavy cruisers and destroyers, and even more crucially it would have deprived them of an operationally significant proportion of their trained personnel. This was the engagement and the outcome that Cunningham was seeking. The strikes from *Formidable* continued, the second managing to damage the *Vittorio Veneto*, the third crippling the cruiser *Pola*. This further slowed down the Italian force, forcing them to leave an entire division of their force behind in order to try to recover the stricken cruiser.

Cunningham used Pridham-Wippell's force to keep up the pressure all afternoon, while at the same time maintaining his distance with his force, and as a result the Italians did not realise just how close and powerful the British force was. In addition, by being careful with his distance, Cunningham knew he could not only react quickly if Pridham-Wippell's cruisers were pressed or other circumstances demanded intervention, but could also choose his direction of engagement for maximum effect. *Mohawk* and *Nubian* made this possible, and could be used in this role because they had the firepower needed to survive on their own as well as speed and seakeeping capability. The two 'Tribals' continued providing the visual link until dusk, after which such communication became impractical: flags being invis-

Mashona was the first Royal Navy vessel to carry the name and was named after the Shona tribe of Rhodesia. She was commissioned straight into service, almost straight into the war, being commissioned on 1 March 1939. She escorted King George VI and Queen Elizabeth aboard the *Empress of Australia* in May, before taking part in the *Thetis* disaster. *(Drachinifel Collection)*

ible, signal lamps far too visible. The 'Tribals' were now recalled to 14th DF stationed to the starboard of *Warspite* and her sisters to provide cover for a strike in the event of a major action.[198] It was also hoped that they could 'illuminate' the enemy by fire, one of the most interesting and pragmatic ideas of British night fighting doctrine.

This idea of using 4.7in shells, exploding against larger enemy warship armour, to highlight them to both the 'Tribals' and any other British destroyer's torpedo crews would, however, go untested at Matapan. As the attack never took form, the destroyers were instead employed later during the rounding-up operation, delivering a *coup de grâce* with torpedoes where necessary, and it was *Nubian* which finally sank the cruiser *Pola*. Cunningham's Battle Squadron had come across *Pola*, with her two sisters *Fiume* and *Zara*, catching them completely unawares and destroying them in short order at close range. It was not what Cunningham had hoped for, but with three heavy cruisers and a brace of destroyers incapacitated, plus further damage inflicted on the wider fleet, Cunningham was not going to complain. Significant as it was, and successful as the plan was in forcing the engagement, Matapan was not as decisive as it could have been. The failure to follow up with the main force and the concentration on the cruisers, due in part to a communication misunderstanding, meant that this battle as said achieved dominance, but not control. As such it represented only the beginning of the 'Tribal' story against the Italian forces; soon they would prove themselves just as they had in Norway against their German foes, but not without losses.

Loss for the 'Tribals' came quickly on the heels of victory when *Mohawk* was sunk by to a torpedo launched by an Italian destroyer, herself severely damaged. This was the same 'Tribal' commanded by Commander Jolly when he received his mortal wound, and

Punjabi at anchor in 1939. *(Drachinifel Collection)*

in a way her end befitted that. The evening of 15 April began, as so many evenings had for 14th DF (comprising the two 'Tribals', *Mohawk* and *Nubian* along with two 'J' class destroyers *Janus* and *Jervis*), leaving Malta in response to air reconnaissance reports of a Tripoli-bound convoy off Cape Bon. This convoy comprised of the Italian *Sabaudia* carrying munitions and the four German freighters *Adana*, *Aegina*, *Arta* and *Iserlohn* loaded with men and vehicles, escorted by three destroyers, one larger 'Navigatori' class vessel, *Luca Tarigo*, and two smaller members of the ill-fated *Folgore* class, *Baleno* and *Lampo*.

Luca Tarigo was an interesting design. Ships of her class had been given a centreline midships mounting, a 'Q' position in British parlance. As such it kept the centre of mass as close to the dimensional centre of the ship's hull as possible. This weapon enabled her to engage from the beam with all six guns, but meant that she had no preponderance of fire either forward or aft. It also kept top weight down because no superfiring positions were required. She was also armed with two triple 21in torpedo launchers (which had replaced the pre-war fitted 21in, 18in and 21in torpedo launchers). *Luca Tarigo* was command ship of the convoy, and the arrangement of her weapons made this the logical position because it permitted maximum freedom of manoeuvre to enable all her guns and torpedoes to bear rapidly on any attack.

The 14th DF located the convoy using radar at 0210hrs on 16 April and spotted the convoy against the moonlight at a distance of about six miles. When they

were about 2,400 yards ahead they launched what might be considered a textbook attack. *Lampo* was taken out by *Janus* and *Jervis* in a hailstorm of 4.7in and 2pdr fire. In return, the Italian vessel fired three salvos from her four guns and launched her torpedoes. *Baleno* had the misfortune to run into *Nubian* which wrecked her bridge and caused so much damage that she was forced out of the fight before capsizing and sinking later that day. The 14th DF then started working through the merchantmen with an efficiency echoing Narvik and Operation Claymore (to be discussed next).

It was at this point that *Luca Tarigo* engaged in the fight. The British destroyers had managed to drive between *Lucia Tarigo* and her charges, and it was as they reduced speed to attack those charges that she entered the fight. She was hit by fire from all the 14th DF, with the two 'J' class vessels firing torpedoes at her. Seeing her successfully crippled, the British carried on finishing off the merchant vessels, but it was now, as she lay damaged and stationary in the water, that *Luca Tarigo* launched her torpedoes. At 0230hrs, twenty minutes after the engagement had begun, and just after avoiding the ramming bow of the leading merchant vessel, *Mohawk* was hit close to 'Y' mount on the starboard side.

This was similar to the damage that *Eskimo* suffered at Narvik. As with *Eskimo*, the guns continued firing and within five minutes her chief engineer reported to her captain, Commander Eaton, that *Mohawk* was ready to move again. However, that was not to be. A second torpedo hit the bulkhead between No 2 and No 3 boiler rooms, causing instantaneous damage. In addition to burst boilers, the upper deck split, causing the torpedo tubes to crash down and crush most of the

Mohawk was one of the 'Tribal' class vessels that served as linchpins for Admiral Cunningham's plan, which depended upon radio silence so that the Italians not realise the extent of the British 'maskirovka' before the Battle of Matapan. *(Drachinifel Collection)*

watch below. It was the end. With no time to launch boats, most of the crew had to swim for it, although some managed to get into one of the six Carley floats which made it clear. All three other ships in the flotilla helped out with recovery of her crew and, including the losses of the other ships, only forty-three British sailors were lost. Then *Janus* launched a torpedo at *Mohawk* which was exhibiting the 'Tribal' class's trademark stubborn buoyancy. Was it worth losing forty-three lives and a very useful destroyer in such a way?

For three enemy destroyers alone, the loss of one might be justified, but for the additional destruction of five valuable merchant ships along with 350 troops, 300 vehicles and 3,500 tons of stores and ammunition from the Afrika Korps, the price was undoubtedly warranted, and such missions were the entire reason for maintaining Malta. As with many of the 'Tribal' class losses, they were risked because it was justified, and it was not only in the Mediterranean that they were being risked during this period; in Norway, in March, the 'Tribals' of the 6th DF took on the role of escorting the landing forces of Operation Claymore into the Arctic Circle.

Operation Claymore

The events of March 1941 around the Lofoten raid were, in terms of strategic importance if not in terms of fighting, not dissimilar to those around the more familiar battle off Cape Matapan.[199] Taking place on 4

March 1941, prior to Matapan, it should probably have been examined first for chronological reasons, but its impact is better understood in the context of Matapan, Claymore, like so many military operations conducted in the twentieth century, was about oil, not in this case crude oil, but fish oil. Fish oil was a key requirement for many of the munitions and lubricants upon which the Nazi war machine depended. Lofoten was a critical point in the chain of production for those supplies. An Allied attack was, however, a long-range gamble. The force would have no air cover; no land aircraft would be within range and no aircraft carriers were available. Furthermore, it would be supported by no ships larger than a destroyer. The force was going to have to be entirely self-reliant and operate in the face of significant potential enemy retaliation.

Four 'Tribals' were to provide 80 per cent of the total fighting force. Carrying by this time a quick firing (QF) 4in anti-aircraft gun in place of an 'X' mounting, they were judged capable of putting up a good defence against anything, and of being a serious threat offensively.[200] Along with the converted Dutch passenger ferries acting as infantry landing ships, *Queen Emma* and *Princess Beatrix* (officially designated Landing Ship Infantry (Medium), LSI(M), they were to be supplemented by *Legion*, an 'L' class destroyer which had 4in guns fitted in all mountings, making her, in theory at least, an anti-aircraft destroyer.[201] The 4in gun was an interesting weapon. While it was primarily intended for AA use, just as the 4.7in gun with which the 'Tribals' were armed was primarily orientated for anti-ship use, it was still an effective general-purpose weapon, especially when used against lighter faster craft such as E-boats – just as the 4.7in was a reasonably potent anti-

Matabele seen in 1939, highlighting the pre-war Home Fleet destroyer look, the peacetime presence shading, and the commonality of the weapons. *(Maritime Quest)*

aircraft weapon, as long as the aircraft were not attacking from too close to vertical. This combination of weapons and ships, supported by a considerable amount of unconventional thinking, was to prove important to operational success.

Operation Claymore had the potential to cause trouble, particularly beyond that area where the force was dependent on Allied assistance and co-operation. The force would refuel from the tanker RFA *War Pindari*, at Skalafjorour, in the British-occupied Danish Faeroe Islands.[202] More significantly, it would be an at-

tack on a key Norwegian industry. If improperly handled it had the potential to cause not only reprisals, economic or worse, on Norwegian civilians by Nazi authorities, but also deaths at British hands, with the attendant political consequences.[203] For this reason the rules of engagement were tight. In fact, compared with some of those used in later operations, they could almost be described as modern with their focus on avoiding civilian casualties and damage to civilian

Matabele was the only ship to ever carry this name to serve with the Royal Navy, and she adopted the Zulu motto *hamba kahle* meaning 'go in peace'. She has accounted for all the name's battle honours, in Norway 1940 and the Arctic 1941–2. *(Drachinifel Collection)*

infrastructure. Partly, the restrictions were due to the novelty of the operation, for it was the first such operation to be conducted. And it was to be conducted against a relatively densely populated area for such a target. It was incredibly important to not upset the Norwegian Government in exile, nor give ammunition to the Nazi propaganda machine.

Operation Claymore was to be the first major commando raid of the Second World War and would set the pattern for many operations to come. It was a departure from the previous small amphibious operations, Valentine and Fork, respectively the British occupation of the Faroe Islands and the invasion of Iceland, earlier in the war. It would make use of specialist shipping and specialist troops, alongside the very special generalists, the 'Tribal' class. Not only was all this assorted equipment to be used, but to complicate matters the landings would not be concentrated; in another parallel with modern operational concepts they were to be distinctly dispersed. Some troops were going to Stamsund on the island of Vestvagoy, some to the islands of Henningsvaer, while others were dispatched to Svolvaer on Austvagoya and still more to Brettesnes on Stormolla.[204] This was by definition a widely distributed operation, something which in the pre-helicopter-assisted era of amphibious warfare was a much bigger risk than it would be today; there was no quick way to concentrate ground forces should unexpected resistance be met, and if such circumstances did arise, the ground forces' dependence on the support of warships was absolute.

Fortunately, this was not put to the test, but the possibility does make the division of warships very logical. It was *Legion* that escorted the commandos to Stamsund, the attack taking place furthest from the mainland and therefore least likely to suffer any surprises.[205] In contrast, the commandos for Hennigsvaer, Svolvaer and Brettesnes were escorted by *Eskimo*, *Tartar* and *Bedouin* respectively, with *Somali* going from port to port to provide support, while at the same time acting as both naval and military command post, having embarked the commander Brigadier Haydon and Rear Admiral Louis Keppel Hamilton.[206] When considering the Namsos experience where air attacks and fast German counter-attack had been critical factors in operations, this is understandable. Although it must have put a strain on the commanding officer at the time, Captain Clifford Carlson, it did not adversely affect his subsequent career, which included command, as Captain, of the battleship *Nelson*, and promotion to Vice Admiral and the running of Singapore for the Navy.

The commandos were able to achieve multiple landings because of the unique davit launching system of the LSI(M)'s Landing Craft Mechanised (LCM(1)), which enabled them to be launched in the same wave as their LCAs (Landing Craft Assault), the standard infantry carrier employed by the Navy throughout the war. This mattered because LCM(1)s could accommodate quadruple the tonnage of a LCA, enabling commandos to take essential equipment with them. It was these little ships, far more than their transports, which needed the escort, and previous experience in Norway had already demonstrated their vulnerability. It was while acting as a ranging shield that *Somali*, the 'Tribal' not assigned for close escort, took part in the only naval fire-fight of the operation when she encountered *Krebs*, an armed trawler, which yielded a set of rotors for an Enigma machine and some code books which were of great use to Bletchley Park. However, the German vessel only managed three shots before being permanently silenced after she ran aground on fire and out of control. The five surviving crew were picked up by *Somali*. It was a very one-sided exchange.[207]

Bedouin intercepted the unarmed coastal ferry *Mira*, which had the misfortune of being in the wrong place at the wrong time. Unexpectedly, however, this vessel continued on her course despite being ordered to stop because an officer in charge of the German equivalent of an Entertainments National Service Association Group had put a gun to the captain's head and wanted to go down fighting.[208] *Bedouin*, in case the ferry passed word to other German occupation forces, had to sink her and then rescue the survivors, including the gun-wielding officer and the captain. At the same time, *Tartar* continued the tradition of efficiency established during Narvik, focussing on the valuable merchant ships with her 4.7in main guns and diligently sinking them. Mostly these were of the coastal variety, but they also included vessels such as the 9,780-ton *Hamburg* (a refrigerated fish factory ship in great demand due the Battle of the Atlantic) and which the naval demolition party had fancied as their prize/transport home to the UK, but they had forgotten to tell anyone else of their plan.[209] Rather unusually for her, *Eskimo* had little to do, and the expected level of opposition did not materialise.

This was particularly true of the air threat, feared throughout the planning, but which only materialised at the end when a lone reconnaissance aircraft appeared. However, it never reached within range of the task force's guns, and nor could it manage to send any report as *Bedouin* jammed its signal.[210] No further aircraft appeared and the force made it home successfully to Scapa at 1300hrs on 6 March. The force had sunk ten ships for a total of 19,350 tons of shipping and destroyed eighteen factories including eight critical to

Maori leaving Malta in 1941 . *(Drachinifel Collection)*

emollient production. Furthermore, 800,000 gallons of oil in seven tank farms were burned. The force had rounded this all off by taking 213 German and 12 Quislings prisoner, as well as 300 Norwegian volunteers. For Combined Operations Command it was testimony to a job well done.

With most of the action taking place primarily on the land, why did the destroyers matter? Simply put, it was the weapons of the destroyers, their torpedoes, 4.7in and 4in guns, that had provided confidence to the force as well as the necessary firepower. The ships and their crews had proved themselves in a mission which traditionally would have been conceived as a cruiser-based operation, but was judged achievable because of the capabilities of the 'Tribals' which made up the force. It was these capabilities which contributed to the operation's success and Lofoten was not the last time these strengths would be called upon; long-range, independent operations would be a feature of the 'Tribal' class experience throughout their war service.

Sink the *Bismarck*

If the Norway campaign can be said to have enabled the 'Tribals' to demonstrate their fighting prowess, especially their ability to give and take punishment while providing cover to more conventional destroyers, the story of the operation to find and sink the *Bismarck*

highlights their cruiser style duties: scouting, fixing and keeping in contact with the enemy.[211] On 23 May 1941 *Cossack*, again under the command of Captain Vian, along with her 4th DF sisters *Maori*, *Sikh* and *Zulu*, a Polish destroyer *Piorun*, and the AA cruiser *Cairo*, were escorting a troop convoy south-bound from the Clyde and were roughly 300 miles west of Ireland.[212] It was then that an alert came through: *Bismarck* and the cruiser *Prinz Eugen* had been sighted in Denmark Strait. The next day they received the shocking news that the pride of the Royal Navy, the battlecruiser *Hood*, following an engagement with *Bismarck*, had been sunk.[213] Vian's first reaction was to order *Cairo* to a station thirty miles in the direction of the enemy to provide early warning, and this is how the convoy proceeded until 0330hrs on the 26th.[214]

At this point Vian received orders to abandon the convoy, with all five destroyers under his command, and to join Admiral Tovey and his flagship *King George V*. Tovey had had to order many of his own destroyers to return to port because they were running out of fuel.[215] At 0800hrs Vian received the sighting report from a Catalina search aircraft giving the actual position of *Bismarck*. Based on this information he decided to head straight for *Bismarck* as he believed his was the best placed force to intercept her. However, he was unable to tell Tovey of his decision due to prior orders for the maintenance of radio silence.[216] Fortunately for both the Navy, and potentially Vian's career, this proved to be a propitious move. When the 4th DF reached *Bismarck*, they arrived 'to join the fray at the moment they were most needed'.[217] The 'Town' class cruiser *Sheffield*, which had established contact during the day and was still shadowing, had suffered damage to her radar and contact would have surely been lost during the night had Vian's force not arrived in time to prevent a potential German rescue mission of the by now stricken *Bismarck*.[218]

Contact would now not be lost thanks to the fortuitous arrival and timing of the 'back pocket cruisers', Vian's destroyers, which carried out the cruiser role and kept in touch with *Bismarck* throughout the night.[219] However, Vian being the leader he was, they were never just going to shadow. It was almost inevitable that the 'Tribals' would attempt to combine the cruiser role of shadowing with the destroyer role of slowing the enemy, although, of course, *Ark Royal*'s Swordfish torpedo bombers had arguably already accomplished this mission with a hit to *Bismarck*'s rudder.[220]

A destroyer slows down an enemy ship in the same way as it seeks to sink it, with torpedoes, and if by aiming to do the former it accomplishes the latter, that is a bonus. After the *Piorun* spotted *Bismarck* at 2238hrs, the flotilla took up shadowing positions, and Vian gave the order 'to attack independently as opportunity offered'.[221]

In total, sixteen torpedoes were launched over the course of six attacks. Three hits were registered, with flames on *Bismarck*'s forecastle visible to all the ships after two of the strikes, although these were quickly extinguished.[222] As dawn broke on the 27th, *King George V* and *Rodney* drew near to finish off the German battleship, escorted by the those 'Tribals' of the 6th DF which still had fuel, *Somali*, *Tartar* and *Mashona*.[223] The subsequent battle was fierce until *Bismarck* was finally defeated and sunk. The duties of the 'Tribals' of the 4th DF were not over for all the ships of the 6th DF had by now all been sent home. This meant *Cossack*, *Sikh* and *Zulu* of the 4th DF had the crucial duty of escorting the battleships *King George V* and *Rodney* back to Scarpa Flow.[224] Had these ships had been lost to the gathering U-boats then the Battle of the Atlantic, in terms of managing the surface raider threat, could have become very problematic and other theatres would have suffered as a consequence.[225] *Maori* remained, together with the cruiser *Dorsetshire*, picking up survivors from *Bismarck* before hurrying to join with the rest of the 4th DF.[226] This was not the last time the 'Tribals' would be involved in hunting 'large prey'.

It was at this moment that a cat, of much myth and some history, mingled its story in with that of the 'Tribals'. The story goes that one of *Bismarck*'s feline crew survived her sinking and was rescued by the crew of *Cossack* and christened Oscar, or Oskar. He did not, however, prove such a good luck charm, though he himself survived the sinking of both *Cossack* and, later, the carrier *Ark Royal*. Re-christened Unsinkable Sam, he eventually found himself assigned to Gibraltar naval base for the rest of his service career.

Mohawk in a photo which seems to be have been taken just on the cusp of war, as she was to become G59 in the autumn of 1940. Taken after March 1939 she is dressed for leaving port, consistent with peacetime practice. (Drachinifel Collection)

Somali at speed. *(Drachinifel Collection)*

Operation Aerial and Convoys from Malta to Murmansk

Convoys, whether abandoned to chase *Bismarck*, protected around coastal waters, or escorted while crossing the Atlantic or Arctic, were a big part of the fighting destroyer story. Even *Gurkha*, the first 'Tribal' to have been sunk, had already taken part in escorting at least six convoys before she was lost in April 1940. The rest of the class were to be equally heavily involved; for example, *Nubian* accompanied at least twenty-three convoys, *Ashanti* twenty-one, *Eskimo* twenty and *Tartar* twenty-five. The class average was roughly fourteen convoys each. These figures do little to describe the experience of any convoy, nor the experience of the least well known of the class, *Punjabi*, veteran of at least eleven convoys, the story of which illustrates the convoy experience well.

Punjabi's early convoy experience included the evacuation of St Nazaire, Operation Aerial. Between 17 and 20 June 1940 she saw constant action, first coming under incessant air attack as she and other destroyers ferried troops from St Nazaire to Quiberon Bay, the closest spot the transports could reach, and subsequently, after escorting the transports home to Plymouth, returning alone to rescue the Polish troops left behind to cover the escape. It was also discovered that there were survivors from one of the transports, the requisitioned liner *Lancastria* which had been sunk with a loss of perhaps as many as 5,000 troops. With German troops closing in on the nearby hospital where the survivors were abandoned, volunteers from *Punjabi* completed several trips by 'borrowed' truck in order to rescue as many of those left behind as they could.

For a 'Tribal' class destroyer, convoy duty did not always assume what is traditionally meant by the expression: close escort work. While 'Tribals' did sometimes perform this duty, they were more often assigned to scouting, being positioned far enough ahead, or travelling the route unaccompanied to trigger traps and either sweep the waters clear of any threat that they could out match, such as destroyers or submarines, and report any threat they could not tackle. This role was crucial to the safety of convoys even after the introduction of Airborne Early Warning systems in the form of radar-carrying Swordfish in 1941. Frequently beyond help from other escorts, 'Tribals', with their excellent mix of capabilities, were well suited to this role.

For *Punjabi* and her crew, life on the Arctic convoys began as it would go on, with a lot of action and plenty of heavy weather. *Punjabi* was one of four vessels which made up Rear Admiral Vian's Force K. The other vessels were her sister *Tartar* and the cruisers *Aurora* and the flagship *Nigeria*. This force was set up on 27 July 1941 for two main roles, though at times it was divided. The first role was to cover Operation Gauntlet between 25 August and 3 September, a raid on northern Norway (to be precise, Spitsbergen in the Svalbard Archipelago) to destroy coalmines and shipping infrastructure, thereby denying coal to Germany. The second was to assess the passage to Russia and try to compensate for the Navy's reluctance to base a surface strike force in Russia despite the diplomatic and political pressure being brought to bear for such an action. Gauntlet was successful: the reassurance of the Russians less so. That would be an ongoing saga, and all the time the Russians could not guarantee the defences of their ports (especially against air attacks) it was judged best to deploy submarines rather than risk surface ships.

From an operational perspective it is interesting to note that, despite the 24-hour daylight, allowing for almost constant surveillance by German reconnaissance aircraft, most were stationed far away in the south with the German Norwegian occupation forces. Consequently, there were no attacks on the forces involved in Gauntlet; but the threat of such attacks was the justification for not basing a surface force in Russia, something which Anthony Eden as Foreign Secretary had promised their Ambassador to Britain, although without first checking with the Admiralty.

Gauntlet was swiftly followed by Operation Strength, in which the oldest carrier in the Fleet, *Argus*, was supported by the 'County' class cruiser *Shropshire* and three 'Tribals', *Punjabi*, together with her sisters *Matabele* and *Somali*. The operation involved the twenty-two Hurricanes of No 151 Wing RAF, aboard *Argus*. Together with fifteen more aboard the merchant ships of another convoy, Operation Dervish, and personnel carried aboard the 'Tribals', it was hoped Operation Strength would provide critical protection for the subsequent convoys as they reached the air support range off the Russian coast. This was part of the Operation Benedict deployment, whereby Hurricanes would be deployed to Vaenga (modern-day Severomorsk) from where they would operate whilst simultaneously training up Russian crews to take over. The goal was achieved and unloading at Archangel was completed by 12 September 1941. The British air crews were withdrawn in November, and the Russians maintained units to cover the ports and convoy approaches for the rest of the war. Following these operations the more routine convoy duties began, although not necessarily so in the case of *Punjabi*.

Punjabi would often be attached to the covering force rather than the convoy, acting as part of the fighting strength that was in place to deal with any major surface threat that might emerge from the Norwegian fiords. One such occasion was during the emergence of the *Tirpitz* during the PQ12 and QP8 'transition window'. This is when both convoys had been timed to be at sea so that the covering forces could be at maximum potential strength to deal with such a threat, but it is also when the convoys are actually passing each other. *Punjabi* was ordered out to sea with a mixed cruiser/destroyer force to try to locate the *Tirpitz*, but the Ger-

man battleship, despite achieving some near misses, was already running south back to Trondheim, and the Navy never caught up with her.

1942 continued to be an eventful period for *Punjabi*. After being part of the covering force for PQ13 (along with sisters *Ashanti*, *Bedouin*, *Eskimo* and *Tartar*), Convoy QP10 would see *Punjabi* as close escort. *Punjabi* had not originally been assigned this role, but after the air attacks on PQ13, she was sent to reinforce the convoy forming up in Kola inlet. They sailed on 10 April in snowy, foggy weather, with bad visibility, and the captain, Commander The Hon J M G Waldegrave, kept a careful watch over the icy waters. Despite the weather, the first air attacks, from the Junkers Ju 88s, arrived the following day. Although a pair were shot down, with the twin 4in AA mount earning an honourable mention, SS *Empire Cowper* was sunk with the loss of nine crew. The following day *U-435* sank two merchant ships, the Russian freighter *Kiev* and the American cargo vessel *El Occidente*. Attacks by Ju 88s continued, with *Punjabi* continually finding herself in harm's way by being positioned up threat. Nevertheless, they successfully fought the attacks until weather, first in the form of fog and then gale force winds accompanied them all the way to Iceland where they arrived on the 22 March. On that occasion fog saved the convoy, but two months later, whilst part of the distant cover for PQ15, more fog, technical failures and navigational mistakes led to a collision with the 35,000-ton battleship *King George V*. *Punjabi* was sunk and only 169 of her crew were rescued, all from the forward half.

Return to the Mediterranean

While escorting convoys was a key role, it was in the cruiser role of surface sweep (the 'offensive' counterpart to those sweeps carried out to secure convoy routes) that the 'Tribal' class contributed to the success of the Battle of Cape Bon in December 1941. Two of their number, *Sikh* and *Maori*, along with a Dutch ship, *Isaac Sweers*, and another destroyer, the 'L' class *Legion*, sank two Italian light cruisers which in design were similar to that preferred by the Mediterranean Fleet's command during the pre-build 'Tribal' discussions as examined in Chapter 1.[227] Cape Bon was a battle which clearly showed both the capabilities of the Navy's destroyer force as a whole and the 'Tribal' class in particular, as the following accounts demonstrate.[228]

Malta – Cape Bon –Tennyson Randle Ford[229]

Commanding Officer, HMS 'Sikh' and the Senior Officer of Group I, including HM Ships 'Legion'

Matabele in 1942 with an altogether more complicated paint scheme than her previous photo. This depicts one of the versions of a 'disruptive paint scheme' adopted as the war went on to make it harder, especially for submarines, to spot ships. This photo is also taken after the 'X' mount was changed to twin 4in guns to provide improved air defence. *(Maritime Quest)*

and 'Maori' and HNMS 'Isaac Sweers'. The Allied force was steaming south in line ahead at high speed in a narrow channel off Cape Bon between the coast and an Italian minefield when two Italian cruisers were sighted ahead steaming on the same course. Commander Stokes was about to overtake and attack the cruisers, when the latter turned 16 points; he therefore reduced speed to avoid showing a big bow wave, kept on the landward side and successfully avoided being sighted by the enemy. 'Sikh' obtained two hits with torpedoes on the leading cruiser, which burst into flames, and attacked the second cruiser so successfully with gunfire that she only fired one ineffective salvo and was destroyed by 'Legion' and 'Maori'. A small destroyer which appeared on 'Sikh's' starboard side was engaged with pom-pom and 0.5inch guns and was damaged; a second destroyer, or E-boat, was probably destroyed by the Allied force

Sikh – Cape Bon – Commander Graham Henry
Stokes RN[230]

3. I immediately reduced the speed of the force under my command in order to avoid showing a big phosphorescent bow wave and led inshore so as to get between the enemy and the land, which, I judged, would give me a chance of getting in unobserved.

4. The manoeuvre was successful beyond my wildest expectations and after passing the customary warning signals to the ships astern, I engaged the leading cruiser with torpedoes and the second with guns at a range of about one thousand yards. Two of my torpedoes hit the leading ship which immediately burst into flames forward and after, and the second ship fired one salvo from her main armament (which salvo burst on the foreshore of Cape Bon) before she was silenced by three well-directed salvoes from 'Sikh' and a torpedo amidships from 'Legion', and she disappeared in a cloud of smoke and I did not see her again. I afterwards engaged a torpedo boat, thought to be of the 'Spica' class, with my short range weapons only as she passed so close and at such a high rate of change of bearing that the main armament could not be brought to bear.

Maori – Cape Bon – Commander Rafe Edward
Courage RN[231]

3. After your torpedoes had damaged the leading cruiser, 'Maori' opened fire with gunfire and a large number of hits were observed on the bridge of the enemy. When she was abeam, 'Maori' fired two torpedoes, one of which was seen to hit; the other was

unobserved. This cruiser the passed astern in flames and was undoubtedly sinking.

4. The second ship was lost sight of, but a sheet of flame was seen away to port and it was presumed that she was sinking.

5. One torpedo-boat was seen and passed, very close, down 'Maori's starboard side. Fire from 4.7in guns was opened but was not very successful owing to the very short range. Close range weapons unfortunately jammed. I did not pursue this torpedo-boat as you made the signal to 'Dis-engage'.

Rate of fire was critical to this action, just as it had been in the fjords of Norway. The manoeuvrability and sheer firepower of the 'Tribals' provided the necessary cover, just as it was thought they would, for a torpedo attack to be pressed home forcefully, aided of course by the element of surprise gained by attacking from the shore side which also made it difficult for the Italians to see them. It was a combination of sudden, concentrated 4.7in fire, momentarily dazzling the bridge and gun crews, with the *coup de main* delivered by torpedoes that disabled the two cruisers *Di Giussano* and *Da Barbiano*. None of this would have been possible though, without the advantages of radar, deployed on an aircraft which had found the Italians, as well as on board the ships. Once again, this attack showed the potency of an aggressively handled destroyer force, which the 'Tribals', thanks to the confidence of their captains and the *esprit de corps* of their crews, epitomised.[232] After taking part in this and other actions, *Maori*'s demise came when she was destroyed by a bomb which penetrated her

Sikh was in many ways a queen of the Mediterranean in her time, operating from Gibraltar, Malta and Alexandria, taking in actions with Force H, various striking forces and the Mediterranean Fleet proper. (Drachinifel Collection)

engine room while she lay at anchor in Grand Harbour.[233] In contrast to *Sikh* and *Zulu*, lost in a brutal battle when taking part in the commando raid on Tobruk in September 1942, it was an ignominious end.[234]

In March 1942 the Second Battle of Sirte took place, a battle which confirmed what the chase of the *Bismarck* had demonstrated: it is not, as the old adage goes, the size of the dog in the fight, but the size of fight in the dog that matters. The 'Tribals', and their successors, were built with a lot of fight in them.

The Second Battle of Sirte

The Second Battle of Sirte is a battle which arouses diverse opinion in relation to both its context and the consequences. But as the historian Peter C Smith makes clear in his work on *Laforey* class destroyers, everyone agrees that it was hugely significant.[235] On one side was the British convoy, MW10, making an urgent run for Malta under the command of Rear Admiral Philip Vian. The urgency was serious because Malta was running out of everything, and the importance of the convoy led to the formation of a sizeable escort force made up of four light cruisers, a dedicated AA cruiser and eighteen destroyers, which included both *Sikh* and *Zulu*.[236] Large it may have been, however, but its potency was compromised due to the damage sustained by major fleet units, such as *Valiant* and *Queen Elizabeth*, and the need to find ships for not just both halves of the Mediterranean, but also the Atlantic, the Indian Ocean and the Pacific. As a consequence the convoy had no battleships and no carriers and was therefore entirely dependent upon destroyers, cruisers and land-based air cover when that was available.[237] In contrast, the Italian force which confronted the convoy – located thanks in large part to the Axis Mediterranean air dominance in March 1942 – was numerically smaller but far more powerful, comprising the battle-

Pujabi would have her career cut short by HMS *King George V* splitting her in two whilst they were operating as part of covering force for PQ 13/ QP 10 Arctic convoys in 1942. *(Drachinifel Collection)*

ship *Littorio*, two heavy cruisers, and ten destroyers.[238] On paper, therefore, the Italian battleship's 15in guns out-matched and out-ranged anything on the British side, making victory all but certain.

During the height of the battle, while the British light cruisers were engaged by the Italian heavy cruisers and some of the destroyers, *Littorio* tried to work her way around the escort force and reach the convoy. Although this was to an extent successful, unfortunately for *Littorio*, it left her in way of the operationally grouped 5th Division, comprising *Sikh*, the *Laforey-* class *Lively*, and two 'H' class vessels, *Hero* and *Havock*.[239] These destroyers hurled themselves at the battleship and its escorts. *Havock* was damaged and out of action quite quickly, but the remaining three destroyers, through sheer aggression, a willingness to expose themselves to danger, and by maintaining a constant barrage of fire from any weapons that would bear, straddling the *Littorio* consistently, managed to hold off the battleship for forty minutes until reinforcements arrived and took up the challenge.[240]

Sikh was the leader of this division, and it was *Sikh* that spotted *Littorio* first, engaging at 16,000 yards, a range at which firing was pointless from a combat damage perspective (although it would not have mattered how close they had been, as anything covered by the

battleship's armour would have been beyond reach of even the 4.7in main guns), but which established them as an 'aggressive' threat in the mind to the battleship. They combined this with a smoke cover which was so dense that it made it difficult for the other destroyers to fire, let alone for the *Littorio* make contact with her quarry.[241] In this battle *Sikh* epitomised those qualities around which the 'Tribals' had been conceived, whether fulfilling either cruiser or destroyer roles. They were designed to fight and, just as importantly, lead the fight.[242] This action is important because, just as the 4th DF did against *Bismarck*, and *Sikh* had done at Cape Bon, she used both her rate of fire and her torpedoes, and her destroyer design capabilities of manoeuvrability, high speed and relatively small target profile, to fulfil the cruiser role of holding an enemy battleship at bay in order to protect the convoy.

Operation Harpoon began like many other Mediterranean convoys, with another convoy starting from the other end of the route; in this case Harpoon started from Gibraltar, while Vigorous set out from Alexandria. Harpoon though, would result in what came to be called the Battle of Mid-June, the nondescript but appropriate name for a battle which took place on 15 June 1942.[243] The 'Tribal' class *Bedouin* was one of five fleet destroyers assigned to convoy protection, the other four being a War Emergency Programme 'P' class *Partridge*, the 'I' class *Itheurial*, and the 1939 'M' class vessels *Marne* and *Matchless*. *Bedouin*'s captain, Commander Scurfield, had been charged by the convoy commander at 0630hrs to lead the destroyers to face the Italian cruisers and destroyers if, but as likely when, they sighted by the convoy.[244] It was a sunny day, and the Italian force of two cruisers and five destroyers were unhindered by the need to protect merchant ships, an unusual boon in Mediterranean actions. In the war in the Mediterranean ships were almost always operating in range of land-based enemy aircraft, but for both sides it was necessary to run convoys. And it was arguably more necessary for the Regia Marina than the Royal Navy as the latter's convoys were mainly for supply of Malta, while the former supplied the entire North Africa campaign. Under those circumstances, when two convoys engaged in a battle each side judged it a success if their convoy got through. However, when only one side had a convoy to escort, then the measure for success for the other side altered.

This scenario was why the division of the escort between a 'Close Escort', comprising the anti-aircraft cruiser *Cairo*, the minelaying cruiser *Abdiel*, a flotilla of 'Hunt' class escort destroyers along with various minesweepers and launches, and the 'Mobile Escort', which comprised of the fleet destroyers was necessary. It would allow for speedy reaction in the event of the force being discovered as it proceeded alone without cover. Commander Scurfield later wrote to his wife: 'This was what I had been training for, for twenty-two years, and I led my five destroyers up towards the enemy. I was in a fortunate position in many ways, and I knew what we had to do. The cost was not to be counted. The ship was as ready for the test as we had been able to make her. I could do no more about it.'[245]

These are words which reflect not only the fighting ethos of Royal Navy destroyers during the war, but also illustrate the conduct of the ship and her crew on 15 June 1942. *Bedouin* and *Partridge* opened fire with their guns at maximum elevation and range, drawing enemy fire to them, enabling their sister ships to get closer.[246] The fleet destroyers fought so well, that even though they were forced to withdraw through their smokescreen because of the sheer weight of enemy fire, the enemy chose not to follow them.[247] These destroyers bought time for their convoy to escape, although it was not without cost; by drawing the enemy fire to themselves *Bedouin* and *Partridge* suffered greatly.[248] As the convoy reformed they were left behind, valiantly attempting to repair and get underway again.

Of the two, *Partridge* had suffered less damage and managed to get underway quite soon, and took *Bedouin* in tow. She had received twelve 6in hits, an indication of the tough nature of the 'Tribal' design.[249] Despite regaining the convoy, damage to *Bedouin* was thought too great for Malta's repair capabilities, and rather than

slow the convoy down the decision was made to turn for Gibraltar.[250] This proved fatal. At 1320hrs they once again found the Italian squadron.[251] At this point *Partridge* slipped her tow, hoping to draw the Italians away from her consort, but it was an unsuccessful ploy. Though *Bedouin* managed to get underway with one engine, her fate was sealed.[252] Not only did the Italians call on two 'Condottieri' class cruisers, the *Raimondo Montecuccoli* (of the sub-class of the same name) and *Eugenio di Savoia* (of the later *Duca d'Aosta* sub-class) along with five destroyers, but they also deployed torpedo bombers, one of which, a Savoia-Marchetti SM.79 Sparviero of 132nd Gruppo launched the torpedo which sank *Bedouin*; in a last act of defiance, *Bedouin* shot this aircraft down.[253] A recurring theme in the story of the 'Tribal' class is the threat of air power, and six of the twelve vessels lost by the Royal Navy were lost to air attacks. Conversely, they consistently acquitted themselves well for their size in air defence roles, particularly after upgrading to the twin 4in mount in X position and fitting extra light weapons. They were frequently used for the transport or transfer of VIPs, such as Winston Churchill and King George, both around the British coast and in the Mediterranean as will be discussed later. It is also why, as with Operation Claymore, when an operation came up in the Mediterranean which was long range and with minimal support, the 'Tribal' class were often the first choice.

Operation Agreement was a commando raid planned to cause massive damage to the ability of the Axis powers to fight in North Africa and took place in September 1942.[254] It came about at the request of the Army, and it was the then C-in-C Mediterranean, Vice Admiral Harwood, of Battle of the River Plate fame, who planned it and oversaw its execution. The plan involved disguising two destroyers, *Sikh* and *Zulu*, as Italian destroyers, by modification of the funnels and their silhouettes, and, under the cover of night, sneak in close to Tobruk in support of a raid which it was hoped would severely damage the facilities of the port.[255] The 'Tribals' had been chosen partly because their gun armament would enable them to provide stronger support for the ground troops than other available destroyers. The remaining force comprised *Coventry*, a 'C' class AA cruiser, the four 'Hunt' class escort destroyers of the 5th DF, as well as sixteen Motor Torpedo Boats (MTBs) and three Motor Launches (MLs). The MTBs, MLs and 'Tribals' would carry out the operation to land and recover the troops. The remaining ships were to act as an escort and supporting force, remaining out of the way to the east during the actual operation.

Unfortunately, this land and amphibious operation proved to be the North African version of Operation Market-Garden in that as much as the risk might have been worth it, it was a bridge, or more accurately a beach too far. As well as the amphibious assault there were to be air attacks, a land-based attack by the Long Range Desert Group and another by the Special Air Service. Fate was not kind however. The commandos, who were supposed to be landed from the 'T' class submarine *Taku*, failed to get ashore because of sea conditions, and so were unable to place the necessary beacons to guide the naval forces. As a result, *Zulu* and *Sikh* escorted the seaborne troops into the wrong beach.[256] The mistake was compounded by the shore garrison being much stronger than intelligence had suggested. The situation was then further exacerbated when *Sikh* was hit by shore artillery while trying to evacuate the troops, and *Zulu* was damaged trying, and failing, to pull her sister out.[257] Unfortunately for the Navy, the operation swiftly turned into more of a rerun of Dunkirk and Crete than the success of Namsos.

Sikh sank during the battle, losing many of her crew. *Zulu* managed to withdraw, but only after being damaged by Italian fighter-bombers and she now needed assistance.[258] She made it to within 100 miles from Alexandria before sinking while under tow, taking thirty-nine of her crew with her; and en route she had had to sink the badly-damaged *Coventry*.[259] So an operation, for which the two 'Tribals' were the best option available, ended in their loss. The operation, in concept at least, was not dissimilar to Claymore and should have worked. The answer to the failure lies in the different circumstances. The Italians were better prepared in Tobruk than virtually anywhere else, and while all available Allied forces had been assigned to it, there were simply not enough to make it viable. This was a key reason why the Navy was losing so many ships: often because they simply did not have enough viable hulls in the water to complete all the necessary tasks that needed doing. Ships were moved from crisis to crisis and mission to mission; the 'Tribal' class destroyers plugged the gaps, a role for which they had been built in the first place.

While the losses of 1942 mounted, it was the losses of 1940 and 1941 which had already persuaded the Admiralty that the 'Tribal' class needed a successor, beyond those further 'Tribals' being assembled and entering service into the Royal Australian and Royal Canadian Navies. Furthermore, cruiser construction was not producing enough ships; there were only so many shipyards which could build the larger vessels and they were overwhelmed. The smaller cruisers, such as the *Dido*s with, for example, the problems with their 5.25in guns, were not proving as good value for money as had been expected during pre-war discussions. In 1942, the decision which had been contemplated in 1941 was finally acted upon. A new design was chosen and the Navy committed valuable and limited resources to the construction of a new class of destroyer. The question was whether it would be built in time to see service in the war.

CHAPTER 4

COMETH THE WAR, COMETH THE 'BATTLE'

If the 'Tribal' class can be said to have had a turbulent conception, then that of the 'Battle' class was even more so. There were those who felt the big destroyer, the 'fighting' destroyer, the 'back pocket cruiser', was not worth it and that it would be better to build more cruisers and more destroyers. Surely specialist ships were better than all-rounders? Furthermore, unlike the 'Tribal' class, the 'Battles' would have no friend with real influence in the halls of Whitehall, the Palace of Westminster or even the Admiralty to fight for them. They were ordered though because, even with the Dominion builds, there would not be enough 'Tribal' class destroyers to carry out all the missions that were required of them, especially as those missions led to heavy losses; and there certainly would not be enough cruisers to carry out all their missions, and the smaller destroyers just did not have the firepower.

The case for new, heavy destroyers to succeed the 'Tribals' had been started by Admiral Sir Reginald Henderson when Third Sea Lord and Controller of the Navy. Almost as soon as the 'Tribals' had been ordered in 1935, he had started the campaign that he would win

Sluys was a fine example of a completed 1942 Batch 'Battle' class. As well as two twin Bofors STAAG mountings she also carried six single Bofors Mk VIII including one mounted abaft 'B' turret which is clearly visible in this photo, as is one of the mounts on the signal deck next to the superstructure. *Sluys* achieved a very respectable top speed of 30.29kts in trials and retained a reputation for being a quick ship. (*Drachinifel Collection*)

in terms of size for their successors the 'J' class. Unfortunately, the case for the armament of the 'J's was still being made and his successor, Rear Admiral Fraser (of Battle of North Cape and British Pacific Fleet fame) was more conventional. Initially the 'Battles' were held up by the hope that light cruiser production could fill the gap between the smaller, more torpedo-focused destroyers and the need for firepower over and above their capabilities. However, it was not long before war experience and need forced the 'fighting' destroyers back on to the agenda. When designs similar to those Henderson had suggested not long previously (as early as 1936/7, but also continually until he died) for the 'L' class were proposed in September 1941, they were granted Admiralty support and ordered with unprecedented speed in October 1941. It was a combination of the urgency of war requirements, and the fact the design had been on the drawing board for some time, which made this possible.

The design reflected the different times it found itself in. The designers of the 'Tribal' class had had the luxury of peace to think about how they might be used when not at war: the 'Battle' class were the built when the nation found itself fighting a second major war less than twenty-five years after the first. This forced decisions to be made which would radically affect the design of the class, the most obvious of these being in their layout. When describing the 1942/3 batches of 'Battle' class destroyers, the focus is often on the decision made to give them only two forward turrets because the aft

R60

Solebay, another 1942 Batch 'Battle' class, in profile. This photo highlights the two amidships deckhouse single Bofors mounts. After trials she almost immediately become the flotilla leader for 5th Destroyer Flotilla, which meant that during Operation Deadlight, she took part in the sinking of German U-boats, including one which required eleven rounds of 4.5in ammunition. (*Drachinifel Collection*)

turret was not needed in combat.[260] Often reference was made to fighting in the Mediterranean and Norway. But as has been discussed earlier, the aft turrets were well used in those battles, so did the Navy misread the evidence? In reality it was a misreading of what was said in the files, or rather the context of what was said. These turrets were the most technologically and materially taxing components of the ships, barring the engines. Reducing the requirement from the four of the 'Tribal' class, or the three of other classes, would ease production and allow more space and displacement for torpedoes and light AA weapons. It was not a case of not needing something: it was a case of whether the lack thereof could be adequately compensated for so as to bring the class more quickly into service.

It was not an easy decision to make. The reason for the pronounced space between 'A' and 'B' turrets and the ship's main structure was the need for the maximum possible firing arcs, and the need to cover as much of the stern as possible. The idea was that if an 80 per cent solution could be achieved then the ships could be procured quickly enough to enter service and have an impact on the outcome of the war which by then was proceeding at pace. However, if any proof was needed about the unease with this decision, it is there with the replacement of the 4in starshell mounting

abaft the funnel, with a 4.5in multi-purpose gun in the 1943 batch. By the time the 1944 batch of 'Battle' class destroyers developed into the 1950s *Daring* class, the vessels were equipped with three turrets including one in 'Y' position. Without the pressure of war, and with the improved capabilities of the weapon systems, it was not only a sound operational decision but also a logical procurement one. And indeed, the design of the 1942 'Battle' class, the first batch of these vessels, was the product of a sound operational concept and logical procurement strategy, at least on paper, for otherwise approval would never have been granted, even under the pressures of war.

HMS *Savage*, a Test Bed

Even in the midst of war the Navy could not avoid some testing, and it was crucial that the guns for the 'Battle' class, as well as the 'Z' and 'C' classes of the War Emergency Flotillas, underwent appraisal. In order to do this, the Admiralty chose to modify an 'S' class destroyer of the 5th Emergency Flotilla, then under construction, and create a ship with the equipment of the fighting destroyer. Her hull was of the Emergency Flotilla destroyers' standard, as established by the 'Q' class of the 3rd Emergency Flotilla, in turn an adaptation of the 'J' class's longitudinally framed hull, which included a 'Tribal' class style bow, but the stern modified with a flatter and broader transom. It had been found that this not only gave more space aft on the upper deck – useful for equipment such as depth charges – but also gave noticeable, albeit not massive, advantages in speed and endurance. Like the rest of her class she had four principal guns, but their arrangement differed significantly from those of her sisters.

Matapan was a 1943 Batch 'Battle' class. The absence of the single Bofors abaft 'B' turret makes the distance between the main armament and the superstructure quite distinct. (*Drachinifel Collection*)

Whereas the rest of her class were armed with four single 4.7in weapons, *Savage* had four new type 4.5in, disposed as a twin mount forward, like those which would equip the 'Battle' class, and two single mounts aft which would be the armament on the 'Z' (10th Emergency Flotilla) and 'C' (11th–15th Emergency Flotillas) classes. Other than this she was outwardly, barring the missing the super firing weapon in 'B' position, a conventional vessel of her class. Below, however, the requirements of the 'tween-deck arrangement necessary to support the twin turret necessitated some changes and rearrangement. In order to expedite completion of her as quickly as possible, the twin mount fitted was modified from a spare from *Illustrious*, the lead ship of the armoured-hangar aircraft carriers which had been one of Admiral Henderson's principal projects. When commissioned, *Savage* displaced 1,734 tons in standard configuration, 2,465 tons when fully loaded, like all War Emergency Destroyers. As a feat of naval architecture, this was by no means the only significant aspect of her design.

The Navy may have conceived *Savage* as a test bed, but she was nonetheless built as a destroyer to fight in a major war. She never had an option other than to serve doubly, both as a test bed and a warship. After successfully going through her trials, her equipment thoroughly inspected and assessed in operation, she was deployed to the Fleet. She would spend most of her service life on the Arctic convoys, as well as taking part in the Battle of North Cape, which is discussed in the next chapter. She took part in at least sixteen trips with Arctic convoys, not many compared to the twenty-five of *Tartar* or the twenty-three of *Nubian*, but still a respectable number. Although the Navy was short of ships, service on Arctic convoys was unforgiving, and it was not a station where inadequate examples of ship types were sent. There were all sorts of places, for example Africa or South America, where a less capable warship could be put to use. It is reasonable to conclude that, despite being experimental, *Savage* was chosen because her unique design was felt to be highly capable. This augured well for the classes which were subsequently built.

The 'Battle' Design

The operational concept of the 'Battle' class was even more orientated to fighting with guns than even the 'Tribal' class. The older class had been conceived in peacetime at a time when thinking about space for general-purpose duties and general-purpose fighting was not just allowed but, in the case of the 'Tribals, but encouraged. In contrast the 'Battle' class came into being at a very different and more difficult time. Losses had mounted and the solution revolved around more armament. This meant that, despite being bigger, they became rather cramped in comparison. They also demonstrated the trend towards specialist ship designs, even for commando raids. Prior to Operation Claymore cruisers and destroyers had provided the necessary lift. With the rise and ready availability of specialist ships such as Landing Ship Tanks (LSTs) and other landing craft, less provision needed to be made on destroyers for a sudden increase in embarked personnel. Furthermore, while the 'Tribal' class could be said to have

Asine, another of the 1943 Batch 'Battle class'. (*Drachinifel Collection*)

been built as cruisers to destroyer lines, the 'Battle' class would be cruisers forward of the bridge structure but destroyers aft. The primary benefit of cutting the 'Y' turret was the doubling of space for torpedo armament. In other matters though the concept was remarkably similar to the brief as written for the 'Tribal' class.

Lagos was a 1942 Batch 'Battle' class and despite not being completed in time for war was rushed to the Far East in January 1946 to replace war-weary vessels. (*Drachinifel Collection*)

The 'Battle' class was conceived with worldwide operations in mind. The ships were to be as potent and as useful in the White Sea as in the Yellow Sea, or, perhaps more likely, in the Barents Sea as they would be in the Philippines Sea. As a result, range, survivability and potential punch were all key areas of the design, although this did not mean significant real-life lessons and experience would only be fitted into the concept as they materialised; some had been predicted before the war demonstrated them. It meant the operational concept of the 'Battles' as compared to that of the 'Tribals' evolved. Space was less of a priority than overwhelming firepower for air defence. This was why every weapon,

Hogue, a 1942 Batch 'Battle' class, had her career cut short in a collision with a larger ship during an exercise in 1959, the 'Crown Colony' class light cruiser *Nigeria,* which had been Admiral Philip Vian's flagship in Force K. By the time of the exercise the ship belonged to the Indian Navy and the ship had been renamed INS *Mysore.* She would go on to take out two more ships in exercises via collision, in 1969 and 1972. (*Drachinifel Collection*)

barring torpedoes and depth charges, was at least dual purpose. They represented a continuation of the 'Tribal' class and, barring the lack of space for peace keeping duties, they were the destroyer which Admiral Henderson would have wished to build.

With an overall length of 379ft (364ft on the waterline), a beam of 40ft 3in and a full load of 3,361 tons, the 'Battle' design was interesting, especially when compared to the 'Tribal's' measurements. The original class had an overall length of 377ft (364ft 8in on the waterline), a beam of 36ft 6ins and a full load of 2,519 tons. The main areas of growth therefore were the beam and the draught, which had also increased by 15in. These hull changes were to benefit stability for the purposes of air defence. The 'Tribals' had been orientated around surface warfare: 'Battles' were surface warfare strong, but they also reflected both the growing threat of air power and the fact that navies in general, but the Royal Navy in particular, were in 1941 still developing and refining the operational tactics needed to counter air attacks. Admiral Henderson returns to the story here, because the ship design that emerged was very similar to that which had been proposed by him in 1937 as the

largest option for the 'L' class in 1937, a similarity which would only grow with each iteration of the design from concept to build.[261] In fact, the 'Battle' class was a product of much of his work, even beyond the hull.

The superstructure and bridge layout were taken from the 'J' class, which itself had been an evolution of that used on the 'Tribal' class. Once again this was a design produced during Henderson's tenure as Third Sea Lord, and most importantly for continuity, Goodall was still in post, and by October 1941 Vice Admiral Sir Bruce Fraser, Henderson's successor, was in a far stronger position than Henderson had been when he had started. This mattered for two reasons. First, it was Goodall whose studies in the earlier part of his career and his interest in foreign destroyer designs had made possible the most obvious structural changes in comparison to the 'Tribal' class, and which enabled so much more weaponry to be carried. Exhaust was trunked out through a single funnel. Furthermore, the engine arrangement to achieve this difference was capable of producing 50,000shp, 6,000shp more than the 'Tribal' class had achieved. Secondly, because there was still the constant view that 'it's better to concentrate on cruisers and to make smaller destroyers slightly more powerful, rather than build bigger destroyers', which was held by many naval officers. However, useful the smaller destroyers were, the bigger 'fighting' destroyers had proved themselves too. A new generation was required, but their value was not simply their size, but what their size enabled them to carry.

As with the 'Tribals' it was sensors which mattered,

Alamein, a 1943 Batch 'Battle' class, is pictured here in a way which highlights the anti-air weapons fit: the two imposing twin 40mm Bofors STAAG mounts, the Squid ASW mortar fitted further back, then a quintuple torpedo launcher, followed by another twin 40mm Bofors, the second quintuple torpedo launcher, then the single 4.5in gun, before reaching the funnel, the single 40mm abreast the bridge structure at the signal deck level and finally, forward, two twin 4.5in turrets. (*Drachinifel Collection*)

sensors and the ability to process the information provided. Carrying four different types of radar, the 275, the 282, the 293 and the 291, the 'Battles' were festooned in comparison to the pre-war ships. The Type 275 was a centimetric evolution of the – by 1941, when design selection took place – quite well developed Type 285 anti-aircraft gunnery radar, a system which had evolved into a more general-purpose gunnery radar by 1944. Therefore, although new in 1944, the year before the class entered service, it was also to a great extent proven.[262] The Type 282 had entered service in 1941. It was a ranging system for Bofors and pom-poms, fitted in the 'Battle' class to the critical Hazemeyer mounts, which will be discussed more fully when guns are examined further on. The Type 293 continued the theme of combining the new with the proven. Its electronics came from the proven Type 276/7 surface search system, while the 293 was a short-range air search radar thanks to the new antenna design. The Type 291, last but by no means least, was designed for destroyers and small ships, including submarines. This system was crucial in enabling Royal Navy warships to find opponents in all weathers.

Electronics, however, is more than simply radar: it also comprises communications such as the varieties of Radio Direction Finding (RDF). This was not an early form of radar, but a system designed to detect enemy transmissions. The most commonly known of these systems, the High Frequency Detection Finder (HF/DF) was more colloquially known as huff-duff. It was designed to detect the communication signals of submarines and aircraft. Along with its counterpart, the less well known Medium Frequency Detection Finder (MF/DF), this proved crucial to class vessels during the Battle of the Atlantic, especially in providing intelligence to support the communication traffic analysis which underpinned many of the key strategic decisions of the battle. It is unsurprising therefore that in the design and specifications their fitting was given great emphasis. It was not only enemy communications that were critical, Identification Friend or Foe (IFF) had grown in importance from its initial developments in the 1930s to the absolutely essential war fighting tool it became for integrated naval and air operations. Whether used for single nation or multinational operations, it was the key enabler.

The third sphere of electronics was the High Angle Control System (HACS). Originally developed for cruisers or bigger ships, it was adapted for the 'Battles' by the time the class was fitting out. It had built-in Type 275 radar and was modified further by being combined with the Fuze Keeping Clock, as had been fitted aboard the 'Tribal' class. This system, by this time called the Mk VI director, was critical though it was by no means perfect. This was principally due to the assumptions

The starboard side of *Alamein*. With her boat deployed alongside and awnings up, she is transformed into a venue, a place to entertain and impress . (*Drachinifel Collection*)

made during the early design phase about the kind of air attack fleets would have to face, and this in turn meant that the engineers developing and the crews manning the systems were to an extent playing catch up, but it was certainly better than nothing. The initial, incorrect, assumption had been that future air attacks would largely be confined to those which could be carried out by heavy bombers (ie level bombing from quite high up) or torpedo bombers. Dive-bombing was discounted, chiefly due the bias of the Air Ministry, but less so by the Royal Air Force which had inherited the technique from the Royal Flying Corps and the Royal Naval Air Service when formed before the First World War. This was not something in which the Air Ministry was really going to invest, nor indeed promote, since they felt the heavy bomber was the more capable weapon system for fighting a war. It was also considered by some to be the best guarantor of maintaining the Royal Air Force as a separate service, something viewed as essential to the security of the United Kingdom in the face of increasing air power.

This is not to say that dive-bombing came as a surprise to the Navy when it experienced it on operations: in fact, barring the few Hawker Hart light bombers that remained in Royal Air Force service at the time, it was the Navy's Fleet Air Arm Blackburn Skua which represented British capability for carrying out dive-bombing. Despite the Admiralty's interest and commit-

ment they had not got far, principally because they had only gained control of the Fleet Air Arm in 1939, and could not really develop capability without getting the Air Ministry on side, which in turn meant they could not develop the counter. It was not only sensors and targeting systems which had to catch up, but also guns and, more specifically, their mounts did as well.

It was this need to counter air attack which really drove the selection of arguably the primary weapon system of the 'Battle' class. The double QF 4.5in Mk IIIs on Mk IV Between Deck, or in abbreviated form 'BD', mounted forward, was certainly prominent. As BD they differed from guns normally fitted on destroyers at this time, which were normally Upper Deck (UD) systems that did not have anything below deck level; simply put they were more battleship style weapons than destroyers'. Moreover, these gun systems were placed so far forward of the superstructure that they made an already aggressive-looking design appear even more so; it seemed as if the guns were so eager to engage the enemy they were stretching their own ship. If the layout of the 'Tribals' made them look impressive in a statesman-like way, the 'Battle' class could be said to have been made to look impressive in a thoroughly threatening way. The reason that these guns were so far forward was to give them as extensive a field of fire as possible, and it was also, at least in part, to make up for the lack of firepower aft. The question is: what did these systems offer to justify the cost in displacement, in complexity of construction and operation, in materials and in design compromises?

This system was selected over the 4.7in guns that

The 'Battle' Class 1942 Batch

Name	Constructor	Laying Down	Commission	Normal Displacement (tons)	History of Name when Bestowed	Initial Flotilla
Barfleur* (Capt. D)	Swan Hunter (Tyne & Wear)	28 October 1942	14 September 1944	2,958	A traditional capital ship name, four predecessors had born it with pride, most were closer to the *Centurion* class battleship in naval ship status	19th DF
Camperdown	Fairfield Shipbuilding & Engineering Company (Govan, Glasgow)	30 October 1942	18 June 1945	2,819	A traditional capital ship name, three predecessors had born it with pride, most like the 'Admiral' class battleship that was its immediate predecessor were more obvious high status ships	19th DF
Armada (Capt. D)	Hawthorn Leslie and Company (Tyneside)	29 December 1942	2 July 1945	2,315 (standard) / 3,361 (full)	One predecessor, a 74-gun Third Rate ship of the line which saw action in the war of 1812, when she was just two years old and which had served the RN till 1863	19th DF
Trafalgar (Capt. D)	Swan Hunter	15 February 1943	23 of July 1945	3,094	A capital ship name which had previously equipped two First Rate ships of the line, and was namesake for a class of battleships in 1887… subsequently has also been namesake for a class of nuclear-Ppowered submarines launched in 1981	19th DF
Hogue	Cammell Laird (Birkenhead)	6 January 1943	24 July 1945	3,211	The original vessel in the lineage was called *La Hogue* and was a Third Rate ship of the line eventually converted to have steam screw propulsion, there was also a *Cressy* class armoured cruiser, sunk in 1914… to date this is the last ship to have carried this name	19th DF
Finisterre	Fairfield Shipbuilding & Engineering Company	8 December 1942	11 September 1945	2,757	A new name in 1942, only ship to have borne this name so far	Gunnery Training Ship
Solebay (Capt. D)	Hawthorn Leslie and Company	3 February 1943	25 September 1945	2,905	Six(Seven) predecessors bore this name, all Fifth and Sixth Rates during the age of sail, originally was allocated to an *Algerine* class minesweeper – but was reallocated whilst that was still in build to this vessel.	5th DF
Lagos	Cammell Laird	8 April 1943	2 November 1945	3,060	A new name in 1942, only ship to have borne this name so far	19th DF
St Kitts	Swan Hunter	8 September 1943	21 January 1946	2,315 (standard) / 3,361 (full)	A new name in 1942, only ship to have borne this name so far	5th DF
Cadiz	Fairfield Shipbuilding & Engineering Company	10 May 1943	12 April 1946	2,806	Predecessor had been a fireship that was used at the Battle of Barfleur, however that and this destroyer are the only uses so far	5th DF
Gravelines	Cammell Laird	10 August 1943	14 June 1946	2,315 (standard) / 3,361 (full)	A new name in 1942, only ship to have borne this name so far	Reserve Fleet
St James (Capt. D)	Fairfield Shipbuilding & Engineering Company	20 May 1943	12 July 1946	2,873	Predecessor had been a ship captured in 1625 and sold in 1628; so far this has been the last ship to carry the name	5th DF

Name	Constructor	Laying Down	Commission	Normal Displacement (tons)	History of Name when Bestowed	Initial Flotilla
Saintes (Capt. D)	Hawthorn Leslie and Company	8 June 1943	27 September 1946	2,315 (standard) / 3,361 (full)	A new name in 1942, only ship to have borne this name so far	5th DF
Sluys	Cammell Laird	24 November 1943	30 September 1946	3,080	A new name in 1942, only ship to have borne this name so far	5th DF
Vigo	Fairfield Shipbuilding & Engineering Company	11 September 1943	9 December 1946	2,757	Three (four) predecessors, a Fourth Rate and two Third Rate ships of the line, a modified 'V&W' destroyer of WWI was also to be namedthus – but was cancelled whilst in build, as such this is currently the last ship to have borne the name	Reserve Fleet
Gabbard	Swan Hunter	2 of February 1944	10 December 1946	3,105	A new name in 1942, only ship to have borne this name so far	5th DF

*= served in WWII Capt.D = Fitted to act as Flotilla Leader ** = as recorded during full power trials unless otherwise stated
Shipyards and launch dates compiled by author from various records including those held at the UK National Archives and the work of Patrick Boniface (2007)

had been the basis of destroyer armament, and were the defining characteristic of the 'Tribal' class. What made it special? What made a barely modified version of the secondary armament of carriers and capital ships the desired system for the new fighting destroyers? Simply put, as the secondary armament on capital ships, they were designed to be both heavy anti-aircraft and anti-surface weapons, with a rapid rate of fire and rotation, but also with an elevation of up to 80 degrees. First and foremost, however, the system was available; it was in service with existing lines of support and training, and a world war was being fought. It was a compromise, but not one that was going to keep Vice Admiral Fraser, or anyone within the Controller's or Constructor's office, awake at night.

Turning to the lighter weapons, in the 'Battle' class

these systems were just as important. They were the reason why, when commissioned, the vessels of the class were considered some of the most powerful anti-aircraft ships in the Fleet. They were also some of the most complex and difficult systems to maintain, but until something better was developed, they were judged to offer the only solution. The gun was the twin 40mm Bofors Mk IV mounting, copied from a Dutch design originally conceived for a class of unbuilt German-inspired battlecruisers proposed for the Far East and

Armada was a 1942 Batch 'Battle' and here is pictured early in her career, when she could have mounted up to fourteen 40mm cannon, although she seems to have had just ten, including the four Hazemayer twin mounts clearly seen arraigned aft. (*Maritime Quest*)

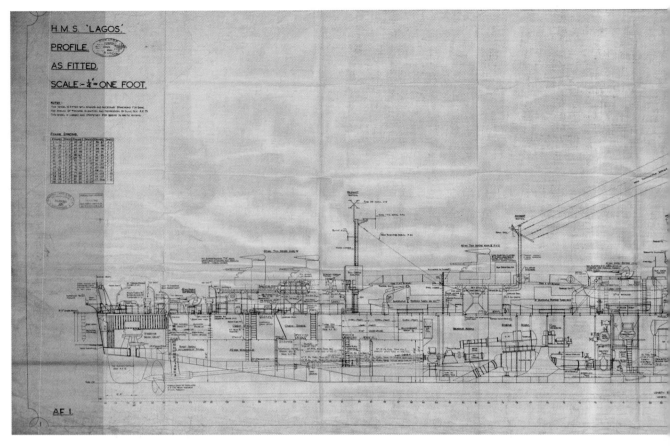

Builders' profile of *Lagos*, as fitted, 1946. (© National Maritime Museum, Greenwich, London)

brought across from the Netherlands to Britain by an escaping minelaying destroyer, HNLMS *Willem Van Der Zaan*. It had been a revelation to British armaments officers. Simply put, it gave a ship stopping power. The increased damage caused by a Bofors 40mm round compared to a pom-pom/Vickers 40mm (especially in terms of range and velocity) coupled with the stability of the platform, thanks to its gyrostabilised three axis system, all combined with its tachymetric targeting set up, made for an excellent system.[263] Fortunately, the Dutch were allies and friendly, so the Hazemayer was quickly in production, the aim being to produce five units a month by mid-1942. The Dutch would require at least two of those, so it would take 17 months to acquire the fifty ordered. The 'Battle' class of 1942 originally carried four, one pair in echelon occupying the 'X' position towards the stern, the other pair arranged on the structure between the torpedo launchers. Enough systems for three 'Battle' class destroyers could

be produced every four months. This added time to the production, but in comparison to the 4.5in guns, the Hazemayer was far simpler.

Since they first evolved, torpedoes had been the mainstay of destroyers, in fact they were the reason for their evolution. First came the torpedo boats, small vessels armed with the 'giant killer' or 'magic bullet' that torpedoes were thought to be prior to the First World War, and which would be the cheap counter to the mighty battleships which then ruled the waves. The response to these vessels was slightly bigger ships, still armed with torpedoes, but also with QF guns to destroy the torpedo boats. These were the torpedo boat destroyers, the appellation soon shortened to destroyer, on which torpedoes were such a significant fixture. The 'Battle' class had two quad torpedo launchers, mounted on the centreline, slightly aft of midships. Each launcher was loaded with four Mk IX 21in torpedoes, ship-killers which were carried by cruisers as well as destroyers and which had been in service since the early 1930s. Displacing nearly 1.7 tons and measuring nearly 24ft in length, it is not hard to see why they were considered such a potent weapon, especially with a top speed of 41kts and a 365kg Torpex

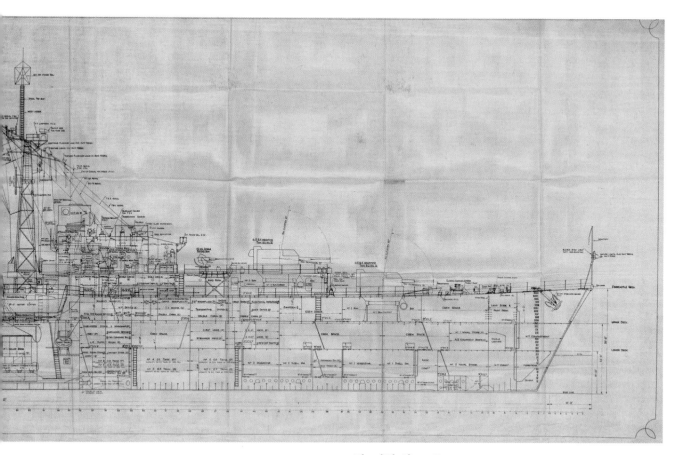

warhead. These were the weapons – though slightly newer, slightly bigger and marginally faster – that would sink the Argentinian cruiser *Belgrano* in 1982. Furthermore, they had been in service since 1929 and used to arm almost all the Royal Navy destroyers from the 'A' class onwards.

However, the torpedo was not the simplest weapon system aboard. That honour went to, by this time very traditional but still effective, ten-pattern depth charge system which provided the anti-submarine capability on this next generation general-purpose destroyer, and had been chosen over the more complex Squid anti-submarine mortar, which was later fitted in the 1950s. It was a standard heritage four-thrower ten-depth charge launch system. This made sense, because the 'Battles', like the 'Tribals' before them, were not primarily anti-submarine vessels. They were general-purpose fighting vessels which would carry out such work when needed. They were there to support and fill in for specialist vessels, as were the 'Tribals'. Anti-submarine work was not their *raison d'être*, so a good, solid and reliable weapon system, rather than one might have offered more but been more complex to operate, was the sensible design decision.

The 'C' Class Destroyer

At the same time as the 'Battle' class was being designed so were other classes, the most important of which were the 11th, 12th, 13th and 14th War Emergency Destroyer Flotillas, the 'C' class destroyers, sometimes termed 'War Emergency Destroyers'. This class is worth examination by way of comparison with the 'Battle' class. They were a traditional destroyer in form and size, at least on paper and in terms of concept, compared with the heavier 'Battle' class's 'fighting' destroyer shape, and they well illustrate the differences of conception for the two types. Technically, there were four sub-classes within the single 'C' class, and they were ordered in four batches of eight ships each between February and September 1942. They were destined to become escorts with torpedo and anti-submarine cover. With 12th Flotilla, the 'Ch' sub-class, the design stabilised with a displacement of 1,900 tons in standard load and 2,535 tons in full, respectively 415 tons and 826 tons lighter than the 'Battle' class. This meant less displacement was available for armour, weapons and machinery, less displacement for everything in comparison to the class which was very nearly a third bigger. However, the 'C' class was larger than

This photograph of *Armada* displays well the rake of the bow and the imposing nature of those 4.5in guns. It also highlights the relative position of the Mk VI director and fire-control system which was the British answer to the American Mk 37. (*Drachinifel Collection*)

previous War Emergency designs, reflecting the fact that more was needed from almost every ship. The increase in size of existing types left space for smaller types to emerge, for example the 'River' class frigates of 1941, a new anti-submarine design which itself displaced the 'Hunt' class escort destroyers of 1939. The growth in ship size offered new opportunities; but in reality more was being demanded of the ships, which was due more to exposure to wartime experience than to the sort of speculative concepts which had driven the initial development of the 'Tribal' class.

The concept for the 'C' was for a conventional destroyer. The Navy needed ships with heavy anti-submarine and torpedo weaponry, capable of engaging other destroyers. It needed the bigger escorts, corvettes, sloops, even the new frigates, but those ships could only do so much and only so many could be built, or more pressingly crewed with enough experienced personnel. While sloops and frigates could be built in the smallest shipyards, they presented a problem for the larger yards, which could not construct multiple frigates or sloops in the same dock, nor build a single small vessel in a dock which would have been a waste of their facilities. But they could be used for the War Emergency

Destroyers of the 'C' class, thereby building ships which could be the 'big destroyers' for work in the Arctic convoys, the Battle of the Atlantic, moving men and materiel from front to front as the waging of a global mechanised war required, or alternatively filling the traditional destroyer role in fleet operations by providing the heavy torpedo strike capability. In all these roles destroyers were needed and they were needed then and there.

The speed with which 'C' class ships were built and commissioned represented one of the principal differences between that class and the 'Battles'. *Caprice* was laid down on 28 September 1942 and commissioned twenty months later on 5 April 1944. *Carysfort*, the last of the first batch, was commissioned on 20 February 1945. The first of the second batch to be commissioned, HMS *Chaplet*, was laid down on 29 April 1943, and only missed the victory over Japan and the end of the war by nine days. In contrast, the 'Battle' class *Barfleur*, the only one to make it to the war in the Far East, was laid down on 28 October 1942, a month after *Caprice*, but was not commissioned until twenty-three months later on 14 September 1944, more than six months after *Caprice*. *Lagos*, a 1942 'Battle', was laid down on 8 April 1943, three days after *Chaplet*, but was commissioned more seven months after her on 2 November 1945.

Slow as the 'Battle' builds might seem, they still represented an improvement on peacetime building times. *Afridi*, the first of the 'Tribal' class, was laid down on 10 March 1936 and commissioned on 3 May 1938,

twenty-six months later, and this difference of three months highlights the urgency applied to war builds, especially considering the relatively more complex build of *Barfleur* compared to *Afridi*. Unfortunately, as *Lagos*'s thirty-two months demonstrate, not everything was always straightforward, even when a design was understood. When days and ship numbers matter, the less capable ship available today is as valuable as the more capable ship tomorrow. This was the balance the

Another early photograph of *Armada*. Photos of the Hazemayer in this configuration are quite rare as it was quickly phased out in favour of the only slightly better, but much heavier and more easily maintained STAAG system. (*Drachinifel Collection*)

Armada in her later configuration, still with ten 40mm, but now they are in STAAG mounts, placed in a little star around the structure and with two pairs securing the stern. It was in this form that she would exercise presence on behalf of the British government throughout her service life. (*Drachinifel Collection*)

Jutland was a 1943 Batch 'Battle' class with a predilection for night action befitting the name. At one point, after recently entering service, she advanced on a suspected Soviet spy ship and then, lighting up the vessel, made the vessel withdraw. It was a classic and recurring role as the world transitioned from World War to Cold War. (*Drachinifel Collection*)

Admiralty was trying to strike. The Navy needed the best destroyers it could come by, as quickly as possible, so it had to strike a balance between the best, the good and the 'it will do'. Destroyers tended to fall into the first or second categories: corvettes, frigates and sloops into the second or third. How did the 'Cs' save six-plus months on their construction in comparison to the 'Battles'?

To begin with, the Admiralty used 'last year's' technology which, while not the best, was mostly good enough. For example, they used the same Fuze Keeping Clock targeting assist system that had been fitted to the 'Tribals', rather than the Fuze Keeping Clock of the 'Battles' which was integrated with radar and a Mk VI director and as such was a generation or more beyond what their predecessors had. Like the Fairey Swordfish and every other torpedo bomber to the Sopwith Cuckoo in the Fleet Air Arm service, the War Emergency Destroyers were the product of a process of the experience of each generation leading to im-

provements in the next one, a process of evolution. A good example of this was the weapons fit. The main guns were four 4.5in single mounts, which had already been tested aboard *Savage* and which did not penetrate the deck. The four mounts were arranged as in the 'Tribals', with mountings in 'A', 'B', 'X' and 'Y' positions. This newish gun armament was coupled with eighty depth charges and two quadruple 21in torpedo launchers, systems which could have come off a pre-war destroyer, but which still packed a punch. These primary systems were supplemented by a twin mounted 40mm Bofors Hazemeyer, like the 'Battles'. Other than that it was either four single QF 2-pounders or two single QF 2-pounders and two single 20mm Oerlikons, a simple but effective armament.

Without the 'C' class and other War Emergency Flotillas coming through the yards, commissioning at a steady and reliable rate, the Navy would never have felt able to spend the time, money and effort on building the 'Battle' class. Reaching for the next generation, the next evolution, the next level, is necessary in war, but only if the country is sure that it has its immediate needs secured. It took until 1942 for the Navy to begin a 'Tribal' class successor programme because they needed to be sure they had enough destroyers before they could start apportioning precious resources to more 'fighting destroyers'. What is more, between the

1942 and 1943 batches, the 'C' class design was changed to reflect the lessons learned during the building of each batch.

The 1943 Later 'Battle' Class

While operational concept, hull and structure were broadly the same between the two batches, the 1943 class incorporated a number of significant changes. Almost imperceptible to the human eye, the 1943 Batch had 9in height added to the bridge, were 3in broader in the beam and, at 3,418 tons fully loaded, displaced nearly 60 tons more than the 1942 Batch. So why make such minimal changes when it was essential to get these ships into service as soon as possible? These changes were necessary to support other changes. The broader beam helped compensate for the higher bridge and it crucially helped with the greater top weight of the weapons load. Torpedoes had been changed from two quadruple, manually-trained systems to two quintuple torpedo tube systems which were much heavier, but did enable a 25 per cent increase in torpedo salvo.

The 4in signal or starshell gun, which had been incorporated amidships just aft of the funnel on the 1942 Batch, was replaced with a 4.5in QF Mk IV 55°, which was also fitted as the primary weapon systems on the 'C' class destroyers. In addition to providing more coverage aft, this increased the 'broadside' 4.5in weight of fire by 25 per cent and provided a weapons system which could be trained manually in an emergency. The in-service conversion of the 1942 Batch would remove their starshell guns as well and all but five ships were completed without them as it was more beneficial to

use the top weight for other weapons, mainly more 40mm cannon. However, the change of gun meant that its platform, in comparison to the 1942 Batch, had to be built up, and it was primarily as a result of this that the bridge on the 1943 Batch was raised 9in. This was very significant when a warship was for the most part commanded from an open bridge, and when the human eye was still the most critical sensor available to a crew, and the closest thing to a tactical command computer processing system was represented by the brains of the captain and executive officers. An open bridge with uninterrupted views was essential. It is only when electronic sensors, and the displays of information gathered by those sensors, take over the conduct of combat, that the need for an enclosed bridge, and later a Command Information Centre buried inside the ship, becomes not only necessary, but practicable.

The ingenious Hazemeyer gun mounts were replaced by STAAG mountings (Stabilised Tachymetric Anti-Aircraft Gun). Still mounting the all-important 40mm cannon, they utilised a more potent and much more reliable platform. The new system was built around the capabilities and requirements of the Type 262 radar, rather than the Type 282 used for the Hazemeyer. The Type 262 was a more dependable system, and when combined with STAAG offered the opportunity to introduce a level of standardisation of system across the fleet. The STAAG's statistics were interesting. The systems weighed twice as much as the Hazemeyer, 14 tons compared to 7 tons. This increase in top weight was justifiable not only because they gained 5 degrees of variance between maximum elevation (92.5 degrees) and depression (-12.5 degrees) or had a 24-volt electric pistol firing mechanism capable of firing under local or remote control, but mainly because of their reliability. A weapon which works, especially after long voyages, is far more useful than a lighter system

Barfleur was not just a 1942 Batch 'Battle' class, she was the first one to achieve operational status and the only one which saw combat with the British Pacific Fleet, although she was originally fitted out for the Arctic. (*Drachinifel Collection*)

HMS *Barfleur* was quite successful as a diplomatic asset and during one five-day visit in Marseilles in 1955 she was toured by nearly 3,000 people – showing the draw of even what was just a 'destroyer'.(Drachinifel Collection)

which does not. It was this reliability that sold STAAG to the Admiralty.

The changes though did not stop there and it is, arguably, the next modification that was the most significant. The 1943 Batch also replaced the depth charges that their 1942 sisters carried with the Squid Mk 1 anti-submarine mortar, allowing both for a more capable anti-submarine profile and the levelling up of the anti-submarine capabilities into the wider fleet. This was the new version of the weapon system that had begun with the Hedgehog. There had been some broadly unsuccessful experimental models prior to the Hedgehog but this was the first weapon that enabled ships to maintain ASDIC/Sonar 'lock' on the target. It was a major breakthrough for convoy escorts. Prior to its introduction, experienced – or lucky – U-boat commanders managed to use the break in contact provided by the conclusion of a depth-charge run, or concussion of the blasts, to execute a rapid random manoeuvre away from the danger zone. This led to the Allied operational tactic of one ship standing and 'fixing' the target and another one or two attacking, making escape less likely, although this tied up more escorts for each individual contact. By eliminating this weakness, the Navy was able to free up escorts and make more contacts simultaneously. This was only one step in the technological battle, but it was an important one. The next decision equally important, and just as with the Dutch Hazemeyer system chosen for the 1942 Batch, demonstrated that the Navy was not precious over national sourcing of equipment.

The major problem with the 1942 'Battles' was that the British fire-control systems which were then available were not that effective against fast low-flying targets. Much pre-war investment had been focused on engaging slow bombers. Undermined by this miscalculation, the Admiralty was faced with a stark choice: either start research and development from scratch to develop a new fire-control system, or import a system. The first option would take time they did not have, so initially they went down the latter route. The American Mk 37 DCT could be adapted and fitted with a Type 275 radar. More importantly, it was lighter than existing British equivalents and was better able to deal with fast-moving high-angle attacks. It was, however, only available in limited numbers, and it was these numbers, minus those needed for certain carriers and the new battleship HMS *Vanguard*, which decided how many 1943 and later 'Battle' class ships could be ordered. Twenty-six of the American type were ordered, which was sufficient for just over three flotillas of 1942 'Battles', but only eight were available for the 1943 'Battles', and only these were completed by the end of the war.

What did this all mean for the mission capabilities of Batch? Up to that point they were the most powerful destroyers designed and built for the Royal Navy. They had the best radars, sonar and command and control equipment available. Of equal importance was the overall design which was large enough, not only to accommodate the equipment and position it correctly, but also to allow it to be crewed and maintained at the necessary levels. These sensors were backed up by an impressive array of weaponry. Despite the fact that it still comprised the Mk IV DP 4.5in turrets, rather than the hoped-for Mk Vs, which would be on the *Daring* class, it was nonetheless highly effective. Thanks to the range and number of 40mm cannon, and the positioning of a 4.5in amidships, the ships were capable of mounting a terrific storm of hot flying metal against any air attack. In addition, a ten-torpedo salvo could be launched. They also mounted the most advanced anti-submarine weapon of the time.

However, they were not without their faults. Being packed with the latest electronics and weaponry left not much room for anything else besides their battle roles and duties. The 'Battles' lost the space and comparative luxury with which the 'Tribals' had started their careers, although they themselves became overcrowded under the pressures of war. Whereas the 'Tribal' class had been good-looking ships, designed for diplomacy, the 'Battles' looked powerful, but did not display the same elegance.

The 1943 'Battles' did not have either the main guns or engines which the Third Sea Lord, the then Vice Admiral Sir Frederic Wake-Walker, would have liked: the Mk VI light turret on the upper deck, rather than the Mk IV BDs then in use, and which did not penetrate the deck. It was the new hope, but would not be ready on time. This will be discussed later in relation to the *Daring* class. Engines, or more powerful engines to be exact, were another issue, and they might have em-

ployed the machinery then being readied for the *Weapon* class, which was heavier than that used in the 'Battles'. In addition, it would have required two funnels, arranged in the USN alternating series style rather than the parallel style preferred by the Royal Navy. The former was felt to offer greater survivability as, in theory, a single hit was unlikely to disable all the turbines or all the boilers; on the other hand, it resulted in more hull and deck space being taken up by engine machinery. In the end it was not to be. These ships were required to be in service as soon as possible and the changes would have almost amounted to designing a whole new class. Which is actually what the Admiralty chose to do, when designing a successor to the 'C' class.

The 'Weapon' Class

One of the most interesting aspects of the 'Weapon' class is the story of their creation. They were part experiment, to show that ships, especially destroyers, did not need to be any bigger than they already were. The argument came from largely the same group of officers who felt the 'Tribal' class were too big, and had argued in favour of the *Dido* class light cruiser over the 'Town' and 'Crown Colony' classes of cruiser. They also felt the *Illustrious* class aircraft carriers were too large and that the 14in gun was the perfect calibre for a battleship. This was not illogical. They believed, rightly, that smaller ships were cheaper to build, run and sustain. They felt that if they made the Navy as cheap as possible, the politicians would interfere less when seeking economies, and there would be sufficient ships to carry out defence duties effectively.

The only flaw in their arguments was that none of

Barfleur had an eventful career and much of it was spent in the traditional Royal Navy theatre of the Mediterranean, including during the 1956 Suez Crisis. Her career straddled not just major political and international upheavals, but also the transition from Destroyer Flotilla to Destroyer Squadron. After starting her career with the 19th DF, she spent most of it with the 3rd DF which became the 3rd DS. (*Drachinifel Collection*)

them could agree what should be removed to make those ships smaller. Neither the ships nor their designs had been growing in size because the DNC and Third Sea Lords were obsessed with big ships. They were growing larger because to achieve greater speed, bigger and more powerful machinery – for example, engines, boilers and gearboxes – were necessary. To achieve a greater range necessitated creating the capacity to carry more fuel. In order to carry more guns, and to deal with the increase in demand for anti-aircraft weapons, there needed to be more magazine capacity, allocated deck space and top weight provision. All this required a larger hull to retain stability and a steady gun platform.

During the late 1930s, Radio Direction Finding (RDF), as in electronic warfare, and then RDF, which was early Radar, came with demands for space. They needed generators, cabling, and tall masts. The latter needed to be particularly carefully designed and positioned to minimise the risk of capsize, the fear of which was not overblown. It was always a risk with the smaller

'Battle' Class 1943 Batch

Name	Constructor	Laying Down	Commission	Normal Displacement (tons)	History of Name when bestowed	Initial Flotilla
Dunkirk	Alexander Stephen and Sons (Glasgow)	19 July 1944	27 November 1945	2,816	Whilst the three predecessors had had a somewhat ignominious start, being a 2-gun ketch captured from the French, the next two had been a 48-gun and 60-gun Fourth Rates respectively; as yet though she is the last to have borne the name.	4th DF
Barrosa	John Brown & Company (Clydebank)	28 December 1943	14 February 1947	2,910	A fifth rate sailing ship, a wooden screw corvette and a Third-Class cruiser all precede this destroyer as carriers of the name; although none since.	Reserve Fleet
Alamein (Capt. D)	Hawthorn Leslie and Company (Tyneside)	1 March 1944	20 March 1947	2,380 (standard) / 3,315 (full)	A new name in 1943, only ship to have borne this name so far	Reserve Fleet
Aisne	Vickers-Armstrong (Newcastle)	26 August 1943	20 March 1947	2,850	A new name in 1943, only ship to have borne this name so far	4th DF
Corunna (Capt. D)	Swan Hunter (Tyne & Wear)	12 April 1944	6 June 1947	2,787	A new name in 1943, only ship to have borne this name so far	Reserve Fleet
Agincourt (Capt. D)	Hawthorne Leslie and Company	12 December 1943	25 June 1947	3,076	There were four(five) predecessors to carry this name, two Third Rate ships of the line, a *Minotaur* class ironclad frigate, and whilst originally planned for an unbuilt *Queen Elizabeth* class battleship – was instead used for the force purchased-battleship *Rio de Janeiro/Sultan Osman* that served in WWI. The name is due back in service soon, having been bestowed on what is currently planned as the seventh and last *Astute* class submarine.	4th DF
Jutland (Capt. D)	Alexander Stephen and Sons	27 November 1944	30 July 1947	3,045	Technically would have been the first *Malplaquet*, but when they cancelled the original first *Jutland*… they transferred the name across to this ship	4th DF
Matapan	John Brown & Company	11 March 1944	5 September 1947	2,862	A new name in 1943, only ship to have borne this name so far	Reserve Fleet

*= served in WWII Capt.D = Fitted to act as Flotilla Leader ** = as recorded during full power trials unless otherwise stated
Shipyards and launch dates compiled by author from various records including those held at the UK National Archives and the work of Patrick Boniface (2007)

The 1943 Batch 'Battle' class *Barossa*. She began her career delivering food and other provisions to the storm-ravaged Isle of Skye and Western Isles before spending much of 1948 filming *The King's Navy*. (*Maritime Quest*)

ships designed to go faster because there was less hull in relation to mass to displace the ship's weight. Over and above these considerations, the new, more complicated equipment required more crew, and larger crews require yet more crew, in terms of the supporting specialties. Furthermore, these crew knew their value and the Invergordon Mutiny was still fresh in any officer's memory. As well as more pay they needed better accommodation, a requirement for yet more space, which all had to be balanced. Mistakes could be very costly. A class built to serve twenty years or more might have to be replaced early, with all the financial and political costs that come with such a decision. Worse still, mistakes could lead to death of crew, without a war and the attention of an enemy.

The answer upon which officers and politicians focused was specialist vessels. An anti-aircraft vessel can reduce its main armament to focus on AA systems, and need not carry depth charges and or torpedoes. This strategy only works when it is possible to guarantee that the anti-aircraft vessel will be operating with anti-surface vessels and anti-submarine vessels, and that none of these ships become incapacitated. To ensure the availability of such a wide range of specialist capability requires more ships and concomitant costs. Such a specialist fleet was not something that was going to be considered in the midst of a major war in which ships were being lost and when every convoy, every operation, every movement could be threatened by enemies who were capable of mounting all-arms attacks, and frequently did so.

As an 'intermediate' destroyer the 'Weapon' class was a compromise in the sense that it was seeking to offer the general-purpose capability that the 'Tribals' had defined and the 'Battles' then embodied, but with 'less' than either, and that is why the chosen design was just smaller than the 'Battles'. The 'Weapons' were not to be the largest destroyers in the Fleet. As they were designated 'intermediate' destroyers, the 'Weapon' class was technically the successor of the 'C' class flotillas, and two of them would take over yard units belonging to the 13th/'Ce' flotilla, *Centaur* and *Celt*. Unlike the War Emergency Destroyers, which had in many ways been made with whatever was available, this class definitely were not. Under such muddled circumstances of conception, where what was wanted was something not a 'Battle', but still a generation beyond a 'C', the quality of the design of the 'Weapon' class might be considered surprising, but for Stanley Goodall and the DNC excellence of design was very much the standard for which he and his department strove.

The success of the design might also have been unforeseen considering how much of it was in flux while the ships were being built. Much the design would be changed and adapted before the ships entered the water and the class shrank dramatically to four units from the nineteen ordered. Originally, they had been specified with six 4in guns mounted in three twin mounts, two twin 40mm STAAG mounts, two single 40mm, a single Squid and two quintuple torpedo systems. Two sextuple systems were considered, but were found to be too heavy. This armament had an all-around capability. The 4in guns had been chosen because they would give sufficient firepower without the need for an increase in displacement and size. Torpedoes were especially important for their anti-ship capabilities. Fitting all this into the design was never going to be an easy task, but it was made especially difficult because it was important that the 'Weapon' class be 'intermediate' destroyers, not 'large' destroyers like a 'Battle', but also not small ships like a 'Hunt'; and nor was it really a continuation of the 'War Emergency Destroyers'; it could be considered the first class built with an eye to the post-war world. One element was strongly defined, the overall length, which should be no more than 365ft. Even this limit had its critics inside the Admiralty.

The reason for the criticism was that the 'Battles' were only 379ft, not much longer than the 'Tribals' 377ft and a lot less than the *Daring*s 390ft; it was the 12ft longer than the 'Weapon' class which made the difference and meant they were the 'big'/'fleet' destroyers, but only just. Which meant detractors declared they were really just a second class of large destroyer, a case seemingly supported by their being beamier than the 'Tribals', at 38ft compared to 36ft 6in. However, the 'Weapons' needed the width in order to accommodate the machinery which, for a displacement of 540 tons,

provided the vessels with 40,000shp (half of what the engines in the inter-war refit of the battleship *Warspite* generated) which gave them a top speed of 34 knots. The alternating engine and boiler rooms, known as a 'unit' arrangement, required two funnels. Trunking, to try to combine the stacks, seems not to have been seriously considered as it would have wasted space and would have cooked the crew in warm climates. The advantage of the arrangement meant that a single hit was unlikely to disable both engines, and even if it did, the greater separation of the systems made the potential for battle damage repairs or routine maintenance work easier. This was never to be tested in combat.

The 'Weapon' class eventually entered service in peacetime, with two commissioned in 1947 and the remaining two commissioned the following year. They entered service not as general-purpose 'intermediate' destroyers, but as prototype fast anti-submarine vessels. They had lost a 4in mount but gained a Squid, and they retained their secondary armament and their torpedoes, which in the pre-missile/post-war age, offered the best mix for surface combat. Adhering to such a heavy torpedo armament may in hindsight seem outmoded, but at the time the last British battleship, *Vanguard*, had only

Builders' profile of *Corunna*, as fitted, 1947. (© National Maritime Museum, Greenwich, London)

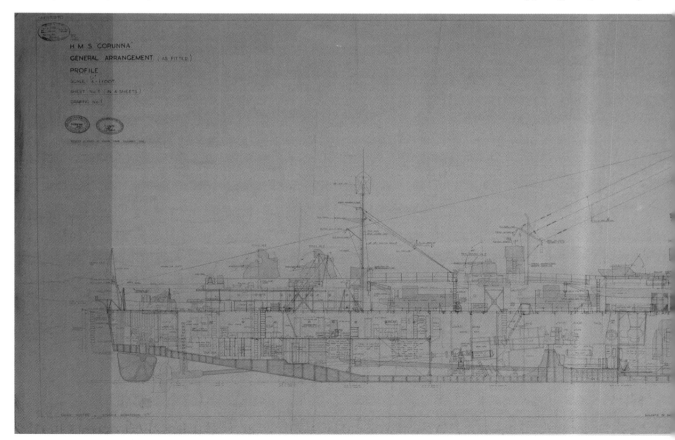

just commissioned (1946) and was considered a critical national asset, as were many older battleships still in service. Although they were out-ranged by aircraft

The 1942 Batch 'Battle' class *Gravelines* would serve a short career. Commissioned in 1946, she had a refit cancelled in 1958 and was scrapped in 1961. (*Drachinifel Collection*)

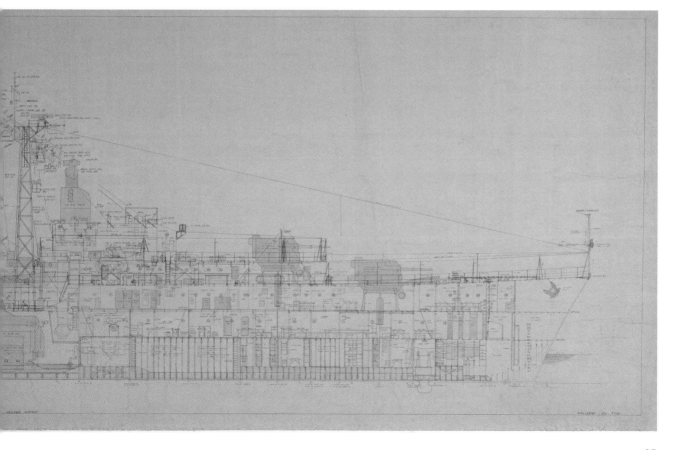

launched from aircraft carriers, they were nonetheless still perceived as the best-value surface combatant available. There had been plenty of opportunities for the decision to have been questioned and changed if deemed sensible, but at each turn they had, at least under wartime conditions, triumphed in the face of their detractors.

The procurement of the 'Weapon' class spanned the periods in office of two Third Sea Lords, the years of fighting a world war and its attendant loss of personnel, and the consequential and constant turnover of staff. When all this change was combined with the rapid pace of technological development, it was not surprising that decisions taken months or years previously were reversed in order to produce a more useful and relevant vessel. The history of the 'Weapon' class is littered with changes of heart. Despite the evolution of their design they retained their principal characteristics, but in a post-war world which was changing fast, the building and commissioning of just four was considered sufficient.

The *Daring* Class

We now turn our attention to the *Daring* class, the largest destroyers then built for the Navy. Some 1944

Saintes was a 1942 Batch 'Battle' class and would serve with distinction. She did trials of the Mk VI 4.5in gun that would equip the *Daring* class in 1947, but after the trials returned to the Mark III 4.5in that the rest of 'Battle' class carried. She would have a long career as a vital member of the 3rd DF/DS, including acting as lead escort for aircraft carriers and the Royal Yacht *Britannia*. (*Drachinifel Collection*)

'Battles' were modified into the *Daring*s that followed in the post-war years. In some cases hulls were lengthened, in others the slip numbers and the materials that had been allocated were transferred. Two were completed to the original plans for Australia. The *Daring*s were redesigned around the new Mk VI twin 4.5in upper deck (UD) turret (which did not penetrate the deck), the quintuple torpedo system, and their machinery was organised in the new 'unit' arrangement as in the 'Weapon' class, which meant a second funnel was necessary. Most importantly these were destroyers designed with radar and electronic warfare systems as a central core around which the ship would be built. As such they could well be described as the first truly modern destroyers: general-purpose and built around a power-hungry, all-seeing electronic eye that became a conspicuous element the design. The most unsurprising, but also most visible, change was the appearance of a third turret aft. The firepower of three turrets provided the opportunity for a transformation of auxiliary weaponry and, coupled with the anticipated arrival of peace, there was a significant reduction in the number and standardisation of the light guns. Compared to the earlier 'Battles', the six, or sometimes four, 40mm Oerlikons of 1944, mounted in two or three twin mounts, was light. Once again the size argument reared its head. These destroyers, at 390ft overall, with a beam of 43ft and a displacement of 3,600 tons or more in full load, had now attained the scale of the First World War *Arethusa* class, and the 54,000shp and 34-plus knots put the *Daring*s' performance beyond it. They were nearly four times the size of the *Acasta* class destroyers which

Hogue in 1945 in Malta as she made her way out to the 19th DF as part of the relief of the forces in the Far East after the Second World War ended. She returned to the UK in 1947 and was deactivated until 1957. She had only been reactivated for two years, and was still a relatively new ship when she had to be stricken off after a collision in 1959. (*Maritime Quest*)

had been *Arethusa*'s contemporaries. In twenty-eight years, destroyers had grown from relatively simple ships, hardly bigger or more advanced than the torpedo boats their forebears were built to counter, into major warships which could have outshone some recent examples of that traditional policeman and shield of Empire, the cruiser.

'The bigger ship makes certainly a steadier platform than the smaller one, and the pitching in the longer ship is of less amplitude and less angle than in the shorter vessel…'[264] These words, spoken in 1934 during a debate on aircraft carriers at the Royal Institution of Naval Architects by Sir Eustace T D'Eyncourt, a former DNC (1919-24), still hold true for destroyers. If a ship's weapon system is primarily its torpedoes then stability is less of a worry because the torpedoes self-stabilise. If guns, especially early generation radar-controlled guns, are the primary weapon system then stability becomes crucial. Taking into consideration all the new systems, and the weight of weaponry required, the size of the *Daring*s, despite them being the biggest conventional destroyers yet built, could be considered

remarkably small. Some proposed designs were bigger and it is due to the skill of the DNC that such a compact vessel was successfully built. To achieve this, they built upon a legacy of previous designs and ideas. The hull was a much-modified form of the 'Battle' class vessels, which had been fitted with stabilisers. Its underwater profile was adjusted to allow better support of sonar. The hull shape above the water, its angles and rake, was inspired by the 'Tribal' class. The length and beam, the proportions which along with their depth of 30ft 9in/22ft 6in, marked them out as a destroyer, a large one, but certainly a destroyer.

This was coupled with power and manoeuvrability, the former a product of the new engine form arranged in the 'unit' fashion, the latter aided by two huge rudders. The engines were developed by the engineers of the Parsons & Marine Engineering Turbine Research and Development Association (PAMATREDA). Propulsion was provided by two units, comprised of a double reduction geared steam turbine, driving one propeller each. The steam came from oil-fired water-tube boilers, one per unit, for *Daring, Decoy, Delight* and *Diana*, which came from Babcock & Wilcox. The machinery for *Dainty, Defender, Diamond* and *Duchess* came from Foster Wheeler. The eight ships were already two batches of four, and were further divided because only four, *Daring, Delight, Defender* and *Dainty* were fitted with the then conventional 220-volt direct current power supply, while the other four, *Decoy, Diamond,*

Diana and *Duchess*, were fitted with 440-volt, three phase, alternating current. In reality, and from a power and mechanical perspective, rather than a class of eight destroyers, the Navy had built four two-unit sub-classes with all the attendant complexity and training issues.

This was partly because the *Daring*s became victims of their own success. As the largest class to be built post-war, the number of 'new builds' gave the constructors opportunities for trialling new ideas, ideas which would be critical if the world changed again and the Fleet had to renew itself in a hurry. This is part of the point though with this class, because of the vessels ordered – on paper at least – in 1945, one, *Delight*, had effectively been ordered in 1943, the yard number having been assigned to the 1943 'Battle' class vessel *Ypres*. The first *Daring*s were not launched until 1949, while the last, *Diana*, was launched in 1952. Commissioning took place over a two-year period from March 1952 to March 1954. Almost a decade passed from the stroke of a pen on an order sheet to the emergence of fully commissioned ships. It was a long time to be at the mercy of changing naval constructors and Sea Lords.

How did these large destroyers come to be built in the face of constant worry over their size and cost? To begin with, as with the 'Tribal' class, these vessels were thought of as different from destroyers, not quite ordered in *Daring* flotillas, but not far of it. Indeed, for much of their service lives they were not counted as being part of the Navy's destroyer strength, but in a category on their own.

Secondly, while many wanted to return to building 'proper' destroyers, in the sense of small, fast, torpedo attack-orientated ships, no one could really agree what was to be cut to make that possible. If the height of the mast was reduced in order to reduce the beam, the radar and gunnery officers would be upset. If the size of the engines was reduced, the Fleet Air Arm would be upset as the new ships would not be fast enough to screen their aircraft carriers. Lots of different groups were keen for the smaller, cheaper, easier-to-build ships, but it would be at the expense of the capabilities which mattered to them.

Furthermore, a return to peace had halted the flood of specialists ships, and this had registered with the Admiralty. What was needed was a well-armed all-rounder, proficient for anti-submarine work, but equipped with anti-aircraft firepower and the capability to destroy surface or land targets. For those making the case for the smaller ships it must have been frustrating when reality and pragmatism got in the way of the pursuit of the more specialist destroyer type.

The *Daring* class were always built to offer a wide suite of capabilities. The standard design is always based around the three main guns with the anti-air, anti-surface and anti-land capabilities. Everything else is built around them. In the 1950s, the Mk VIs could fire shells up to 14,000yds at an elevation of 80 degrees; at an elevation of 45 degrees they could reach nearly 21,000yds, or 19km, which was in excess of the pre-war calculated maximum effective cruiser fighting range.[265] These were excellent weapon systems, which needed to be provided with the best possible platform to enable them to live up to their capabilities. Therefore, the hull, in length, breadth and depth, was of destroyer proportions, as defined by the needs of the guns, but crucially, in terms of politics, was not a cruiser. The *Daring* class were built in peacetime for both war and peacetime duties, for example by using naval diplomacy either as a deterrent or to shape potential conflicts.

This is clearer when some designs aspects of the vessels are considered, and they demonstrate how they were built for the deterrence of war. An electric galley, fluorescent lighting and a laundry are not cheap and for a ship which was still to make use of depot vessels, where normally destroyers would regularly restock and get a lot of their 'hotel' functions carried out; but they offered facilities for taking on the cruiser roles of diplomacy. This was augmented by the three 'structures' of the vessel. First was the 'stepped' forward structure, containing the Mk VIs; the two STAAG 40mm weapon systems; and the large open bridge of a new design (up until the *Daring*s all destroyer bridge structures had been based on the design of the 1936 'H' class), with the principle director and the base of the tripod radar mast that rose high up above it all. The forward funnel, fitted with a cowl, was enclosed within the lattice mainmast. Lines were solid, angled and stylised, demonstrating great attention to detail, all of which sent an important message that if this was a nation prepared to invest in appearance, imagine what it would invest in fighting. Next was the first torpedo launcher, followed by the middle structure which contained the second funnel and the single non-STAAG twin 40mm. There followed another torpedo launcher and the aft structure, containing the auxiliary director and third Mk VI. Finally, between that and the stern nestled the Squid anti-submarine mortar. At first glance the ship looked good, while further scrutiny revealed all the detail confirming first impressions. These ships were built to be statements, just as the 'Tribals', together with the 'Town' and 'County' class cruisers, had been. It is a feature of ships expected to perform naval diplomacy.

It is interesting that, even with a weapon system covering the rear, Stanley Goodall apparently con-

The *Daring* Class

Name	Constructor	Laying Down	Commission	Normal Displacement (tons)	History of Name when Bestowed	Initial Flotilla
Diamond	John Brown & Company (Clydebank)	15 March 1949	21 February 1952	2,950 (Standard) / 3,580 (full)	With ten ships having preceded this vessel bearing this name and one since succeeding it (that is currently in service), this arguably one of the most storied names in RN history.	5th DF - Partnered with HMS *Swiftsure*
Daring	Swan Hunter (Tyne & Wear)	29 September 1945	8 March 1952		With five (seven) ships having borne the name prior to this ship, including the lead ship of another destroyer class in 1893, and it having been planned for a *Laforey* class destroyer and a *Danae* class cruiser, before given to the 'D' class destroyer that immediately preceded her (and which was lost in WWII), it's rather fitting that this name has since gone on to christen the name ship in a third class of destroyers within the RN.	2th DF
Duchess	John I. Thornycroft & Company (Southampton)	8 July 1948	23 October 1952		Five previous bearers of the name in RN service, including a paddle steamer in WWI and a 90-gun Second Rate ship of the line.	5th DF- carrier guard
Defender	Alexander Stephen and Sons (Glasgow)	22 March 1949	5 December 1952		Started life as *Dogstar* which would have been the first use of that name, but was changed to *Defender*, which had been borne by six ships previously and a shore establishment. Like *Daring* and *Diamond* it has since been used for a vessel which is currently in service with the RN.	2th DF – but deployed to Far East to substitute for cruisers
Dainty	J. Samuel White (Cowes)	17 December 1945	26 February 1953		This was the most recent of ships to carry the name, one it's three predecessors had been a 4-gun 'Pink' sailing vessel. Which probably made more sense, than one of the largest destroyers in service at the time of commissioning.	2th DF
Decoy	Yarrow Shipbuilders Ltd (Glasgow)	23 September 1946	28 April 1953		Would originally have been *Dragon*, a name which was brought back with the latest (Type 45) *Daring* class destroyers. *Decoy* was chosen because it had the greater connection with destroyers, having two of its five predecessors being a destroyer and torpedo boat destroyer respectively; *Dragon* conversely was considered more of a cruiser name.	2th DF
Delight	Fairfield Shipbuilding & Engineering Company (Govan, Glasgow)	5 June 1943	9 October 1953		This was this vessel's (or rather yard number's) third name, it started as a 1943 Batch 'Battle' class called *Ypres*, but then became *Disdain* before eventually becoming *Delight*. That was an exceedingly storied name to choose, having been used by eleven (twelve) vessels previously, mostly smaller sloops, a 'D' class brig and Sixth Rate sailing ships, but a destroyer had carried the name more recently. So when the ship which was to have been *Delight*, was cancelled, Disdain was renamed to continue this tradition.	5th DF
Diana	Yarrow Shipbuilders Ltd	8 July 1948	29 March 1954		Was originally ordered as *Druid*, but that name lost out to *Diana* and the eight predecessors who had carried that name when the original *Diana* was cancelled. Whilst most had been smaller vessels, those predecessors had unsurprisingly included a 'D' class 1930s-built destroyer and just as interestingly an *Eclipse* class second-class cruiser.	2th DF

Shipyards and launch dates compiled by author from various records including those held at the UK National Archives and the work of Neil McCart (2008)

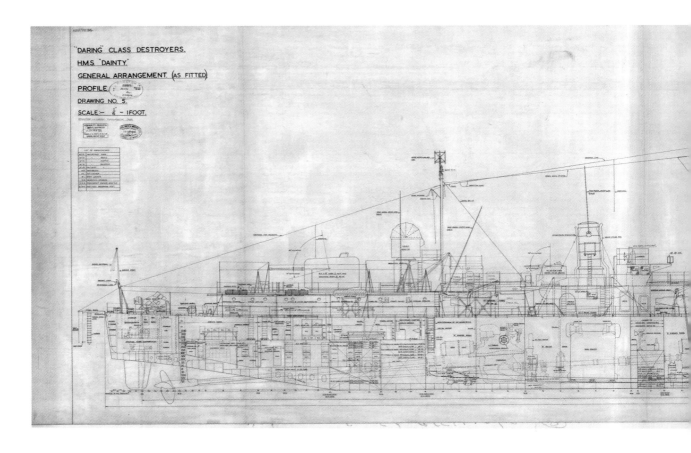

Builders' profile of *Dainty*, as fitted, 1955. (© National Maritime Museum, Greenwich, London)

sidered extending the hull and mounting the forward Mk VI's well forward of the bridge structure, as in the 'Battle' class, in order to provide as much weapons coverage aft as possible. This was a further riposte to the explanation that, for the 1942 'Battles', there was no need to worry about the main armament's field of fire not covering the stern because operational experience demonstrated that destroyers always fought towards an enemy.

Too many in the Admiralty, especially those from cruiser and battleship-orientated careers, were fixated on displacement, as if by returning it almost 1922 Washington Treaty standards, would engender again what they regarded as the key attribute of a destroyer. Indeed, so obsessed were some with this aspect that at one point the naval constructors were prevailed upon to consider reducing the deck heights to save weight. Fortunately for their crews this idea was squashed. The design was nurtured by the naval constructors, shielded by successive Third Sea Lords, and the former Third

Sea Lord, Admiral Sir Bruce Fraser, when he became First Sea Lord. When they finally commissioned, the visual impact of their design endowed them with status and strength to spare. They had a tenacious presence, without the 'straining to destroy' aspect struck by the 'Battle' class design.

Surprisingly, given the precedent, but not surprisingly considering the context of the time, the sensors were far more an evolution of the 'Battle' class than a revolution in electronic wizardry. Type 262s were back in the STAAGs and also on the 'auxiliary director', the Close Range Blind Fire Director (CRBF) – another engineering committee-named system – which was also very effective. There was a Type 275 mounted on an HACS director unit, a Type 274 for navigation, a Type 291 for air warning and a Type 293Q for target indication. All, barring the Type 274, or a version of them, had been fitted to the 'Battle' class. Some of the systems together with their earlier versions had been used in combat by the 'Tribal' class. This was sensible, considering these were very good radars for the period and the Navy had limited funds to spend on radar systems which might be shortly rendered useless by the advent of missiles. It also meant the risk was lowered in a high-

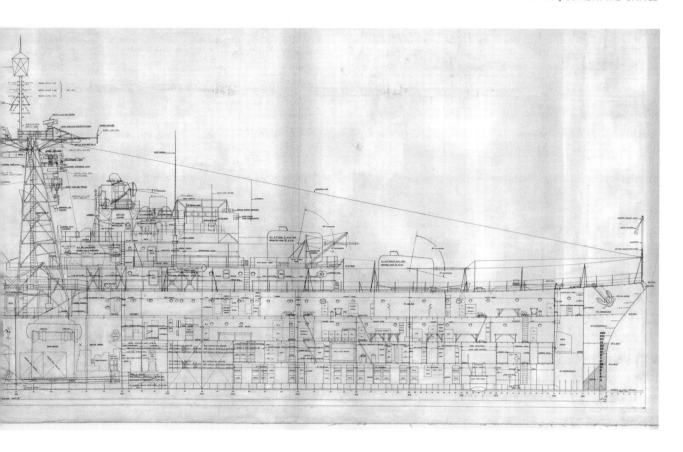

risk area; they had a proven track record, while at the same time their machinery and power supplies meant there was the potential to upgrade them with relative ease if needed.

Conceptually, the ships of the *Daring* class were the heirs of the 'Tribal' class. They had destroyer proportions, and were almost built to a light cruiser's bearing, displacement and scale, with the ability to be a presence and carry out diplomatic as well as combat duties. They were ships of their time, but their time was one of transition, and even if they offered the useful characteristics needed to provide the Navy and the nation with an aptitude for diplomacy, when the *Daring*s entered service there was a worry they would quickly become outdated, for the dawning of the missile age was on the horizon.

Stanley Vernon Goodall, Director of Naval Construction

The person behind this design, Stanley Goodall, Director of Naval Construction, was a consummate and professional builder of ships of all sizes and duties. If Admiral Henderson had been the driving force of the concept of the fighting destroyer, the person who had provided both inspiration and political communication at its genesis, then become its articulator and translator from concept to reality, was Stanley Goodall, alongside his team of naval constructors, naval architects and shipwrights – the details and drawing men – who were employed directly by the Admiralty to oversee naval construction. They were the craftsmen charged with turning Henderson's ideas into a reality that could be understood by the yards that would build them. Goodall survived his friend Henderson by many years, a fact which doubtless explains the greater amount of available material on him than on Henderson.

There is also his own writing, particularly his contributions to the proceedings of the Royal Institution of Naval Architects. Goodall had a wealth of experience upon which to draw. He joined the constructors straight after graduation from the Royal Naval College in 1907. He was appointed Director in 1936, having accrued twenty-nine years' service, just as the 'Tribal' class were being finalised, With the support of Henderson, he would serve in the role until 1944, a period spanning the service of three Third Sea Lords. Goodall was, without doubt, the institutional memory for he was the constant which kept the department running during transition periods, when Third Sea Lords were finding their feet. He was succeeded by Sir Charles Swift Lillicrap, but continued to advise the next two Third Sea Lords, was consulted extensively by the department and, as Vice President of the Royal Institution of Naval Architects, gave freely of his time and lobbied hard for projects about which he was passionate.

Goodall was a details man, judicious in his use of language, a good example of which is a post-war piece in which he described the some of the difficulties building the vital convoy escorts essential to the Battle of the Atlantic.

One important matter in planning, a word that has become rather unpopular of late, is the psychology of the people called upon to carry out the plans. We have heard a great deal about prefabricated ships in the United States. There the shipyard labour was new and had to be trained so that the methods adopted were readily accepted. But in our case, the prefabricated parts were assembled by men used to normal practice. They may vote progressive in elections but they are conservative in their work. It was very trying after all our efforts to see work absolutely stopped because two unions could not agree which should put together the pre-fabricated parts to make a fair ship. Eventually, that difficulty was overcome but we lost some valuable time.[266]

One can imagine the intense frustration this must have caused, having poured so much time and energy into pushing designs forward to get them into the war as quickly as possible so they could serve the nation to which he was devoted. Yet only a little of this is apparent. It is wryly observant, and it contains the sort of information useful for arming potential successors with the necessary understanding to enable his role to be carried out in the future.

From a study of his work, many might consider Goodall a battleship man, but he had, prior to becoming DNC, spent much of the 1920s and 1930s as head of the Destroyer Design Section, and he presented a paper on *Ark Royal* to the Royal Institution of Naval Architects in 1939. He had seniority and experience and, having had regular contact with him prior to his selection, it is clear Henderson knew the abilities of the man. Not least of these was Goodall's ready use of his knowledge and experience to argue the Admiralty's case in places which mattered. For example, in 1936, at a meeting of the Royal Institution of Naval Architects, he responded to Rear Admiral Thursfield's paper, *Modern Trends in Warship Design*, and the discussion it created, with a long statement which included the following.

I listened to Lord Cork's remarks on the carrying of aircraft in men-of-war with considerable dismay. Admiral Thursfield dismissed this question rather lightly by comparing the carrying of aircraft with the carrying of boats. But the two problems are not at all comparable. Admiral Thursfield stated that space and weight are required for the catapult from which aircraft are flown off. Lord Cork spoke of the difficulty of getting the aircraft back into the ship, but neither mentioned the subject of gunblast. Aircraft are large and fragile, and the greater part of the deck area of a capital ship is swept by gunblast, hence to provide such accommodation for the aircraft that after action they be available for use in the air is a problem that is extremely difficult…

But apart from this fact I feel that naval officers do not comprehend sufficiently clearly the effect on displacement of those weapons which had not been limited by treaty as the gun has been limited. I refer to the mine, the torpedo, and the bomb, protection against which affects the size of the capital ship. There have been great technical advances since 1921 – I should like to refer particularly to the advances in marine engineering – which would have enabled some reduction to be made in the displacement limit of capital ships, if at the same time a limit had been placed on the size of the torpedo, the mine, and the bomb. Until such a limit is imposed I fail to see any hope for a reduction in the displacement of the capital ship.[267]

These are two paragraphs taken from one-and-a-half A4 pages of tightly packed script, neither of which applies explicitly to destroyers; but in fact they are highly relevant. Aircraft can be substituted with radar, and other delicate equipment, which became key during the war. For capital ships a direct substitution of a destroyer works just as well. The world of the 1920s and 1930s had changed the calculations for what a capital ship needed in terms of torpedo defence and secondary armament. Those years also changed the facts of life for destroyers, as did wartime experience, and constructors sought to wrestle with the same challenges they faced with the larger capital ships, but in destroyers with even less space to play with and often far more exacting demands. A destroyer had to retain its speed otherwise its *raison d'être* was gone. And just as the tonnage had to be watched, so too did the cost. Capital ships, even carriers and cruisers, were national status symbols, steel ambassadors of presence and power. Destroyers were not. They were the workhorses of the Fleet, wanted in bulk and at bulk prices, and designers were supposed

A fine view of *Jutland* taken by P Woodyard RN, with her crew manning the rails. It highlights the distribution of firepower: the eight 40mm cannon, the five 4.5in guns, the ten torpedoes, and the two Squid launchers. (Maritime Quest)

to fit in all the trimmings. As Head of Destroyers and then DNC for a combined total of more than three decades, Goodall was responsible for delivering that to the Navy.

What probably complicated the role more than anything was his position. While advising the Admiralty Board he was not a member of the Board. Therefore, the role was to an extent reliant upon the qualities of the Third Sea Lord, who as Controller was the voting member responsible for construction. Therefore, Goodall's job was as much about managing upwards, as downwards, as much about personalities as detail. An active Third Sea Lord like Henderson would require one style of communication from him – more action rather than bureaucracy – while a more conservative officer, such as Admiral Fraser who succeeded Henderson, required a different style again, an often more outspoken one. This was also true of Admiral Wake-Walker, and the relationship evolved still further with Admiral Daniel and Admiral Denny by which time he was no longer DNC, but an advisor.

The Balancing Act and Summary

A constant refrain in this era, seen in the reports and memoirs of officers, was that British ships were under-armed in comparison to their opponents. It was thought this was due to undue conservatism on the part of con-structors and Controllers. What is most striking, for those familiar with debates about ship design of the Napoleonic Wars, is the similarity between the two eras. If building for the same displacement, more weapons can only be carried if something else is cut. The Navy was building ships to fight a global war and they not only needed weapons but also fuel, spare parts and all the other things a ship needs when operating around the globe far from its home base. And in wartime these factors are exacerbated.

In wartime, while the pressures on the purse strings may be reduced because making the case for the procurement of weapon systems is much easier with a visible threat, it does not make procurement easier. The questions still remain as to what exactly should be procured. Is it best to procure the latest, most high-tech products of research and the biggest and best design that can be built, or is it better to stick with tried and tested, off the shelf and easily procured gear? Neither route, taken exclusively, is the right one. The first route leaves a nation open to simply being outnumbered and pretty much steamrolled by larger forces at the time of the latter's choosing. The second may lead to a nation's forces taking the figurative 'knife to a gunfight'. A balance must be sought and in such a complex design as a warship, quality and reliability have to be encapsulated in one system. The engines chosen, the layout selected, the shape of the hull, these are all major choices to be made, even before weapons or sensors can be considered. They all combine to create a critical asset.

Admiral Henderson, to an extent, conceived and championed the 'fighting' destroyer. It was Stanley

Goodall who transformed the concept into a design, not just once, not just twice, but many times and with many designs. That is why a chapter in a book about three classes of destroyer has discussed five. The 'Battle' class, both 1942 and 1943 Batches, like the 'Tribal' class before them and the *Daring* class which sprang from the 1944 Batch, were not produced in isolation. To evaluate them without the context of their construction, whether historical, technological or political, would be to strip them of a large part of those intangible qualities which made their designs work so well for the Royal Navy and other navies which employed them. Warships are part of a whole, a navy, and are not just individual vessels. Each ship gives that fleet particular capabilities. Build

Barfleur in 1945 in her fighting form. There were eight 40mm Bofors in four twin Hazemayer mounts on the stern, with six 20mm cannon (twins mounted in the bridge wings, one abaft 'B' turret and a sixth on the quarterdeck) arranged around her. In this form she was one of the most powerful destroyers to serve with the Royal Navy in the Second World War. (*Maritime Quest*)

enough of those ships and they furnish the nation which possesses them with high degree of both destroyer and anti-destroyer fighting capability. This will be discussed further in the next chapter which picks up the events of operations where it left them in the previous chapter, in November 1942 and Operation Torch.

CHAPTER 5

THE SHIELD AND THE CANNON 1943–5

In his *The Navy at War*, Stephen Roskill quotes the words of Churchill, who proclaimed on 11 February 1943, that 'The defeat of the U-boat … is the prelude to all effective aggressive operations.'[268] It was a succinct appraisal of the war's direction at the beginning of that year. But it was not, however, entirely accurate. It is true the U-boat menace had to be dealt with, but there were other priorities. 1943 was to be a year of a range of campaigns and events, all of which required timetabling, plans, and, regardless of cost, the war had to be taken to the enemy in other theatres.

In North Africa, in early 1943, *Ashanti*, *Eskimo* and *Tartar* continued to represent the 'Tribals'' participation in Operation Torch. These three destroyers had joined the Force H during October 1942, when it was reformed following Operation Ironclad (the invasion of Madagascar) that had taken place earlier in 1942. They had come to the Mediterranean to take part in Operation Pedestal where they were part of Force X and Force Z. Their initial duties as members of the reformed Force H were to screen the larger ships, including the sister battleships *Nelson*, *Rodney*, and the far

newer *Duke of York*, the last battlecruiser *Renown* and the carriers *Victorious*, *Formidable* and *Furious*. Leading Force H from the Admiral's bridge aboard the *Duke of York* was Acting Vice Admiral Edward Syfret. Vice Admiral Borrough was in charge of the Allied Fleet aboard the Landing Headquarters Ship *Bulolo*, with Admiral Cunningham, commanding from ashore, leading as Naval Commander, Allied Expeditionary Force. These command arrangements mattered little to the 'Tribals' as they forged through the water on their way to another amphibious operation.

Torch was very different in many ways from previous amphibious operations. It was not a commando raid, a trial run or an evacuation. It was planned as a fully supplied and supported assault against a committed enemy. Only the most optimistic believed that French soldiers would not defend French territory; after Mers El Kebir and Madagascar it was unlikely that they would be welcoming. But hopes that resistance

Ashanti featuring her 1943 paint scheme. The camouflage was intended to make visual tracking difficult. (*Drachinifel Collection*)

Corunna was a 1943 Batch 'Battle' class which, like many of her sisters, arrived much too late for war, but took the opportunity to fight for hearts and minds, a role that typified much of the naval diplomacy of the Cold War. On one occasion she became the post boat at Christmas between Sicily to Malta, making up a Royal Mail sign and dressing a crewman as Santa Claus to deliver the post. (*Drachinifel Collection*)

would be less than total were to some extent vindicated by an opportunistic deal made by General Eisenhower with the captured Admiral Darlan whereby the Vichy Forces would not surrender, but rather retain rank and privileges and transfer to the Free French. This was, however, more of an issue for the land forces. For the warships, Operation Torch represented another critical Mediterranean convoy battle along with the possible added duty of delivering naval gunfire support. There were other tasks such as *Ashanti* at one point during the night of 7/8 November, along with the *Dido* class cruiser *Argonaut*, being used to make false signals and pretend to be lost merchant ships in an attempt to mislead the Vichy French and other Axis forces in the area into attacking Force H rather than the convoy.

On 8 November 1942, guided by a Fairey Albacore, *Ashanti* and *Tartar* sought to engage a surfaced U-boat just to the east of Algiers. After being illuminated by *Ashanti*'s searchlight, the U-boat turned inside towards the destroyer and dived, coming too close for 'B' mount to bear, but giving *Ashanti* the opportunity to launch depth charges.[269] Unfortunately, *Tartar* was bearing down as hard as she could and suddenly found herself

forced to go full astern using maximum rudder to avoid collision with *Ashanti*, something which would have taken place just where the Albacore's depth charges exploded and the U-boat had dived. In the midst of this mêlée, with the sea transformed into a swirling and foaming mass of water, the U-boat escaped, with a story to tell.

Ashanti's next job, on 9 November, was as part of the screen for the carrier *Argus* which was providing support to the troops ashore. However, as soon as Mers-El-Kebir was secured and cleared, by 11 November *Ashanti*'s job became one of gate guard, to prevent German E-boats, or more likely Italian torpedo boats, from trying to gain entry to the harbour; but also the occasional coraller of circling torpedoes, dropped or accidentally launched by damaged enemy aircraft and ships, and on occasion taking on the role of tugboat when an ocean liner went rogue slipping her own and severing *Ashanti*'s mooring cables.[270] *Ashanti*'s charmed existence, whereby she had managed thus far in the war to avoid major damage, continued, partly thanks to the boom-defence erected around her berth to protect from torpedo attack, but also to luck. For example, the petrol store next to her berth in Oran was hit during an air raid on 14 November very soon after she had left for a patrol, causing an explosion which would have surely destroyed her. In January 1943 she managed to damage a propeller when moving in alongside the battlecruiser *Renown* in Gibraltar to have her feed-water tanks repaired. This of required more time in dock for repairs before her return to work in March 1943 escorting a

Barossa was another 'Battle' class which suffered collision damage, although hers was inflicted by her sister ship *Corunna* responding to orders too quickly and ramming her. Luckily, and thanks to some quick reactions of the watch, it was only the stern starboard quarter that was impacted, though it damaged nine frames and flooded of the spirit compartment, the latter problem quickly solved by an emergency jackstay transfer of rum from another sister, *Agincourt. (Drachinifel Collection)*

convoy of LSIs heading for the Cape of Good Hope.

Eskimo also suffered damage when in harbour, on this occasion alongside the battleship *Nelson* at Mers El Kebir, and though the feed-water boiler room had a fire, the major damage was done to her main electrical cables. This kept her out of the war for a week, but after a herculean feat by the dockyard workers, naval personnel from *Vindictive* and her own crew, *Eskimo* was back to the normal duties of a critical fleet destroyer, principally with Force Q, a cruiser and destroyer task force tasked with operating in the Western Mediterranean. However, this was not for long for the world was about to change.

Cadiz looks still incomplete in this photograph. A 1942 Batch 'Battle' class, she was delayed and eventually completed without many of her 40mm weapons because after the war was over the Navy just needed ships in the water to replace so many damaged ships. *(Drachinifel Collection)*

Tartar was the 'Lucky' ship during Operation Husky. She started her career, pre-war, as one of the escorts of *Empress of Australia*, and she was also the lead escort for *Queen Elizabeth* on her maiden voyage. These duties were followed by a hard fighting war. (*Drachinifel Collection*)

By 7 May 1943, the Axis armies in North Africa were no longer fighting, but withdrawing on all fronts as rapidly as they could; it was naturally assumed that there would now be an attempt to evacuate their troops, as the British had done at Crete, Dunkirk and Namsos. On 8 May Admiral Cunningham, intending to take full advantage of this, issued the order to the Fleet to 'sink, burn and destroy. Let nothing pass.' With these words Operation Retribution commenced.[271] After such an impassioned inception, the anticipated evacuation proved an anticlimax. The German and Italian high command were both unwilling as well as unable to recover their forces without serious risk of losses. As a result, Retribution was less a ferocious battle than a rescue exercise, often of small craft, one of which was towing an RAF sergeant pilot in his dinghy. The highlight for *Eskimo* was capturing a Panzer division's Chief of Staff. Despite its limited scope, the operation was not without risk. The destroyer *Laforey* was hit by a shore battery and a 'Hunt' class escort destroyer, *Bicester*, was bombed by an RAF Spitfire while carrying out minesweeping duties, despite her upper works being painted red and sporting a large Union flag.

Very Special Operations

On 19 June 1943 five warships sped across the Mediterranean, preceded by minesweepers and under the densest possible fighter cover. While the minesweepers and the fighters were a little out of the ordinary – normally there would be a couple of the former and at a

most a flight of the latter – the ships at the heart of this operation had been chosen to match the nature of the occasion: the four largest destroyers available, *Eskimo*, her sister ship *Nubian*, together with the 'J' class *Jervis* and the 'L' class *Lookout*, escorting the small *Arethusa* class cruiser *Aurora*. This group could have been mistaken for a destroyer sweep, and an enemy pilot, especially one engaged with fighter cover, could have easily missed the presence of a small cruiser in a pack of large destroyers. The degree of care and attention on this occasion was warranted by the presence of the King aboard ship, who was going to Malta. Setting out from Tripoli, the little force arrived safely in Grand Harbour, Valletta, at 0800hrs on 20 June. The King was given fourteen hours to tour the island before being whisked back to Tripoli. The ships were on maximum alert the entire time, for although the Mediterranean was now safer, for this mission nothing was safe enough in their minds. The orders to the destroyer captains having been clear, that any and all measures necessary to protect the cruiser would be justified. After leaving the King at Tripoli and a short respite, they returned to Malta and, almost immediately, into the jaws of the enemy. It was from Malta that the ships would proceed with the next phase of the Mediterranean war.

For *Nubian*, having been assigned to the reformed Force K in December 1942, and earning her laurels the hard way, Malta was by this point practically her home port. Fortunately, while operations were intensive, the opposition was frequently less than equal to the task and below the fighting standard which might have been expected. The force actually deployed consisted of poorly-armed merchant ships, schooners, torpedo boats and a trawler with a single 66mm Stromboli gun. The trawler, combusted under a maelstrom of shells provided by a welter of 4.7in destroyer guns, the explosion showering *Nubian*'s deck in oily soot and jagged shrapnel, possibly causing more risk of injury than her gun had.[272] As time went on, Operation Retribution offered ever slimmer pickings and even these started to dry up within a couple of weeks.

Elite crews expect to be in the action, although they too enjoy a respite, and if too many days are spent at sea to no avail it can weaken morale or, worse, crews might become overconfident. But in this case the ferocious pace of operations (Operation Retribution had after all come on the heels of Operation Torch, which itself had come on the heels of a slew of operations) did not let up the entirety of 1943, and that level of intensity can have an impact of its own. It is possible that the pace and constant activity of operations was telling on the crews, because *Nubian* suffered her own accident in April. A 4in graze fuze shell, fired from 'X' mount, proved faulty and exploded alongside the 40mm pom-pom, instantly killing two ratings and wounding another who later died in Bighi Hospital on Malta.[273] It was a sad loss, but a sort of harbinger of what was to come.

Two events now occurred involving hospital ships. The first concerned an Italian hospital ship which *Nubian*, along with the two 'P' class destroyers, *Paladin* and *Petard*, encountered on 4 May 1943. This encounter took place at an extended range, because the British destroyers having destroyed a convoy consisting of a merchant ship *Campo Basso* loaded with munitions and vehicles, and an escorting *Spica* class torpedo boat *Perseo*, off the coast of Kelibia, Tunisia, the night before were eager to get back to Malta. They let this vessel go having signalled her as to where they expected survivors to be from the previous night's action; some officers

wished they had inspected her to make sure she was what she claimed to be.

Later that week they encountered another hospital ship, this time flying the Nazi merchant ensign. It was a converted yacht shadowing the British destroyers, *Nubian*, *Paladin* and *Petard*, as they carried out a patrol. A boarding party was despatched and and after a thorough search of the vessel, which revealed no signs of sick or wounded personnel, but plenty of arms and ammunition, the yacht was taken as a prize of war and her crew put under armed guard. However, the crew still tried to cause trouble and it was found they were carrying iron in their pockets with the intention of upsetting the compass. The return journey to Malta took three days, with a diet of black bread and tinned pears as sustenance for the prize crew.[274]

In June 1943 *Nubian* paired up with her sister *Tartar* for island-storming operations to clear the Fleet's path from North Africa to Sicily in preparation for Operation Husky, the invasion of Sicily. Beginning with Pantelleria, and in the company of other destroyers and cruisers, Rear Admiral Rhoderick McGrigor (a future First Sea Lord), commanded the forces from aboard *Tartar*, providing another instance of 'Tribals' being used to command operations, even if they were not openly (officially) chosen as flagships. The operation, which began on 11 June, went well. The island was secured quickly with minimal resistance, and sub-

Camperdown was a classic example of the 1942 Batch 'Battle' class. She was rammed by the 'Flower' class corvette *Coreopsis* during the filming of *The Cruel Sea* and had to be towed to the 1953 Coronation Review. (*Drachinifel Collection*)

Finisterre was another of the 1942 Batch 'Battles' which had been rushed into service for the 19th DF, although she ended up being retained in home waters and would spend most of her career in the 1st DS. Here she is in Malta, a regular haunt of the 'Battle' class units. (*Maritime Quest*)

sequently most of the force was sent to Lampedusa where again their efforts met with similar success. It was then decided that a single 'Tribal', *Nubian*, was sufficient to tackle Linosa, while the majority of the remaining force moved on to Lampione.[275]

Commander Holland-Martin, captain of *Nubian*, received a signal on 12 June: 'Deal with Linosa tomorrow. Defences unknown.'[276] *Nubian* approached the steep and rocky island at 0530hrs on Sunday 13 June 1943. The landing party was taken ashore by whaler, as her motorboat was still in Malta being repaired and *Nubian* began her conquest of the island. In response to the sounding of her siren to alert the garrison and the people, there was a flourish of white flags waved from all sorts of vantage points. *Nubian* continued to steam slowly round the island, menacing it with her guns and picking up Italian soldiers from the garrison as they rowed out to her in whatever craft they could find.

Ashore the landing party had more difficulty. The commandant was not where he was supposed to have been, and when he was eventually located, he declared it beneath his dignity, both as a commandant and a gentleman, to surrender. He was then informed that his 168-man garrison was already aboard *Nubian* under guard and that his gesture was thus futile.[277] He signed the surrender at 0615hrs. Linosa had been conquered in less than 45 minutes and the crew of *Nubian* celebrated with breakfast. Unfortunately, not all amphibious operations were so easily executed, as *Tartar*'s story shows.

Tartar, the 'Lucky' ship during Operation Husky

Tartar was christened 'Lucky' *Tartar* by her flotilla mates because, despite taking part in many of the Royal

Navy's most high profile and risky operations such as Operation Husky, she survived.[278] *Tartar*'s involvement with Husky and the invasion of Sicily is a good point from which to examine her history, which demonstrates so well the utility of the class, and the facilities that their design offered.

From D+1 *Tartar* was primarily on amphibious duty, joining with the ACID assault convoy (the assaults for D-Day in Operation Husky were called ACID, BATK, CENT, DIME and RESERVE) aiming for the Augusta to Catania area of eastern Sicily. On the night of D-Day she escorted the landing craft in, leading them to the correct position despite the failure to pick up the sonic buoys placed by submarine.[279] As the landing craft approached two powerful enemy searchlights were switched on. They were immediately engaged by *Tartar*, using all her guns to extinguish them before they could be of use.[281]

On D+2, 10 July 1943, *Tartar* took a break from supporting the amphibious operations to join Force H in a sweep of the Sicilian Channel, the strait between Tunisia and Sicily, and the sweep was entirely without incident, barring a false ASDIC contact which resulted in the dropping of a single depth charge.[280] This is testimony to how successfully the Navy had sanitised the Mediterranean by that time. The Italian fleet was still a presence, but Mare Nostrum had become, as it had largely been since the Battle of Trafalgar, a decidedly Royal Navy body of water. After completing the sweep, *Tartar* returned to her previous station providing supporting fire and air cover for the amphibious operation until late on D+2 when an air attack disabled her sister ship *Eskimo*. *Tartar* assisted her back to Malta.[282]

These were not the most perhaps the most significant aspects of *Tartar*'s involvement with Husky. Because of its success, it was hugely important beyond its immediate impact in the Mediterranean for it was a proving a ground where lessons were learned, especially with regard to Operation Overlord the following year, and the fact that *Tartar* had on board Major J Michael Lind made her contribution particularly important.[283]

It was Major Lind's report which emphasised the need during training to accustom 'by practice to the motion of their craft' the troops who would be used in an assault, and which provided the necessary confirmation for what had already been suspected and which would inform a lot of the training for D-Day.[284] In addition, he recommended the need for those directing the guns with the landing parties ashore and those firing them from ships to have met in order to be able to better understand each other.[285] He drew directly on his experience of *Tartar*, having watched gun crews do

Cadiz looks a lot more finished here, although all the 40mm Bofors mounts and searchlights are under covers. (*Drachinifel Collection*)

their best to understand what was needed by the troops when the two sides were not used to talking to each other. Unfortunately, this was a lesson which was forgotten soon after the end of the war, and had to be re-learnt in 1982 during the Falklands War, testimony to the importance of institutional memory.[286] Finally, Lind enunciated clearly the difficulty of unloading merchant ships and the potential consequences which would have occurred had the enemy had more assets, especially artillery or aircraft.[287] These were crucial lessons which were to have an impact on D-Day. Most significantly, perhaps, is that although Dieppe had previously shown the need for the Mulberry harbours, the experience of Husky emphasised this as a priority which could not take even a day; it needed to be ready to go the moment the beaches were secured. This was not to be *Tartar*'s

only involvement in Overlord, although the duties of the 10th Flotilla will be discussed later. Furthermore, it was also not her only experience of carrying a very special passenger.

On her next amphibious operation, Operation Baytown, which could be called a precursor of Operation Avalanche, the main landings at Salerno, *Tartar* was carrying Admiral Cunningham.[288] Having read Lind's report, he wanted to make his own assessment of the amphibious operations for which, as Commander-in-Chief Mediterranean Fleet, he was largely respon-

Sikh at Malta before the Second World War when she was a pristine, white, the elegant presence ship with her crew lining the rails and giving little indication, beyond 'B' mount's painted stripes, of the frantic rescue of refugees from Cartagena displaced by the Spanish Civil War, or the global conflict she herself would soon be swept up in and which would eventually overwhelm her. (*Drachinifel Collection*)

Gabbard was a 1942 Batch 'Battle' class built by Swan Hunter and entered service in 1946, but due in part to the manning crisis did not achieve real operational activity till 1947. Her career would have high points and low points, and in 1949 she was called upon to tow the damaged carrier *Albion* into port after the larger ship had collided with a collier. (*Maritime Quest*)

sible.[289] *Tartar* was the ideal vessel. As a destroyer she could get closer inshore, allowing a better view, and her speed allowed a wide area to be covered. Most importantly, however, the space provided by the 'Tribal' class design meant both the C-in-C and a small staff could be accommodated.[290] 'Lucky' *Tartar* may not have had the blessings which her sister *Ashanti* experienced, but she had earned her own reputation for good fortune. This, combined with a 'Tribal's' inbuilt toughness,

made her a 'relatively safe' ship for a VIP. The report on Avalanche by Cunningham, written very soon after it was over, makes interesting reading, especially in light of D-Day.

Particularly pertinent was why the Gulf of Salerno was chosen over the Gulf of Geata further north, despite the presence of *Unicorn* acting in the capacity of a light fleet carrier, together with four escort carriers being made available to support operations. They made up Force V, under the command of the by then Rear Admiral Vian, and were in addition to two existing fleet carriers and battleships of Force H of the Mediterranean Fleet. Despite this air cover the Gulf of Salerno was favoured because single-seat fighters could reach there from bases in Sicily.[291] Furthermore, due to the Italian Armistice, Force H spent most of its time either covering the escape of the Italian fleet or providing air defence for Force V, which took the lead in providing essential combat air support.[292]

The problems experienced with the loading of stores during the operation was something which would again be experienced by naval forces in the Falklands War,

Finisterre was one of the ships activated when the submarine *Affray* was lost in the English Channel. Eyewitnesses watched as she went astern from her berth, turned on her axis and then shot out of Portsmouth Harbour with every knot she could muster. (*Drachinifel Collection*)

St Kitts was a 1942 Batch 'Battle' class and when she had been in service just three years, she and *Gabbard* were sent to take part in Operation Rusty, an exercise intended to determine how well the new ships stood up to arctic ice, especially their crucial electronic equipment. (*Drachinifel Collection*)

although in the case of Avalanche it actually put four Landing Craft Tank out of action, causing problems beyond just logistical issues.[293] Loaded stores had to be carefully balanced because of the stresses that could put on the hulls, something that was possibly better understood by Merchant Navy crews than wartime naval personnel. In addition, the right stores had to be loaded at the right time and in the right order to support the operations ashore, something that required careful co-ordination.

Through all the details of the report there appear little asides which seem to have been added in later in the war by Admiral Cunningham. In a section on Gunnery and Bombardment, Point 33, has been added 'The gunnery lessons learnt in this operation have been applied in operations in 1944 and 1945'. By that point in 1945, Cunningham was First Sea Lord and many of the lessons drawn from his own earlier observations and the reports of others, had been applied.[294] This shows how useful was his experience on *Tartar*, and that his first-hand knowledge helped him face the weighty decisions he had to make later with more certainty.

Force K

After *Tartar*'s involvement with Baytown, she continued to play a part in Operation Avalanche. With her sister ship *Nubian* and the other destroyers of the 19th Flotilla,

she was assigned to the 15th Cruiser Squadron in Force K.[295] Force K was to have served as the 'supporting force' if there had been a fleet action, and would have been recalled to Force H. If the assault forces needed fire support, they were to charge in and provide bombardment. Basically, these ships were grouped together as the 'forward reserve'. This was a role for which the 'Tribals' were eminently well suited, and which would comprise most of *Tartar*'s subsequent war experience.

By 1943 Force K was well into its third incarnation. Its first had been as an Africa based anti-surface raider formation in 1939; the next two were spent as surface raiders. Their role was simple: to operate from Malta and cut off all supplies to North Africa by whatever means possible. The second had unfortunately to come to an end following a nasty experience in a minefield on 19/20 December 1941, not far from Tripoli, when the *Arethusa* class cruiser *Aurora* was damaged, and the *Leander* class cruiser *Neptune* and the destroyer *Kandahar* sunk. The third incarnation of this force came to a conclusion after the successful completion of Operation Stone Age in November 1942. *Nubian* was a key part of this convoy operation which brought important supplies to Malta.

Arguably, one of Force K's most critical successes took place the following year, on 3 May 1943. It has already been mentioned briefly, but now is the time to consider it in more detail. *Nubian*, along with the 'P' class sisters *Petard* and *Paladin*, tracked down the Italian transport ship *Campo Basso* with her torpedo boat escort, *Perseo*, heading for Tunisia. Engaging their quarry at 2347hrs, they fired ten salvos at the merchant ship.[296]

Mohawk was lost to torpedoes, fired from a sinking Italian destroyer, after taking part in the destruction of an entire Axis convoy bound for North Africa, but even before the war had begun she had faced the threat of Italian torpedoes during the Spanish Civil war. (*Maritime Quest*)

Laden with a cargo of vehicles, bombs and landmines, it is not surprising that the 60 4.7in shells and 120 4in shells that hit the *Campo* reduced her to a fireball so huge that the destroyers, which were three miles off, felt the effect of the blast. It was so violent it was claimed stacks of signals sheets were whisked off tables in the Wireless Telegraphy (W/T) room, while the stokers manning the boilers 'complained that it felt as though their ears were being drawn out'.[297] Nor did the *Perseo* escape. First *Nubian* engaged her, and then the other two destroyers joined the fray even after she was out of control and belching smoke and steam; soon she exploded and sank. What is perhaps most illustrative of the relentlessness of Force K's activities and duties, is that during this engagement, *Nubian's* engine room artificers were repairing the evaporator distiller, completing the job on their way back to Malta.[298]

After Operations Husky, Avalanche, Baytown and Slapstick (the September 1943 landings at Taranto) in which Force K had consistently been called upon to provide a mobile, high-speed, hard-hitting reaction force, it was time for a change to suit changing circumstances. The Italian fleet had surrendered, along with their government, on 9 September 1943. Most of the fleet went on to form the Italian Co-Belligerent Navy (the Marina Cobelligerante Italiano of the Italian Royalist forces) which was probably not to be wholly trusted, but it did mean the Allies could, with these Italian forces fighting on their side, restructure their own Mediterranean forces. Force K was placed under the command of Force H. The latter included at this point *Nelson* and *King George V*, used largely to provide support for the Army and to deal with any remaining units of the Italian navy which had either been taken over by the Germans or were still loyal to the Fascist regime of Mussolini. By January 1944 it was no longer necessary. Force H was disbanded and its ships proceeded to the Home and Eastern Fleets to continue the war on those fronts.

Battle of North Cape

December 1943 witnessed an engagement of huge import that saw the Canadian 'Tribals' *Athabaskan*, *Huron* and *Haida* representing the class, although *Ashanti* was involved as well. Furthermore, *Savage*, the 'S' class test bed for the 'Battle' class, was also an important participant. But before considering the Battle of North Cape and its real impact, it is necessary look back almost a year, to December 1942 and the Battle of the Barents Sea, to understand its context and potential impact. This action involved Captain Robert St Vincent Sherbrooke, a 'Tribal' class alumnus, who had commanded both *Cossack* during the Battles of Narvik and *Matabele* prior to his command of *Onslow* and the 17th Destroyer Flotilla, which provided the bulk of the escort of Convoy JW15B during the Battle of the Barents Sea. There was distant cover available from the 'Town' class cruiser *Sheffield*, the 'Crown Colony' class cruiser, *Jamaica*, and two more destroyers under the command of Rear Admiral Robert Burnett, though they were many hours away.

The scene was set when the Kriegsmarine heavy cruisers, including the *Deutschland* class *Lützow* (formerly the *Deutschland*, which under her previous name had provided not only the class name, but also the less successful Northern Waters counterpart to the cruise of the *Graf Spee*) and the *Admiral Hipper* of the class of that name, along with five destroyers, including three vessels from what the Allies referred to as the 'Narvik' class; two Type 36A, *Z29* and *Z30*, and one Type 36A (Mob) *Z31*, as well as the pre-war destroyers, one Type 1934A *Friedrich Eckholdt* (Z16) and two Type 1934 *Richard Beitzen* (Z4) and *Theodor Riedel* (Z6), all hove into view between 0800hrs and 0820hrs on Thursday 31 December. What would unfold was described in the VC citation which appeared a little over a week later in the Third Supplement to *The London Gazette* on Friday 8 January 1943.

The KING has been graciously pleased to approve the award of the VICTORIA CROSS, for valour in the defence of a convoy, to:

Captain Robert St. Vincent Sherbrooke, DSO, Royal Navy.

Captain Sherbrooke, in HMS *Onslow*, was the Senior Officer in command of the destroyers escorting an important convoy bound for North Russia. On the morning of 31st of December, off the North Cape, he made contact with a greatly superior enemy force, which was attempting to destroy the convoy. Captain Sherbrooke led his destroyers into attack and closed the Enemy. Four times the Enemy tried to attack the convoy, but was forced each time to withdraw behind a smoke screen to avoid the threat of torpedoes, and each time Captain Sher-

St Kitts was completed in 1946 and escorted *Vanguard,* Britain's last battleship, to South Africa on the Royal Tour which included King George VI, Queen Elizabeth and the Princesses. (*Drachinifel Collection*)

booke pursued him and drove him outside gun range of the convoy and towards our covering forces. These engagements lasted about two hours, but after the first forty minutes HMS *Onslow* was hit, and Captain Sherbrooke was seriously wounded in the face and temporarily lost the use of one eye. Nevertheless he continued to direct the ships under his command until further hits on his own ship compelled him to disengage, but not until he was satisfied that the next Senior Officer has assumed control. It was only then that he agreed to leave the bridge for medical attention, and until the convoy was out of danger he insisted on receiving all reports of the action.

His courage, his fortitude and his cool and prompt decisions inspired all around him. By his leadership and example the convoy was saved from damage and was brought safely to its destination

Captain Sherbrooke's available destroyers included, in addition to his own ship *Onslow*, *Achates* and *Onslow's* sisters *Orwell*, *Obedient* and *Obdurate*; this number was further reduced as *Achates* was left with the convoy. This whole operation was about aggression. The Kriegsmarine force, which had been brought together under Vizeadmiral Oskar Kummetz, should have routed them. However, there were two problems. At the time Kummetz was one of the most unlucky commanding officers in the Kriegsmarine; it had been his cruiser *Blücher* which had been sunk during the invasion of Norway. Most importantly no one had told Sherbrooke that he was meant to lose. For an officer who had been inculcated into the culture of the 'Tribal' class flotillas, such a concept would have been as foreign to him as

the idea of withdrawing. Furthermore, no one instructed him to scatter the convoy, as had been the case with PQ17. Six big German destroyers and two oversized heavy cruisers should have overwhelmed the four British destroyers, and previously, on occasions when those circumstances were feared, such orders would have been issued.

Sherbrooke, mostly using aggressive feinting, gunfire, the threat of torpedoes and the liberal use of smoke, drove Kummetz and his ships off. In effect, the British destroyers held off the German force through intimidation rather than actual strength, just as *Sikh* had against the Regia Marina's *Littorio* earlier in the war. However, the greatest impact of this action was not the saving of the convoy, although that was important. Of greater effect was the psychological impact on Hitler of the resignation of Admiral Raeder and replacement by Dönitz, and the threat to the continued existence of the Kriegsmarine's large surface raiders. If Hitler had scrapped them at the beginning of 1943 the impact on the rest of the war could have been enormous. It would have freed a great many ships from the Home Fleet to reinforce the Mediterranean and Eastern Fleets, including almost every battleship and cruiser not needed for D-Day, every aircraft carrier bigger than an escort carrier, plus most of the smaller utilitarian vessels, together with most of the Navy's cruisers. Dönitz successfully headed off this domestic political attack, and it was principally due to this that in December 1943 a battle-

The 1942 Batch 'Battle' class *Trafalgar* carries out a series of high-speed manoeuvres, typifying the handling qualities of the class. (*Maritime Quest*)

ship, the *Scharnhorst,* was sent out to intercept Arctic convoys.

This is what made the Battle of North Cape matter, not only from the British point of view, but also because of the high stakes involved on the German side. It was the last throw of the dice, an attempt to provide *Scharnhorst,* together with her sister ship *Gneisenau,* an opportunity to repeat the successes of previous operations, including the 1939 North Atlantic cruise which sank the *Rawalpindi,* Operation Berlin of 1941, and the Channel Dash in February 1942. This time, however, she was alone. Following the Battle of the Barents Sea, the work to repair the damage *Gneisenau* sustained during the Channel Dash ceased. Furthermore, *Scharnhorst* had only five *Narvik* class destroyers accompanying her. However, prior to the battle they were sent off by Konteradmiral Eric Bey to search for the convoy but lost contact with the flagship. With no cruiser, she was on her own, a true surface raider, but without the benefit of being far from the enemy's main fleet. As it turned out, the events of December 1943, shared a month and a geographical area with those of December 1942.

Onslow was once again the lead ship of the convoy's ocean escort, that of JW 55B, which was drawn principally from 17th Destroyer Flotilla, by now under the command of another 'Tribal' class alumnus, Captain James Abernethy McCoy, a former commander of *Bedouin.* The convoy also had a close escort, which included two Canadian 'Tribal' class destroyers, *Huron* and *Haida,* the latter now the last surviving 'Tribal' class destroyer. preserved in Hamilton, Ontario. There was also a UK-bound convoy in the area, RA55A, with a

Trafalgar is a name which carries a lot of a weight, and the Royal Navy does not bestow the name lightly. Prior to this 'Battle', it had been carried only by two First Rates and a battleship, so the naming of this ship demonstrated the status of the class in the minds of the Admiralty. (*Drachinifel Collection*)

similar-sized escort which included two more 'Tribals', *Ashanti* and the Canadian *Athabaskan*. In addition, there was Force 1, a cruiser formation made up of the 'Town' class cruiser *Belfast* (now another preserved ship, based in London), as flagship for Vice Admiral Robert Burnett, her older sister *Sheffield*, veteran of the Barents Sea Battle and the 'County' class heavy cruiser *Norfolk*. This was not all. Admiral Sir Bruce Fraser, the C-in-C Home Fleet, the man who had succeeded Admiral Henderson as Third Sea Lord, was at sea in his flagship the new *King George V* class battleship *Duke of York*, armed with ten 14in guns, and with an escort comprising *Jamaica*, a light cruiser and veteran of the Barents Sea action, and the 'S' class destroyers *Savage*, *Saumarez* and *Scorpion*, together with the Royal Norwegian Navy's *Stord*. Put in simple terms, Konteradmiral Bey was advancing into a contested sea with one of the lower capability battleships in service at the time, mounting only 11in guns. He faced a newer, bigger, more heavily armed and armoured battleship, a heavy cruiser, three light cruisers and four destroyers, with potential availability of a maximum of twelve more destroyers, giving odds of between nine to twenty-one versus one.

Bey twice managed to find RA55A on Sunday 26 December but he was driven off both times by Burnett's cruisers and the convoy's destroyers. This was not without some cost to both sides. *Norfolk* had a turret and radar disabled by two hits from 11in shells. *Scharnhorst* also lost her radar, which prevented her from learning when engine problems with *Norfolk* and *Sheffield* left *Belfast* as her sole pursuer. *Scharnhorst* was not going to escape. Fraser was deluged with radio traffic updating him as to *Scharnhorst*'s position, and this allowed him to refine his own attack from the south and to call in further destroyers then escorting RA55A. Simultaneously, he ordered his attendant destroyers to surge ahead and attack with torpedoes. At 1617hrs *Scharnhorst* was detected by *Duke of York*'s Type 273 radar; fifteen minutes later the Type 284 radar had her. Sixteen minutes later at 1648hrs, *Belfast* fired starshell to illuminate the German battleship. *Scharnhorst* was unprepared for what was coming. *Duke of York* opened fire at a range of nearly 12,000yds which, in terms of a 14in shell, is virtually point blank. The first hit disabled *Scharnhorst*'s 'A' and 'B' turrets, a second destroyed the aircraft and their hangar. Bey turned north, hoping to outrun *Duke of York* but *Belfast*, with *Norfolk*, was waiting. *Duke of York* was joined by *Jamaica*, and at 1724hrs Bey sent the message, 'Am surrounded by heavy units'. An hour later, at 1820hrs, *Duke of York* disabled the valiant German ship's No 1 boiler room.

This caused an immediate drop in speed and Fraser was able to send in his destroyers. Now they could attack, pairing up, alternately approaching from each side, while *Scharnhorst* tried to weave and drive them off in turn like a tired and wounded bison driving off wolves. The first set of destroyers scored roughly four hits, further reducing the battleship's speed. *Belfast* and

Jamaica joined in with their torpedoes, before, finally, *Opportune*, *Virago*, *Musketeer* and *Matchless* arrived to unleash a further nineteen torpedoes at her. Despite her motto of *Immer Voran* – ever onward – the mighty *Scharnhorst* went ever downwards into the depths, taking most of her crew with her. The destroyers had struck again. After his victory, and the threat of the large German surface vessels reduced, it is altogether unsurprising that Fraser soon found himself in command of the British Pacific Fleet, accompanied by many of the ships he had led in the Home Fleet.

This battle was significant for the 'Tribal' class. In the Barents Sea action their aggression and training which was brought to the fore. During the Battle of North Cape, their presence provided sufficient capability and reassurance to allow Fraser to denude the convoy of almost everything else, and for not an inconsiderable amount of time, reasonably confident that they were safe. More critically, he could commit what forces he had with 100 per cent certainty that if the Germans had found a convoy with a reduced escort – a Kriegsmarine cruiser of which Fraser was unaware, or a well co-ordinated U-boat attack was launched – the general purpose destroyers would provide a safety net in the face of any such eventuality. They were what gave Fraser and all the Fleet/Force commanders the freedom to take risks. In addition, the 4.5in weapons of *Savage* were absolutely savage, proving to be a good choice and worth the wait for the *Battle*s.

1944: The 10th Destroyer Flotilla and the Battle of Ushant

D-Day or Operation Overlord, the invasion of Normandy, is famous for many reasons, not least for the ferocity of the sea battles which took place around its ragged coast. 'Tribal' class vessels were committed before the start. Unsurprisingly, in view of their capabilities, they had been overwhelmingly selected for the 10th DF which was charged with clearing the seas from Plymouth to the West. The flotilla was made up of *Tartar*, *Ashanti* and *Eskimo*, two Canadian 'Tribal' class destroyers, *Haida* and *Huron*, the 'J' class *Javelin* and two Polish destroyers, the 'N' class *Piorun* and the *Grom* class *Błyskawica* (built by Samuel White, Cowes, and now preserved in Gydnia), and provided force security and ocean control. At various time the 10th also included two Canadian 'Tribals', *Athabaskan* and *Iroquois*, together with the remaining 'Tribal', *Nubian*.[299] They quickly made a name for themselves, so much so that in 1944 a poem, or possibly song, *The Fighting Tenth*, was composed in their honour by Wrens based at Longroom Signal Station.

There are specks on the horizon
As familiar as can be
D10 with his flotilla
Proceeding in from Sea.

Battle ensigns at all mastheads
An impressive sight to see
The *Tartar* with the 10th DF
Come in triumphantly.

The pendants now come visible
Four Three, Five One, Two Four,
Tartar, *Ashanti*, *Huron*,
Astern there loom five more.

Błyskawica, *Javelin*, *Haida*,
Piorun, *Eskimo*,
Buntings on the signal bridge,
Stokers down below.

Proceeding through the gate at last
They move more cautiously
The same old signal flying
Act Independently.

We hope we'll always see you
(Not calling pendant Three)
The Fighting Tenth's a lovely sight
When coming in from sea [300]

In the run up to D-Day the Fighting 10th were employed extensively on channel sweeps, often called 'tunnels', as they were 'a straight run in the dark'. While they avoided following E-boats (Schnellboote) into shallow waters, they could use their radar and guns to reach places into which they preferred not to run. Though *Ashanti* and *Athabaskan* were both occasionally summoned away for others tasks they always returned. On one such trip *Ashanti* was twice fired at by *U-739*; both torpedoes missed and the blessings of the Asante tribe held. On the 'tunnels' the destroyers were often joined by a cruiser; occasionally by *Apollo*, the *Abdiel* class minelayer with a top speed in excess of 40 knots and a bad habit of leaving her escort behind in the middle of night as she full steamed ahead. More frequently, however, it was *Black Prince*, a *Bellona* sub-class *Dido* class cruiser, with a top speed of 32.5 knots, which accompanied the destroyers. A typical 'tunnel' operation was that of 25/26 April 1944. *Black Prince*, *Ashanti*, *Haida*, *Athabaskan* and *Huron* intercepted four *Elbing* class fleet torpedo boats, which at 1,294 tons were virtually small destroyers and carried six torpe-

St James was a 1942 Batch 'Battle' class with the distinction of having unintentionally sunk another ship using her primary gun battery during calibration trials, when instead of hitting the target she hit the tug *Bucanneer* instead with a single 4.5in round. (*Drachinifel Collection*)

does, together with four 4.1in, four 37mm and nine 20mm guns.

While *Black Prince* kept firing starshell until 'B' turret jammed, the 'Tribals' pursued the German ships through rocks, smoke and shallow water in pitch darkness along the coast of France. They worked in pairs, one alternately firing starshell to supplement *Black Prince*'s efforts, the other concentrating on hitting the Kriegsmarine vessels. One was sunk while the other three were damaged. Unfortunately, *Athabaskan* would be lost three days later, when she and *Haida* were a covering a minelaying operation; with intermittent intelligence they investigated what turned out to be German torpedo boats. *T24* hit *Athabaskan* and many of the crew, including the commanding officer Lieutenant Commander John Stubbs who refused rescue by *Haida* while trying to swim back to rescue more crew, were lost. The missions continued until 2/3 June when the flotilla was placed on the Hurd's Deep patrol (a position to the northwest of the Channel Islands and the deepest place in the Channel) and the Flotilla Commander given almost unprecedented powers.

In October 1943, another *Dido* class cruiser *Charybdis* and the 'Hunt' class destroyer *Limborne* were sunk by German destroyers during an earlier 'tunnel' operation.[301] Taking this and the critical nature of the cross Channel activity into account, the 'Tribals' and their colleagues in 10th DF were employed as a blocking force to prevent German surface vessels interfering.

This continued even after D-Day, as the great fear was the Germans getting in amongst the lightly armed, slow moving, numerous transports and landing craft – which give them plenty of targets and make engaging them a nightmare for the British.

The closest it came to happening was on 9 June, when the 10th DF engaged the German 8th DF.[302] The result was a hard fought action where the 10th DF carried out their orders successfully, though it was largely overshadowed by the scale of the other events which had started three days earlier and were ongoing. This action, the Battle of Ushant, as some call it, or the 'action off Île De Bas' as it is referred to by the Royal Navy in their records, was significant.[303]

The 'Tribals' had not been selected just because they carried more guns and had a well-established reputation for doing whatever was necessary to win. Their size and dimensions made them the perfect candidates for the integration and upgrading of radar throughout the war. This meant that, on 9 June, all eight vessels incorporated good radar. While all carried Warning Combined Type 291 (as was being fitted to the 'Battle' class) it was seldom used because it could be monitored by the enemy to reveal their positions. The Warning Surface units were for the most part better. The reason for this qualification is that while *Ashanti*, *Eskimo* and *Tartar* were fitted with the latest Type 276, which could detect smallish destroyers at a range of about 12 miles, the other two Canadian vessels, *Haida* and *Huron*, were equipped with the Type 271Q, which was older and had, theoretically, a far less useful display, only capable of detecting destroyers at nine miles. This latter fit was repeated on the Polish *Błyskawica* and *Piorun*, as well as the British *Javelin*.

The Type 276 had the further advantage being a powered rotation unit. This enabled it not only to per-

Solebay was something of a special guardian for the Royal Yacht *Britannia*, especially during the early 1960s when she was her escort for visits to the Mediterranean as well as West Africa where they visited *Ashanti*'s favourite port, Takoradi, and where she was described as stealing the show whilst all lit up in Freetown at night. (*Drachinifel Collection*)

form constant horizon scanning, but to support a Plan Position Indicator (PPI) display. This was critical for night operations because it enabled relative positions to be shown in real time. This is why ships fitted with Type 276 had the better display. However, there are some reports, based on night actions in which the 10th DF were involved, that suggest it might not have been so simple. In fact, it appears that 10th DF may have had PPI fitted to more than just those ships with the perfect radar set up for it. It is even possible that they had somehow modified their radars themselves to work with the displays. After all, the fitting of a small electric motor to rotate a radar, which was already manually rotatable, would not have been a complicated task for a ship's crew. Actions such as these were seldom divulged, and not just for reasons of national security, but because of the sensitivity about where the electric motor might have been sourced. It is unsurprising there are conflicting reports. However, considering the frequency of night operations, their operational doctrine (which will be examined next) and the critical tasking of the unit, it would have made sense for the unit to 'adapt' their kit where possible.

The need and willingness to adapt is made clear in the service history of 10th DF. Commander St John Tyrwhitt was the only son of Admiral of the Fleet Sir Reginald Tyrwhitt, who had commanded the Harwich force in the First World War. After the war St John would follow in his father's footsteps, rising to Admiral and Second Sea Lord. He handed over to Commander Basil Jones in March 1944, and the 10th DF soon developed new tactics. Tyrwhitt, like his father, had already been experimenting not only with different options for night operations and during the hunting of the *Bismarck*, Vian had famously and convincingly made use of the box formation. Jones considered this, but after careful analysis of the 25/26 April operation discussed earlier, instead tried something new which would take advantage of the 'Tribals" specific qualities: their heavy forward gun arrangement, their radar and the quality of their crews.

It was desirable that all destroyers should have their forecastle guns bearing, their Radar unimpeded ahead, and ships capable of individual action comb enemy torpedoes. Only a reasonably broad and shaken-out line of bearing formation [in this case, line abreast] could satisfy these conditions. It was realised cruising at night for lengthy periods in such a formation was a strain as regards station keeping, although the P.P.I. removed much of the strain [for those who had it]. Accordingly Line Ahead for comfort, and Line of Bearing for action, was the order of the day.[304]

The traditional or standard formation had been line ahead. It was safe and kept the force together during a night battle. It had been used at the Battle of Cape Bon and it was why the two ships at the rear had such little impact on the action. It was also more difficult to avoid torpedo attacks and, additionally, when turning away from an attack the destroyers often lost their prey. Line abreast manoeuvring changed all that and it was the quality of the crews that made it possible. It also explains the use of the word 'comb', in that the ships in formation abreast would act like the teeth of a comb, forcing the water between them which, it was hoped, would suck torpedoes and possibly mines into the confluence between the ships, rather than hitting them.

It was a change in tactics which, had it had happened earlier in the war, would certainly have been used to justify the weapons arrangement of the 'Battle' class. That though is ancillary to the action currently under discussion. With this tactical change and the fitted radars, in addition to the innate firepower included in Henderson's original design and handling characteristics of 'Tribal' class vessels, the scene was set for an English Channel version of the Pacific campaign destroyer battle of Cape St George.

The action took place of Ushant while the Allies were still coming ashore. If the German destroyers had made it to the lanes which the supply ships were crossing in order to bring more soldiers and materiel to the fighting effort ashore, the Allied operations would have been severely disrupted (possibly even halted temporarily) with all the consequent knock-on effects on the land operation. Instead, the three Kriegsmarine destroyers,

Solebay in 1945, just after being completed. It was broadly in this form that she would start for the Far East, only to be recalled to the 5th DF to take on the role not just of Flotilla Leader, but also German Waters Guard Ship, visiting Wilhelmshaven, Cuxhaven, Kiel, Flensburg and Hamburg taking part in what was a post-war northern European presence mission. (*Maritime Quest*)

two Type 1936A *Narvik* class vessels *Z24* and *Z32*, along with a captured Dutch vessel, the *Gerard Callenburgh* (renamed *ZH1*) and a single torpedo boat, the *Elbing* class destroyer-sized vessel *T24* (which had sunk *Athabaskan* in April) of the 8th Zerstörer-flotille that the Germans sent never reached their target.[305]

Thanks to intelligence both from Bletchley Park Enigma, and from the aptly named Headache, the C-in-C Plymouth, Admiral Leatham was able to coach the 10th to an optimal position. The Headache system was fitted to destroyers which allowed them to tune into enemy radio communications. It was aptly named Headache because it sometimes caused trouble and misunderstandings. But on this occasion it worked well and, combined with other assets, helped Leatham to direct his forces. At 0114hrs on 9 June, *Tartar*'s Type 276 displayed contact, bearing 241° at a range of 10 miles. In contrast, though the Germans received some warning from their radars, it was only because of the moonlit night they knew the Allied destroyers were almost upon them. Immediately, the element of surprise having been lost, the German vessels swung and launched their torpedoes before trying to make good their escape. They took aim at the 19th Division. Each flotilla was grouped into two divisions, also given ascending numbers as a rule. In the 10th DF there was the 19th Division, built around Jones in *Tartar*, and the 20th Division, assembled around the less experienced Namiensniowski in *Błyskawica* and formed from the more recent additions to the flotilla. With ample warning from Headache, and advancing in line abreast, the 'Tribals' of the 19th Division just kept advancing, avoiding the torpedoes and, having lost no speed through diversionary tactics, were soon upon the German vessels.

This allowed Jones and the 10th DF to begin the action at a fast pace as the two forces engaged each other. Once the initial contact phase was over, *Z32* turned north to the waiting embrace of the 20th Division, while the 19th Division split, with *Ashanti* teaming with

Sluys, soon after she was completed, making minimal speed and appearing almost serene. (*Maritime Quest*)

Tartar against *ZH1* and *Z24*.[306] *Z32* managed to get away from 20th Division, which had been in line astern and had had less time to organise themselves for the fight. The captain of *Z32* deserves credit for the handling of his ship, managing to surprise and score some hits against *Tartar* before disappearing into the resulting smoke. This did little to help the rest of the Zerstörerflotille, and just at this point *ZH1*, emerged from the smoke (traditionally something with gave an attacking destroyer an advantage) straight into a fusillade of fire from *Ashanti* and then *Tartar*. Thanks to radar and their firepower – possibly involving two torpedoes from *Ashanti* – she was soon disabled, at which point both 'Tribals' closed in and finished the job with more gunfire.

South of this action, *Z24* and *T24* were being given undivided attention from the Canadian 'Tribals', *Haida* and *Huron*, a move which forced the German vessels to flee into a British minefield that had not been properly charted. That it proved only successful in halting the Canadian pursuit was not well received when reported back to Admiral Ramsay. However, the night was not yet over and *Z32*, having evaded the 'Tribals' three times, was now to meet her end. Initially, when they encountered each other at 0230hrs, both sides

thought the others were part of their force. The Canadians became suspicious first and, using radar, opened fire with star shell from their 4in 'X' mounts and blazed 4.7in gunfire from 'A' and 'B' mounts; for the second time that night a German destroyer took refuge inside a British minefield. However, this time the Allies maintained a radar lock and were able to follow until, at 0444hrs, they opened fire again. Seeing the 'Tribal' silhouette in the flashes of their guns, *Z32* believed themselves to be engaging cruisers. By 0513hrs, with his ship enveloped in flames, and in a repeat of the Battle of Narvik, the captain ordered her to be run aground off Île de Batz.[307]

Fortunately, for the 10th DF's next critical operation, which took place in the eastern Indian Ocean in the approaches to Singapore, they had charts with accurate locations of minefields, and once again they were employed clearing the path for an amphibious operation; this one, however, never took place, and this time it was *Nubian* rather than *Tartar* forging the path.

Nubian, a virtually unmatched service

Calabria 1940, Norway 1940, Mediterranean 1940–3, Libya 1940, Matapan 1941, Sfax 1941, Greece 1941, Crete 1941, Malta Convoys 1941, Sicily 1943, Salerno 1943, Arctic 1944, Norway 1944, Burma 1945–5

'The dominion of the sea, as it is an ancient and undoubted right of the crown of England, so it is the best security of the land. The wooden walls are the best walls of his kingdom.' These are the words of Thomas Coventry, Baron and Lord Keeper of the Great Seal, in a speech to judges on 17 June 1635 when justifying a ship money tax. Three hundred and ten years later he would have replaced 'wooden walls' with 'steel walls' and *Nubian* would have been firmly in his eye, for her battle honours read like a list of the Royal Navy's campaigns in the war. *Nubian* was a ship which thanks to record as much as design could easily lay claim to the title of the Royal Navy's 'Swiss Army Knife Destroyer', though the records of *Ashanti*, *Eskimo* and *Tartar* were not far behind.[308] Only *Warspite* would exceed her in battle honours, and she had been in another World War. *Nubian* has already been mentioned a number of times, but there is still much to tell; and she was, in many ways, a quiet achiever, not acquiring the fame of some others in her class.

The understated report compiled by the Royal Navy of *Nubian*'s service after the war rather confirms this. After taking part in the landings at Salerno and Sicily,[309] *Nubian* 'had a busy time helping to stop supplies from reaching Rommel, and sank at least two big merchant ships and one destroyer'.[310] While conducting what was considered 'probably the best work of her career' during a ten-day period in September 1943 she regularly bombarded Pantelleria, Lampedusa, Catanai, Augusta and Salerno, expending thousands of rounds in support of Allied troops – nearly 2,000 rounds into Salerno alone.[311] Despite all the reports on her service, when writing in response to an enquiring cadet unit officer, the head of the Royal Navy's Historical section gave only a minimal summing up of her service:

> H.M.S. Nubian was a destroyer of the 'Tribal' Class, completed in 1938, which served with distinction throughout the Second World War. She was in the Mediterranean until after the end of the war with Italy in September, 1943, taking part in the Battle of Matapan, the defence of Crete, the capture of Sicily, and other operations. Following a refit in the Tyne in the winter of the 1943-1944 she served in the Home Fleet for the rest of 1944, and in the Far East in 1945. She was placed on the disposal list in 1949.[312]

This is not entirely accurate. While *Nubian* started the war in the Mediterranean, along with the rest of the 4th DF to which she belonged, they did not stay there.[313] As previously told, the 4th DF was called back to Britain and almost immediately thrust into operations around Norway. Shortly after Norway *Nubian* and her sister *Mohawk* were transferred from the 4th DF to the 14th DF, and by 17 May 1940 were back in warmer waters.[314] By March 1941 they had become the reliable fleet units which Admiral Cunningham felt comfortable using in critical roles such as at the Battle of Matapan, previously discussed.

Matapan is an interesting battle, mostly because it has the distinction of being one of the few battles ever fought which conformed to one side's pre-war doctrines, at least in outline. The RN did manage to use air attacks to slow down the enemy, and it did use cruisers to then track that enemy, while the battle fleet closed in; and it did fight its main action at night. What is often forgotten about this battle is that it was a convoy protection battle. At this time the Royal Navy were heavily involved in protecting convoys overflowing with British Army personnel, equipment and supplies to Greece, a too tempting a target for the Italian Navy to ignore.[315] However, as so often with chases, the British forces started to spread out. Needing to concentrate his cruisers on the enemy, Cunningham turned to *Nubian* and *Mohawk* to fill the gap, 'to form a visual signal link between Pridham-Wippell's cruisers and the Battle-fleet'.[316] This served two purposes: it kept the need for 'noisier' radio communication to a minimum, and it also provided a means of stopping the Italians slipping unnoticed between the two groups of the British Force, with the intention of either escaping or surprising the main force.[317]

Despite conforming to pre-war plans and exercises, the battle was not all the British hoped it would be. Rather than the battleship *Vittorio Veneto*, damaged but not crippled by an air strike from *Formidable's* Swordfish, they had to make to do with three heavy cruisers, *Pola*, already crippled by aircraft, *Zara* and *Fiume* which Admiral Iachino had despatched back to recover *Pola*.[318] During the night action the destroyer's role was to find and fix the enemy with searchlights, to enable battleships to engage while reducing the risk of a torpedo attack.[319] It was a short sharp battle. The Navy had prepared extensively for night fighting, practising regularly with the available technology such as flashless charges for their guns to minimise exposure of their position and avoid blinding gunners.[320] Despite the focus on support of battleships and the subsequent mêlée action that developed, the British destroyers, including the *Tribal*s, were not as prominent as they might have been in a larger action.

It was, however, *Nubian* which delivered the final blow in the battle, firing a torpedo into *Pola* and sinking her at 0403hrs on 29 March, following the evacuation

Lagos in the 1940s. She returned to the UK after her Far East deployment in 1947 and would be placed in reserve till 1957, during which time she was regularly inspected and overhauled to keep her ready for operations at short notice. (*Maritime Quest*)

of her crew by British ships.[321] Despite going roughly to plan, and despite debate about a poorly-worded signal from Cunningham, the action could never have gone exactly as hoped. To have caught up with the main Italian fleet would have left the British force close to the Italian coast, and exposed it to its air force and having to fight in daylight. Victory might have been theirs, but not one with practically no losses. As it was the Navy lost two Swordfish and crews. Cunningham, given the opportunity, would probably have wished such an outcome for the next operation, one which was on the same scale as Dunkirk in terms of risk and necessity, but even more fraught.

Crete was a direct result of Matapan. Without that victory it would not have been possible to deploy troops and supplies to Greece at the same level, and when German and Italian forces invaded, the British would not have been as exposed. The first evacuation was from the mainland to Crete, which was straightforward. However, on arrival on Crete the forces did not form a cohesive defence.[322] Despite the set-up of a naval defence by Cunningham, which successfully prevented, with some help from the Luftwaffe and the Italian navy's reluctance to commit heavy units, enemy forces approaching, this was ultimately pointless, because the enemy finally came by air. With no organisation in place, the ground forces were quickly dislodged – requiring further evacuation.[323] It was a far more difficult task, which moved Cunningham to make his most famous pronouncement: 'You can build a new ship in three years, but you can't rebuild a reputation in under three hundred years.'[324]

On 26 May, as the destroyers of the 14th DF were escorting *Formidable* and other main fleet units following a successful strike against Scapanto airfield, which lies between Rhodes and Crete, the force was attacked by Ju 87s and Ju 88s. The Stukas went for *Formidable*, hitting her twice.[325] The Ju 88s, which were trying out the new technique of skip bombing, similar in principle to the method employed by the Dambusters, focussed their attack on *Nubian*.[326] They missed, but one bomb, dropped by a Ju 87, hit 'Y' mounting and the resulting explosion caused the loss of her stern and started a number of fires, similar to the damage suffered by *Eskimo* at Narvik, though at the other end of the ship.[327] As with *Eskimo*, *Nubian* was saved by excellent damage control and a miracle, for despite losing her rudder, her props and her propeller shafts were unscathed, and she could manage 20 knots, steering by her main engines. She was escorted back to Alexandria by her flotilla mate, *Jackal*.[328] Her survival was all the more remarkable considering that four cruisers and six destroyers were lost, in addition to damage to *Formidable*, two battleships, four more cruisers, another destroyer and a submarine. Nineteen vessels were put out of action, ten permanently. It was a sacrifice which almost erased in one operation the advantages won by Taranto and Matapan.[329]

Cyprus – 26 May – extract from Commander Ravenhill's report:

The Action

At approximately 1320 on May 26th, when *Nubian* was in position 'B' of screening diagram No.6A screening the Battle Fleet, an attack was made on our forces by a large formation of enemy aircraft consisting of J.U.87s and J.U.88s. As the attack developed *Nubian* opened fire over the Fleet with umbrella barrage. It soon became apparent, however, that the leading enemy units were attacking the screen and two definite attacks were made on *Nubian*, one by a J.U.87 and one by a J.U.88. Speed was increased to 26 Knots (maximum available) and the ship manoeuvred to avoid the bombs which missed.

The Fleet was then attacked and the umbrella barrage was recommenced. Shortly after fire was opened it was observed that *Formidable* had been hit. A number of enemy aircraft then passed down *Nubian*'s port side at a fairly low elevation and fire was transferred to them. At this moment one of the signalmen pointed out a J.U.87 which was approaching the ship at a low level from astern, I put the wheel hard to starboard and directed the guns on this target. The machine was, however, fairly close and before effective fire could be developed it had reached its position and dropped a bomb. This bomb hit No.4 mounting and exploded heavily.[330]

After such damage it is not surprising *Nubian* was out of action for some time. While in Bombay for repairs the Navy took the opportunity to upgrade her, fitting radar, finally changing 'X' mount to a twin 4in high-angle AA system, along with some 20mm Oerlikons and moving the depth-charge throwers, to mention a few.[331] By October 1942, after 16 months, *Nubian* returned to the Mediterranean where she served there until 1944.[332] She became a permanent fixture of operations, as elaborated earlier in the chapter, capturing the entire island of Linosa, together with its garrison, single-handedly in June 1943.[333] At the end of the war in the Mediterranean, *Nubian* returned to northern European waters, Arctic convoys and Norway. Her war, however, did not end in those waters. She earned further honour off the coast of Burma, for instance clearing the route to Singapore for the planned Operation Mailfist.[334]

The post-war service lives for the surviving 'Tribal' ships were cut short by the extent of their wartime service. According to her captain, Commander Holland-Martin, by September 1943, *Nubian*, for example, had travelled 53,556 nautical miles, been underway for a total of 2,985 hours, used 16,726 tons of fuel oil and had averaged 18.5 knots. With such wear on the ships and a change in vision for the post-war era, it was inevitable that their careers would come to an end.[335] With lessons from the war and the reassurance of the numbers it had achieved during those years, the Navy was focused on achieving capability through commonality, for example the 4.5in and 40mm guns would become standard, and maintaining a force of 'specialists' as best it could. Cruisers, destroyers and frigates all had a purposeful role: a worn out comparatively small class which straddled those duties was a complication. Especially with the 'Battle' class still coming into service and the *Daring* class on the 'stocks'. So the Royal Navy put to one side the experience of capacity and capability that the inter-war general-purpose designs had provided it with.

The decision might have been different had surface raiders continued to be a threat, but in the immediate post-war years of the 1940s such a threat did not exist. It was only in 1949, the year in which 'Tribal' class vessels were scrapped, that submarines ceased to be the only major sea threat and surface battles once again seemed possible; the date marked the commencement of the building of the Soviet Navy's *Sverdlov* class cruisers.[336] This might partly explain the survival of the Australian and Canadian 'Tribals', a decision that was vindicated by their excellent service in Korea.[337] Whatever the case, it is certain that *Nubian*, despite wanting to be useful to the very end, did not get either the preservation or even the honourable end she deserved. By 1948 she was being used as a target ship in Loch Striven prior to being sent for scrap at Briton Ferry in June 1949.[338]

Construction Goes On

All the operational reports, and all the ongoing feedback from officers and petty officers, were constantly fed back into the design and construction of the Navy's new destroyers, feedback which required the offices of the Third Sea Lord and the Naval Constructors to walk a tightrope while delivering ships which were both needed and then up to date on entering service. This was especially true of the 'Battle' class which were conceived at the moment of the greatest losses for the Navy's destroyer force, but were built as the war changed, and entered service when the Mediterranean was nowhere near the high-risk theatre it had been. From their conception radar had been a big part of their design, but as it became increasingly not just an extra sensor, but also a critical part of the ship's navigation system, and also employed in flotilla co-ordina-

St James (R65, ex-D65) is seen alongside *Vanguard*. 'Battles' were often used for such escort duties because of their powerful anti-air armament, along with their strong all-round capability. They could adapt to any role a destroyer might be called upon to fill within a task group, from distant picket to close quarters guardian. (*Drachinifel Collection*)

tion, changes were necessary. This was most visible in the growth and structure of masts. There were other aspects of their design that had to be developed.

Barfleur, the first of the 'Battle' class to enter service, was well prepared for Arctic conditions and was to be one of the critical destroyers escorting essential convoys to supply the Soviet Union when the war in Europe no longer required her services. This meant she had all sorts of modifications, including a huge amount of stor-

age space of anti-freeze and lubricants for protection of such fragile things as radar; more obviously, she was painted for the Arctic. As the war wound down in the West it continued to build in the East, towards the amphibious operations still to come, notably the envisaged retaking of Singapore (Operation Mailfist), and the invasion of Japan (Operation Downfall). The Navy needed its best ships, forged by the experience of war, stationed in the East.

The developments in naval warfare between 1939 and 1945 had been enormous, and it is fair to say that some things had been foreseen correctly, some things had been prepared for well, but there is nothing like the experience of war to push forward technology, doctrine, design and the philosophy of war; none emerged in 1945 quite the same.

TO THE EAST AND THE WAR IS OVER

When examining the deployment of 'Tribal' and 'Battle' class destroyers, it is worth looking at why it took so long to send them to the Pacific. Why was there not more haste placed upon the construction and deployment of the 1942 'Battle' class? In answer to the first, while the Royal Navy destroyers took their time getting to the theatre, the RAN 'Tribal' destroyers were already out in the Pacific proving themselves. This, coupled with the ample numbers of cruisers and destroyers within first the Eastern Fleet and later the British Pacific Fleet's order of battle, offers the main explanation. However, with the expansion of operations anticipated prior even to the defeat of Nazi Germany, it now was imperative to get these vital force multipliers into theatre.

Unsurprisingly, considering their recent duties in the Mediterranean and Normandy, it was not the Pacific Fleet they joined, but the East Indies Fleet, the force tasked with retaking, or assisting in the retaking, of Singapore. By 1945 the East Indies Fleet was not as important, from the perspective of the Alliance, as the British Pacific Fleet, which was viewed as the critical

means for Britain – and by extension the British Empire – to make a meaningful contribution to the war against Japan. The recapture of as much lost territory as possible was also imperative. This was the mission of the East Indies Fleet and, by extension, the 'Tribal' class destroyers which joined its strength in May 1945. For an understanding of how important they were as assets in this force, it is necessary to consider what made up the force in May 1945. Its single most powerful unit was the venerable, refitted but still capable battleship, *Queen Elizabeth*, the name ship of the *Queen Elizabeth* class. She was also the only unit of, and consequently flagship of, 1st Battle Squadron. Often overshadowed by her younger sister ship, *Warspite*, she was, with her eight 15in guns, a linchpin of many planned operations, and also the most eminent ship of this force.

This photograph of the 1943 Batch 'Battle' class *Agincourt* in the English Channel in 1951 highlights the American Mk 37 Fire Control her batch were fitted with, but also the range of small craft and floats carried aboard these ships both for regular operations and crew survival. (*Maritime Quest*)

Agincourt after conversion to a radar picket. The photograph shows both the size and scale of the radar structure (and which has continued to the modern Type 45 *Daring* class destroyers with their 'conehead' radars). It also highlights the structural changes that the transition necessitated: the loss of torpedoes, and much of the 40mm armament. The number of personnel was also considerably reduced. (*Drachinifel Collection*)

The strike power of the East Indies Fleet was provided by escort carriers. These do not have the same lustre as a fleet carrier, or even a light fleet carrier. However, the nine vessels of the 21st Aircraft Carrier Squadron, *Activity, Ameer, Attacker, Emperor, Empress, Hunter, Khedive, Shah* and *Stalker*, were operationally potent. Their squadron flagship was usually one of the two *Dido* class AA cruisers on station, *Royalist* and her sister *Phoebe*, which were sometimes needed for more than their 5.25in guns in this fleet, often being used as Task Force flagships. In addition, there was also the virtually unmodified *Cradoc*, a First World War 'C' class cruiser, the smallest cruiser on station, and which served as the East Indies Flagship.[339] Chosen instead of the *Dido* class vessels in large part because she did not need to move around much, it avoided tying up a valuable asset. The bulk of the naval gunfire support for any amphibious operation would come from the four 8in armed

'County' class heavy cruisers, *Cumberland, London, Suffolk* and *Sussex* (which left the East Indies in July 1945); and two 6in-armed light cruisers, the 'Crown Colony' class *Nigeria* and the Free Dutch *Tromp* (which left in August). While there were a number of reasons given, the main reason that neither *Queen Elizabeth* nor any of the larger cruisers were flagship was because they could thus be easily transferred should the British Pacific Fleet find itself in a crisis.

The East Indies Fleet was one which was dependent upon escort carriers for its reach and smaller ships, especially destroyers, for its planned fighting strength. By May 1945, in addition to the three 'Tribal' class vessels *Eskimo, Nubian* and *Tartar*, there were twelve other destroyers present: *Penn, Paladin, Scout, Rocket, Saumarez*, the French *Le Triomphant*, HMAS *Vendetta*, which left in August, *Venus, Verulam, Vigilant*, two of which had left by August, and *Virago* and *Volage*. In addition, there were approximately fifteen frigates, six corvettes and seven sloops. This was the 'fighting' strength of the Fleet which could, in theory, be called upon to do what was necessary, but in practice it was a force with very limited scouting and surface action capabilities, capabilities essential for clearing out the Japanese forces remaining between it and its target destination. The duties of the 'Tribals' were to act as the 'reliable' independent ships

Asine, also after conversion to a radar picket. The scale of the equipment is clearly demonstrated by comparison to other ships and the dockyard crane. (*Drachinifel Collection*)

on station, scouting, clearing the path, and commando operations – though without the commandos – as typified by Operation Irregular.

Operation Irregular 1945

While serving in the Far East, the trio of the remaining 'Tribal' sisters, *Tartar*, *Nubian* and *Eskimo*, or 10th DF as they had remained, became involved in Operation Irregular, a little over a year after their action off Île de Batz during the D-Day operations.[340] Irregular was an aggressive patrol in the area between the Andaman Sea and the Strait of Malacca, specifically between the

Nicobar Islands and Sabang (an island off the coast of Indonesia), an area directly on the line from the main Indian Ocean base of Trincomalee to Singapore.[341] The purpose of this mission was to find and destroy the enemy in order to prevent the resupply of island garrisons or the operation of forces in an area through which an amphibious assault force heading for Singapore would have to navigate. Force 65, as it was known for the operation, was made up of the three 'Tribal' class vessels along with the 'P' class destroyers, *Paladin* and *Penn*. The five destroyers left Trincomalee at 1800hrs on 5 June 1945, a little over a month after VE Day.

Corunna during her working-up period in 1948, when she was based at Chatham before her deployment with the *Colossus* class light fleet carrier *Vengeance* to South Africa. (*Drachinifel Collection*)

On 7 June *Paladin* was sent on a special patrol while the other four destroyers remained together. On 9 June, following two days of aggressive patrolling, they met up with Force 64, the resupply group, made up of the tanker RFA *Olwen* and the 'River' class frigate *Test*.[342] *Penn* was not refuelled until early on 10 June, at which point she was despatched on her solo mission. On the 11th Force 65, or specifically the 'Tribals', split from Force 65, which remained near that area because *Paladin* was expected to call in shortly. Acting on intelligence received from *Trident*, a submarine operating in the area, the remainder of Force 65, *Tartar*, *Nubian* and *Eskimo*, proceeded line abreast at a speed of 25 knots and spread over a front of seven miles, towards position 06° 45' North, 93° 50' East, just south of the Great Nicobar Island, near the entrance to the Strait of Malacca.[343] Just as with the Île de Batz action, information and operational doctrine enabled the destroyers, still under the command of Commander Basil Jones, to seek out the enemy.

The 10th DF was certainly successful. At 0526hrs on 12 June 1945, near the island of Rondo just north of Sabang, two small radar echoes were detected at a range of 26,000yds, nearly fifteen miles. Six minutes later there was visual confirmation. Their targets had been found.[344] At this point, the reason for sending 'Tribals', especially wartime upgraded 'Tribals', became apparent. Before they were able to intercept the enemy ships, the destroyers were engaged by, reportedly, a 'Tess' (a Japanese domestically-produced version of the Douglas DC-2 airliner), and the gunfire alerted the enemy ships to their presence.[345] This did not, however, stop the interception. At 0552hrs, and at a range of 6,500 yards, the 'Tribals' opened fire on what proved to be an enemy Landing Ship, Tank (LST), armed with a 3in gun and several 20mm cannon, and a sub-chaser of the PC 40-44 class armed with a 6pdr and a single 20mm cannon.[346] Initially, the Japanese vessels attempted to flee, but then decided to fight. After initially staying together, at about 0603hrs the enemy ships tried to separate, so that *Nubian* concentrated on the sub-chaser leaving *Tartar* and *Eskimo* to focus on the LST. As more enemy aircraft appeared on the radar the decision was made to use torpedoes as well. *Tartar* fired first but the torpedoes ran underneath the shallow drafted LST. More semi-armour piercing (SAP) rounds were fired, which stopped the LST, and caused a list of 30-degrees. By 0619hrs, less than an hour after first contact, *Eskimo* was able to finish off the LST with torpedoes, while *Nubian* despatched the sub-chaser No 57 with heavy gunfire.[347]

However, the fight was not over. A group of four 'Lilys', two 'Dinahs' and an 'Oscar' – or to give them their Japanese names, four Kawasaki Ki-48 twin-engined light bombers, two Mitsubishi Ki-46 twin-engined reconnaissance /light bombers, and the Japanese Army's A6M Zero lookalike, the single-engined Nakajima Ki-43 – kept up an intermittent but persistent series of attacks, necessitating several burst of anti-aircraft fire to keep them at bay. The fight was further complicated when four Liberator aircraft 'joined company' with the destroyers, but for the first 30 minutes did not show up on Identification Friend or Foe (IFF). By 0845hrs the destroyers had managed to lose the harassing aircraft and had a successful mission mostly behind them.[348] *Paladin* was still on her detached duties, as was *Penn*. The 'Tribals' refuelled from *Olwen* on 13 June, a move made urgent by the discovery of water in two of *Tartar*'s tanks, and reached Trincomalee on 14 June. On their return, it was found that the three 'Tribals' had between

Aisne, 30 August 1954 in St Helen's Roads, just off the Isle of Wight at the entrance to the Solent and Portsmouth. She was travelling along the coast from Chatham to Portsmouth to join up with other ships in preparation for the transit to Norway to take part in Exercise Morning Mist. (*Drachinifel Collection*)

Daring demonstrates the big difference with the 'Battle' class, and the reason the class could do away with so many of the 40mm cannon was the capabilities of the Mk VI 4.5in turrets. Their rate of fire, their range and ceiling provided these vessels with a significant area of effect against aircraft, whilst also providing a boost in relative anti-ship and anti-land capabilities. (*Drachinifel Collection*)

them expended 748 rounds of SAP, 336 rounds of 4.7in High Explosive (HE), 45 rounds of High Explosive Variable Time (HEVT) and 189 rounds of 4in HE, a very high rate of, albeit approximate, fifty-five rounds fired per gun. This is of further interest in view of the fact that *Eskimo*'s Type 285 radar developed a fault (a broken lead in an input plug caused by the firing salvos of her main battery), which meant she was firing by Fuze Keeping Clock aid alone. It was particularly exasperating that this had gone wrong because, unlike the Type 293 and Type 291 sets with which the 'Tribals' had been fitted before proceeding to join the East

Indies Fleet, it was the latest and best radar they could have. In fact, it was virtually the same system as that installed in the 'Battle' class on their entry into service.

This account has so far omitted much mention of the activities of *Paladin* and *Penn*. They had joined up, and it was partially to distract from what they were doing that the 'Tribals' had pushed so far and hard to try to draw the hornets' nest of aircraft on to them. The 'P' class destroyers had been despatched to provide cover for *Trident*, which was aiming to recover a clandestine party from the Batu Islands. They arrived by 9 June but were unable to make contact with the party, although the destroyers managed to account for a Japanese landing craft on 12 June. On 18 June, *Trident*

Gravelines in 1952. Her crew are lining the rails fore and aft, and this photograph was probably taken during the period when she was shuttling back and forth between the UK and the Mediterranean as the Navy tried to manage its duties in the emerging Cold War. (*Drachinifel Collection*)

Relatives line the dockside while crew line the rails as the 1943 Batch 'Battle' class *Dunkirk* arrives home to Devonport from a deployment to the Mediterranean on 21 April 1959, for what were the extensive exercises and diplomatic events that comprised NATO's tenth anniversary celebrations at Malta. (*Maritime Quest*)

herself destroyed a second landing craft with gunfire, which was found upon inspection to contain radio equipment belonging to the clandestine party. The files contain little more information about the party or their fate, and in fact this was made as a separate report from that which was submitted about the more planned aspects of Operation Irregular. The destroyers had wanted to pick up Japanese survivors, but the presence of enemy aircraft and the Japanese reluctance to be rescued prevented it.

Operation Irregular was another illustration of how the 'Tribals' could be deployed and used. It was a mission without much fanfare and it was not the only mission accomplished in the Far East by the class. Had the war continued for longer, the operation to recapture Singapore would have been launched, and under those circumstances the softening up and weakening of the Japanese island defenders by the erosion of their re-

supply lines would have severely impeded their ability to defend it.

The End of the War

Irregular typifies the operations in which the 'Tribals' and the 10th DF took part in the East Indies and in the wider, hard fought war at sea. In September 1944 *Ashanti* went in for a major refit at Palmer's Yarrow Yard, at a cost of quarter of a million pounds, yet when she came out she still suffered from mechanical problems. The years of unremitting sea time and hard fighting had caught up with the 'Tribals'. In *Ashanti*'s case the failure of the refit led to her being put into reserve, followed by damage control tests in Loch Striven in 1948, and finally her breaking up at Troon in 1949. This was hardly a fitting end for a ship after such a distinguished career during which she had brought her crews safely home from every mission, but it was not untypical.

In *Eskimo*'s case the war had taken an even heavier toll. There are not many ships which are on to their third bow before they have been completed six years in commission. First, the wishes of her officers and crew to continue fighting rather than have a refit in Durban (because they had had one in Bombay on arrival in the Indian Ocean) had been overruled. Instead of being present at Victory over Japan Day, *Eskimo* was in Diego Suarez, Madagascar, en route for a refit in South Africa, the purpose of which was largely to keep the South African workforce employed. In November, on completion of the refit, *Eskimo* made her way home, visiting a number of ports including Takoradi, where, before the war, *Ashanti* had been blessed by the Asante on the way out, and where *Eskimo* was likewise welcomed and fêted by the Asante. She reached home on the Friday before Christmas 1945 and might well have been left on a midstream buoy in order to save the higher weekend wages of the dockyard workers if the Press had not wanted photos of the unloading of Christmas puddings, amongst other things, which she had brought with her from the people of Cape Town. Early in 1946 her torpedo tubes and screws were removed, and she ended her days as a depot, accommodation and headquarters ship for minesweepers and other vessels which were clearing the Thames and Medway of war detritus. Later she was used as target in the Gare Loch, before being sent to Troon in 1949 for scrapping.

For *Nubian* the war never quite ended. As one of the most decorated ships it is no surprise that after what she had been through she was present for the surrender

Matapan spent little of her career as a destroyer, but she was critical after her 1961–71 conversion (it was held up due to lack of money) to an underwater trials ship, to test new sonars, especially a new bulbous bow unit. She would spend six years and notch up several records doing this work before being paid off in 1977. (*Drachinifel Collection*)

of Penang in western Malaysia. She might not have lost a bow, but in 1941, while protecting *Formidable* off Crete, she had lost her stern. Although she had lost her rudder and most of the compartments aft of 'X' mount, her shafts had remained undamaged, enabling her to do 20 knots and steer by main engines, ensuring her survival. After Penang, *Nubian* and *Tartar* helped with the evacuation of prisoners of war from Singapore, before returning home in 1945, crossing the Mediterranean with a sister ship as she had often done before, but this time with no aircraft dogging their passage. It was a smooth voyage which allowed the crew to relax. For a while *Nubian* served as a Reserve Fleet accommodation ship at Whale Island in Portsmouth, until July 1948, when she was, like her sisters, sent to Loch Striven to serve as a target vessel. Less than a year later she was scrapped at Briton Ferry. *Tartar* also went to Loch Striven and was scrapped in February 1948. But she would have the most appropriate retirement party before this.

The party, however, was not for *Tartar*, but for Aunty May, the American widow Mrs Hanrahan who, during the war, had adopted the 'Tribals' as her 'godsons'. After years of support, on 6 May 1946, she was finally able to visit one of the class. In 1939 she decided that while her country, the United States, might remain neutral, she would not, and being a forthright woman of action as well as words, she was not to be persuaded otherwise. It is not certain why she picked *Somali* for the receipt of her care, but care she lavished on the ship. Thick winter clothing for the crew, together with chocolate, sweets, cigarettes and personal gifts were soon despatched. Upon learning that *Somali* was a flotilla

leader, she immediately despatched similar supplies to all the 'Tribals'. Her husband, Captain D C Hanrahan, had been a destroyer and Q-ship captain in the US Navy during the First World War, which gave her genuine insight into the needs of sailors. She was also a very wealthy woman with the means and opportunity to provide those extra comforts.

Parcels quickly became a regular, at least monthly, part of the life of the ships, and were delivered wherever the destroyers went, no matter how far away. She not only sent presents to the ships, but food for the families of the men at home; and she hosted parties for them at her homes in London and New York throughout the remainder of her life. In 1946, she was welcomed aboard *Tartar* for a thank you, and it was estimated that be-

tween 1939 and 1946 she had had 3,500 'godsons' and had spent some £50,000, nearly two and a quarter million in today's money, a figure many believe to be an underestimate, though she never confirmed the sum herself. When presented with a silver model 'Tribal' she declared it 'her most precious possession'. She died in 1953, unhonoured by the British Government but a woman much loved by the Royal Navy's destroyer men and their families for whom she had so diligently striven during six years of war.

In the years after the war ended the Australian 'Tribals' made a name for themselves, operating with American Task Force 74 and proving themselves of great value; the exploits of the Canadian 'Tribals', already covered, were also significant. And their service continued, chiefly because for these navies the 'Tribals' were not only virtually brand new but were still entering service as the war ended. HMAS *Bataan* was completed on 25 May 1945, HMCS *Micmac* on 18 September 1945, HMCS *Nootka* on 7 August 1946, HMCS *Cayuga* on 20 October 1947 and HMCS *Atha-*

Corunna (D97) working with a Whirlwind from *Eagle* (R05). This photograph was taken in 1953 and illustrates the difficulty and complexity of working with early helicopters. It also highlights the scale and size of the 40mm mounts arraigned aft. (*Michael Rainsworth, Maritime Quest*)

Gravelines during the early 1950s when she still carried Hazemayer 40mm mounts. By 1951 she would lose these in favour of two twin 40mm Bofors Mk 2 STAAG mounts. It is also just before she would lose her depth charges for a Squid A/S Mortar. *(Maritime Quest)*

baskan on 20 January 1948. So in 1950, at the outbreak of the Korean War, the 'Tribals' found themselves at the forefront. *Haida* spent much of the war deployed inshore where her task was to eliminate trains running along a coastal line. The engine of the first train they engaged escaped their attack and thereafter *Haida* always aimed at the engine first. In contrast, *Athabaskan* and *Cayuga* were present at the Incheon landings in

September 1950, continuing the 'Tribals' association with major amphibious operations.

The 'Battles' and the Royal Navy

The high point of the post-war years for the 'Battle' class was not the part played by the 1942 Batch *Hogue* standing in for the 'Tribals' for the filming *Sink the Bismarck* – although there was a nice symmetry there. Nor was it *Barfleur*'s redoubtable efforts to join the British

This profile view of *Daring* shows off her rounded lines and sweeping foredeck, designed to give her the best possible performance at sea. *(Maritime Quest)*

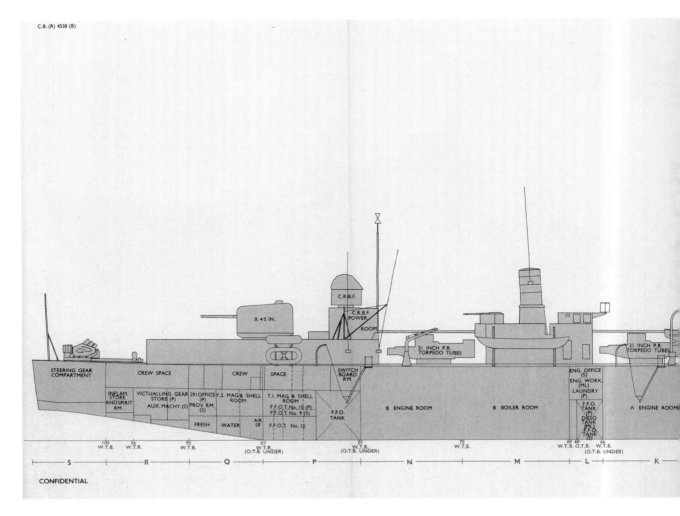

C.B. (R) 4538 (B)

CONFIDENTIAL

Daring class illustrated in profile as part of the ABCD guide to the class (ADM 239.428). The emphasises the sub-division and organisation the Navy was aiming for, especially between the all-important engine room/boiler room spaces and the use of liquid stores to help give them greater protection/division from other parts of the ship. (*UK National Archives*)

Pacific Fleet in time to see combat with the 19th DF and take part with Task Force 38 in attacks on Tokyo and Yokohama. It probably came with 19th DF's continuing post-war operations in the Far East, particularly when *Armada* stood up against pirates in large, sea-going Chinese junks. *Armada* had joined *Barfleur*, along with *Camperdown*, *Lagos*, *Hogue* and *Trafalgar* roughly six months earlier. *Finisterre* had been recalled to home waters which, with the end of the war, was considered more appropriate, and so the flotilla's strength was never complete. On 16 June the merchant ship SS *Taiposhan*, owned by the Tai On Steam Navigation Co Ltd of Hong Kong, ran aground on a sandbank roughly a

hundred miles north of Shanghai whilst bound for Tsingtao (Qingdao). Finding herself being circled by pirates, she called for help. *Armada* rushed to the stricken merchant ship's aid, and the pirates were successfully driven off, but the destroyer was unable to free *Taiposhan*, so stayed on watch for two days until a tug arrived from Shanghai to complete the task. The faithful 'Battle' then escorted both merchant ship and tug to Shanghai and safety. It was a satisfying assignment for a ship designed for independent cruising.

This was not, however, a taste of things to come. For Britain, the First World War had been damaging enough, but the subsequent crippling Depression and the Second World War were financially devastating. Britain might have overcome the Depression and, won the wars, but it was at a terrible cost in citizenry, materiel, infrastructure and, most importantly, financial cost. The Royal Navy now needed not only to find a way to save money, but also to preserve a force to fight a war they feared was brewing with the Soviet-led com-

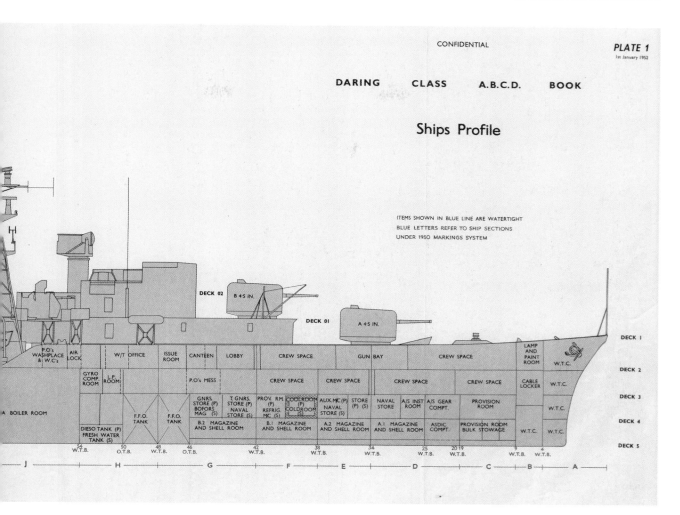

PLATE 1
1st January 1952

DARING CLASS A.B.C.D. BOOK

Ships Profile

ITEMS SHOWN IN BLUE LINE ARE WATERTIGHT
BLUE LETTERS REFER TO SHIP SECTIONS
UNDER 1950 MARKINGS SYSTEM

munist powers. It was neither wanted nor sought, but Britain had an Empire to protect, a Commonwealth to which it owed a debt of honour, interests to defend and the constant requirement of its strategic position to maintain freedom of movement of goods and capital. More importantly the Royal Navy could consider a number of options.

In the numerically smaller forces

Daring's 40mm STAAG AA mount, with one fitted either side of the superstructure position on O1 deck, the same level as 'B' turret. This was intended to provide overlapping complementary fire position to the 4.5in guns in the overall anti-air protection of the ship. (*Drachinifel Collection*)

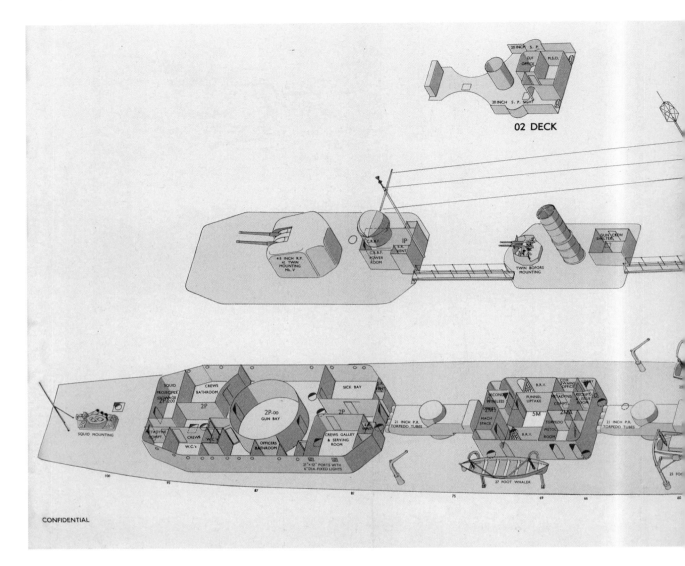

CONFIDENTIAL

Daring class illustrated overview of Decks 02, 01, 1 and 2 as part of the ABCD guide to the class. The sick bay is at one end of the aft superstructure, the Squid projectile stowage and crew's bathroom at the other end, all built around the space for the Mk VI gun that occupied 'X' position. (*UK National Archives*)

at the beginning of the twenty-first century the only option in the face of the Treasury's desire to limit running costs is to invest in and run top-of-the-line warships to carry out a wide range of duties. In the late 1940s one solution was put the best of their ships in long-term refit/reserve so they would be available when needed. Alternatively, they could keep War Emergency Destroyers going and wear them out with peacetime duties, or simply get rid of the vessels as some had supposed would happen during the course of the war. By early 1947, the 19th DF had been mostly recalled and

placed in reserve, some of which would hardly be used, while some would not emerge from reserve for the best part of a decade. All this was done to preserve their value for the nation.

However, this did not mean that all twenty-four members of the class were placed in reserve. The 5th DF, the Home Fleet 'Battles', remained at sea. Again, this was about cost. To deal with a surging proactive Soviet Union required cruisers or similar vessels, a like-for-like balance approach. Although it was cost effective to deploy the available cruisers around the world to cover distant stations, it created other problems as there were far fewer cruisers than prior to the war, which made the coverage of all stations virtually impossible. The 'Battle' class made sense for the busier home waters where the range was usually shorter and there was far more infrastructure available nearby. The

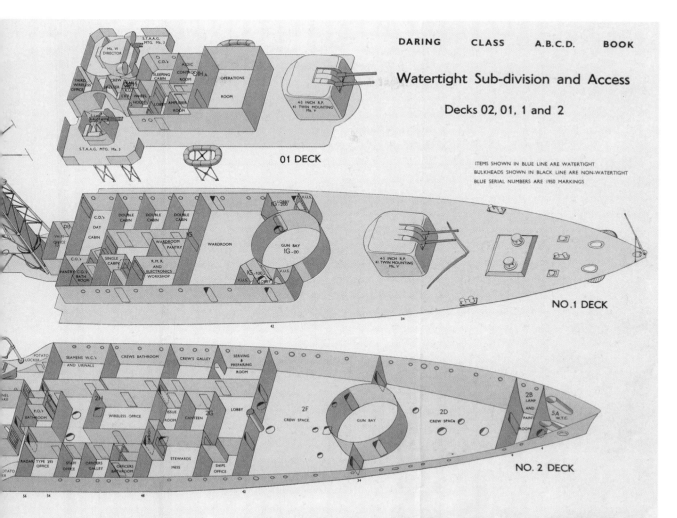

DARING CLASS A.B.C.D. BOOK

Watertight Sub-division and Access

Decks 02, 01, 1 and 2

ITEMS SHOWN IN BLUE LINE ARE WATERTIGHT
BULKHEADS SHOWN IN BLACK LINE ARE NON-WATERTIGHT
BLUE SERIAL NUMBERS ARE 1950 MARKINGS

'Battles' could provide the numbers, and if the situation required more 'muscle' something else could quickly be deployed. This was also true of the Mediterranean Fleet, though the 'Battles' often were the 'muscle'.

It was not just money and international relations which were affecting things. 1947 also brought with it a manning crisis, a long-term con-

Daring's Squid being loaded. The weight of the rounds, combined with a desire to make rapid reloading as practical as possible, governed the layout of these weapons. (Drachinifel Collection)

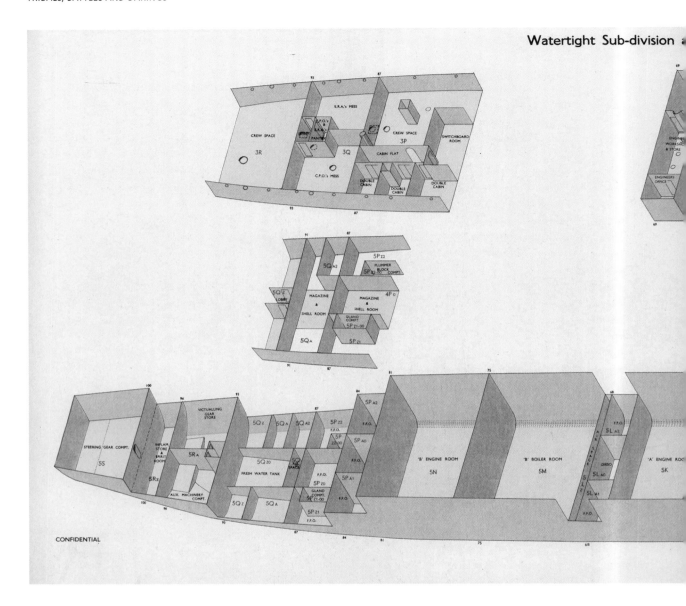

Watertight Sub-division

Daring class illustrated overview of Decks 3, 4 and 5. This illustrates the space required for provisions, the relative thickness of the 'cool' rooms, the way the shell storage and diesel generators are distributed within the space of the hull to try to assist with damage control. (*UK National Archives*)

sequence of the war with its prolific short-term enlistments and commissions. By the end of the 1940s the Navy was dealing with a second wave of war-time service personnel losses, the first wave having consisted of the duration-only personnel who departed in 1945/6. Even more critical was the loss of experienced officers and sailors who had extended their post-war service.

Under such circumstances it was probably a good thing that National Service numbers were reducing, because without experienced personnel who could train them to an acceptable standard, it would have been immensely taxing on an already stretched system. A combination of all these factors meant the 'Battle' class found itself severely disadvantaged just as it was getting into its stride.

By the late 1940s and early 1950s this was compounded by fear of the fast submarine and the corresponding need to get as many fast anti-submarine assets as possible into service. This might have been the death knell for the class for despite their all-around strengths, their ASW capability was, even after refits to

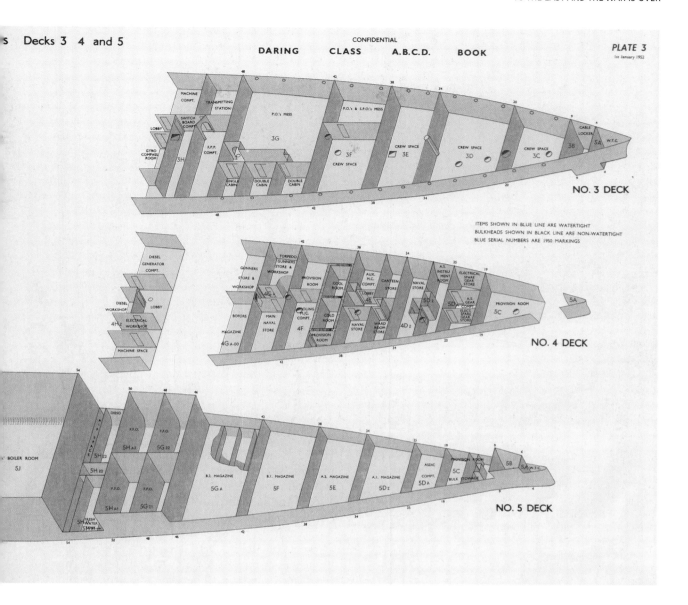

DARING CLASS A.B.C.D. BOOK

CONFIDENTIAL

PLATE 3
1st January 1952

the 1942 Batch and the addition of a single Squid mortar, unimpressive. Fortunately, at the time the Navy had to worry about more than one threat, which is where the 'Battles' had the edge. They were the multi-purpose asset with the most potential for development in other areas, namely air defence, and the ships were brought into service for the Mediterranean. So *Saintes*, *Armada*, *Vigo* and *Gravelines* – the latter replaced by *Barfleur* – were deployed to the Mediterranean, staying through the administrative transition that turned Flotillas into Squadrons, and serving with Navy until 1958. In a sense, and despite this service, the class never fulfilled its potential. The war was over, to be followed by recession, and when they could finally be put to use as pres-

ence multipliers (or cruiser substitutes), and begin building a name for themselves the *Daring* class appeared. The 'Battles' never became wholly active, despite events at the time which suited them, their clear operational potential, and the Navy's appreciation of their strengths. With an ample supply of specialist vessels, both cruisers and allied 'Tribals' in Korea, these general-purpose assets were not able to be used in a way which would gain attention. For example, in late 1951, while part of 4th DF (the 1943 Batch unit), *Agincourt* found herself in the Mediterranean.

Later we were seconded to the Mediterranean Fleet and journeyed in the Persian Gulf with stops at Gi-

Daring at speed, showing the pitch of the ship that the gun mounts would have to deal with. These ships were designed to be as stable as practicable as platforms for their guns, but the reality of high speed manoeuvring at sea as well as rough weather is that both the fire-control mechanism and the guns themselves have to be built to compensate for an unstable environment. (*Drachinifel Collection*)

braltar, Malta and Cyprus. While at Cyprus the crew practised landing parties at Larnaca. We proceeded to Port Said where they refused to refuel us so Captain Evans sent away a landing party, took over the fuel station and pumped our own oil. I remember there was a dockyard strike and I believe at about this time, the statue of Ferdinand de Lesseps – the builder of the Suez Canal – was tipped over. We helped berth merchant ships which were waiting to pass down the Suez Canal. We eventually reached Port Suez and entered the Red sea but we were then recalled, arriving back in Portsmouth in March 1952.[349]

Although these were essential duties, they did not make headlines, and certainly inspire no roles in movies. It was the fate of the 'Battle' class to be continually in-

volved in more the conventional experiences compared to their sister classes. A further example of this is the story of *Barossa* – another 1943 Batch unit – during her 1962/3 Indonesian patrol. 'The Indonesian confrontation was well advanced by this time and along with other naval units we were required to patrol the seas around the coast of Malaya in an attempt to prevent incursion by hostile groups of Indonesian terrorists, regular soldiers and saboteurs. They would normally travel by night and used small wooden boats, called kumpits, to carry arms, explosives and intelligence information.'[350] No action took place, but both these examples illustrate the kind of presence, when combined with a possible mission, which Britain could project to the world.

Daring Class Dawn

'Though built as destroyers, these vessels were later officially described as the "*Daring* class ships" thus becoming neither fish, nor fowl, nor good red herring! They have now become destroyers again.' So wrote Captain Manning RN (ret) in 1961.[351] The arrival of the *Daring* class represented the biggest possible threat to the 'Battles'. The ships were everything that a post-war, uncompromising design could produce for a general-purpose fighting destroyer. They were big and, for their size, impressively proportioned and, despite theoretically being destroyers, they were high status ships. However, this did not mean everyone loved them. Captain Manning's quote is a good example of this. The bounty of war, and the freedom to build as many specialists as necessary, was still a legacy which had to be dealt with. The reality was that the Navy could not build enough of those sorts of specialist ships, so it needed ships which fill the cruiser roles of presence, naval gunfire support and command, while also being able to carry out the destroyer/frigate duties of air defence, anti-submarine warfare and surface attack. As Neil McCart wrote in his recent work:

> For the Royal Navy of the early 1950s, however, the new class represent the ultimate in warship design, comprising eight powerful destroyers which were capable of carrying out duties normally assigned to light cruisers. Each of the *Daring* class ships was in commission for less than 20 years, but during that time they saw the final transition from the big-gun era, to the age of the guided missile. During their early years of service at least one ship of the class operated with the Navy's last big 15-inch gun battleship, HMS *Vanguard*, and in their closing years they

operated with the Navy's first guided-missile ships, the County-class destroyers. As their Official Logs, which are preserved at the National Archives, proudly proclaim, they were originally classified not as destroyers, but as warships of the 'Daring Class'.[352]

In their own ways both these views are right. However, the reality is that this was a concept introduced just prior to the Second World War, and originally was conceived because of, and to, the artificial limits imposed by treaty. That twelve of the sixteen original 'Tribal' class were lost would appear to justify the detractors, though the circumstances of those losses would suggest that the other option of risking cruisers might well have led to greater losses. The same could have happened to regular destroyers without the necessary firepower. As a result the 'Battle' class had been built but they had problems fulfilling the peacetime cruiser role of presence, rather than simple intimidation – the 'Battles' just looked too aggressive. To establish a presence, a ship has to balance its profile of power and visible strength with poise and a statesman-like profile. It is the X-factor that can be designed for, but which cannot be measured until the class is in service. The *Daring*s had the power with their high bow, the steps of the forward turrets leading up to the open bridge, the director and finally the radar-mounted lattice mast. They displayed power, but the angles of the structure and the lines of the hull

Dainty, having lost her torpedoes for more accommodation space over the course of two major refits in six years. This was in many ways their final form in Royal Navy service. (*Drachinifel Collection*)

Dainty pictured in final form as before, this time viewed from the stern. It shows that while space had been taken for accommodation, plenty of deck space needed to be left for boats and other necessities of warship life. (*Maritime Quest*)

gave them their poise and presence. In many ways the *Daring*s were the quintessential post-war warship. They represented the lessons learned and, despite being *Daring*s, because they were grouped with destroyers it meant that, unlike cruisers, carriers and battleships, they were relatively free of scrutiny, that is, until the Navy wanted to use them as intended, as officially outlined below in June 1953.

In your minute of June 2nd you asked for the history of the Class.

2. The *Daring*s were included in the 1944/45 New Construction Programme as Destroyers and were laid down between 1946 and 1950.

3. The class totals eight ships; five have recently joined the Fleet, one is being placed direct in Reserve because of naval manpower shortage, and the remaining two will join the Fleet this Autumn.

4. These Ships carry six 4.5-inch guns with a high rate of fire and good accuracy against both aircraft and ships.

5. Their torpedo armament (ten torpedoes) gives them a good offensive striking power.

6. In addition they carry an ahead-throwing anti-submarine mortar (SQUID), and with their twin rudders these ships, despite their size, have the small turning circles essential for anti-submarine operations.

7. *Daring*s are in fact the smallest hull (3,500 tons) in which it is possible to fit the complicated armaments necessary for a 'maid of all work', and their offensive power far exceeds that of the light cruisers of the past.

8. In a future war *Daring* Class ships will be required:
   a) for use in screen of the British carrier striking forces (Atlantic Station) and for inclusion in light surface action forces when needed;
   b) at the spearhead of light forces to seek out enemy light forces (destroyers and below) in:

Decoy in profile, showing off the lines of the *Daring* class. This picture was taken half way through the process of stripping away torpedoes and represents the transition from the period when the torpedo was the primary stand-off anti-ship weapon, to when the missile would take over that role. (*Drachinifel Collection*)

i) the Scandinavian area
ii) Turkish Waters

For such a role their organisation as separate units working as light cruisers is more appropriate than the standard destroyer squadron organisation. To employ them so at present helps to offset the shortage of cruisers in commission, a shortage that cannot be remedied while the manpower remains acute.[353]

The last paragraph is especially revealing. In wartime they are to be used along the same lines as cruisers, and in peace will be used as cruisers to prepare them for this. During the 1930s, Treaties had been the driving force behind the 'Tribals'. In the late 1940s and early 1950s, it was manpower and the consequential costs which were driving not only their use, but also their form. If they had had the money there is no doubt the Navy would have preferred more cruisers, but if there were not sufficient funds it aimed for the best 'maid of all work' possible within all the limits.

Destroyers Filling in For Cruisers? The Far East and Churchill's Second Term

The 'Battles' had not taken part in Korea, although the Commonwealth navy 'Tribals' certainly had. These two destroyer classes were not the only 'back pocket cruisers' which featured in the war or 'peace' which followed after the ceasefire. On 16 June 1953, following the Coronation Fleet Review, *Defender*, the fourth of the *Daring* class destroyers, left Spithead for the Far East, arriving in Hong Kong on 27 July in time for a truce to be declared, but not knowing about the confrontation she had left behind in Whitehall, nor what battles were to come. The debate in Whitehall was between the

Decoy was the only Royal Navy ship of the class to have missiles, eventually being fitted with Seacats. If this had been extended to other ships of the class there is a definite chance some of them might have still been in service during the Falklands War, when their 40mm STAAG mounts and Mk VI fire-control systems would have been very useful in San Carlos Water, and their Mk VI 4.5in main guns of real value for shore bombardment. *(Maritime Quest)*

Defender, one of the four direct current ships and one of four ships fitted with Foster Wheeler boilers, a combination she shared only with her sister *Dainty*. This did have consequences for her operation and upgrades as time went on, but these complexities were all part of the politics of their construction. By patronising two boiler manufacturers the 'benefit' had been spread and by using two forms of electric current the risk associated with a new system had been balanced by retaining the established system. *(Drachinifel Collection)*

Defender in 1953 in the Far East on her first deployment which would in prove to be demanding and included taking part in the final stages of the Korean War, and being part of a deterrence action in the Formosa Strait between Taiwan and China. (*Maritime Quest*)

Prime Minister, Winston Churchill, First Lord of the Admiralty James Thomas (1st Viscount Cilcennin), and the First Sea Lord, Admiral of the Fleet Rhoderick McGrigor, continuing to the natural conclusion of what had been begun by the latter's predecessor, Admiral of the Fleet Bruce Fraser. This was the solution to the on-going manning issues, and issues of presence, in which frigates were not enough, but cruisers were just too much. For the First Lord his argument can be summed up in paragraph 3 of his paper dated 28 May 1953.

> 3. *Defender*, one of the new *Daring* class, had been allocated to the Mediterranean Fleet, but I have now decided that she shall go to the Far East Station immediately after the Naval Review, and shall relieve the cruisers in turn. Ships of the *Daring* Class are already being employed with the cruisers of the Home and Mediterranean Fleets, and, as I said when introducing the Navy Estimates debate, they are to all intents and purposes light cruisers. To employ her in

Korea will provide valuable experience of this class of ship in active service conditions.[354]

Churchill's argument comes in paragraphs 4 and 5 of his response dated 31 May 1953.

> 4. Please supply me with the legends and complements I have asked for, and meanwhile do not suppose you can mislead the other side by pretending that overblown destroyers are light cruisers or frigates. You have, I am sure, a good deal to play with in complements so long as no hostile fleet is involved.
> 5. On the whole in present circumstances of world naval strengths which are overwhelmingly on our side, I would feel inclined to favour a big ship undermanned to a little ship with full war complements. After all, the Chinese are not going to board any ships we may have in their waters and firing with four guns out of six may do whatever is needful.[355]

For a while the debate was heated but petered out as Churchill became distracted by other things. It also served to illustrate both Churchill's familiarity with the Navy and his distance. At this point the Navy had very few six-gun cruisers in service, most vessels being 'Town', 'Crown Colony' or subsequent classes, often sailing with one triple gun turret crewed, whilst the

Defender later in her life, with no torpedoes and no missiles fitted. In this form she epitomised gunboat diplomacy being, with some of her sisters, some of the last all-gun armament ships to serve in any major navy. (*Drachinifel Collection*)

other two or three turrets were mothballed to save on cost and relieve accommodation pressures. The final note was from W Marshall of the Admiralty to John Colville, Churchill's Joint Principal Private Secretary dated 29 June. 'Thank you for your letter of 28th instant about the *Daring* Class. I confirm that *Defender* has already left for the Far East. The First Lord has no points on which he requires further clarification.' [356]

This typifies both the beginning of the story in 1934/5, when the 'Tribals' were conceived, as well as the story post-war. General-purpose fighting destroyers were not so much a compromise with naval requirements, as with political and foreign policy ones. The need and quality of a presence in order to influence events was of great importance to the leaders of the nation. For the Navy the provision of the tools, on the budget allocated by those leaders, was difficult. The story did not end with this exchange, although, on 27 July 1953, when a truce in the Korean War was declared, Churchill might have thought he had been proved right.

The warring parties on the Korean peninsula might have stopped exchanging gunfire, but that did not mean the Far East was either peaceful or could be described as being at peace. There were still patrols to carry out. In fact *Defender* would partner with the 'Town' class cruiser *Birmingham* and HMCS *Iroquois*, a Second World War-built 'Tribal' class destroyer of the Canadian navy. Sometimes they also took the *Colossus* class light fleet carrier *Ocean* with them. On 1 October 1953 *Defender* was visiting the USN joint base at Yokosuka, Japan, in preparation for a planned joint exercise which, in the event, never happened. [357] Instead of a run ashore, her crew did not even make it to the liberty boat. Communist Chinese forces were thought to be massing in preparation for an invasion of Taiwan across the Formosa Strait. *Defender* was despatched immediately, conducting a five-day patrol which finished in Hong Kong. Until the third week of January 1954 she kept up a constant series of patrols of the Strait, a visible and potent British sentinel and a tangible sign of British interest in events. Once the government was sure no threat would materialise, *Defender* was sent to Sasebo, to join one of *Birmingham*'s sisters, *Newcastle*, for a final patrol of Korea's west coast. Interestingly, it was *Birmingham* and *Newcastle* that *Defender*, rather than another cruiser, had originally been sent out to cover for while they were in refit. [358]

CHAPTER 7

THE LESSONS AND LEGACY OF THE 'BACK POCKET CRUISERS'

Grand strategy is often confused with being a concept or idea which magically makes everything fit and work, and will serve as a solution to every problem; in reality this can never be the case because the future cannot be predicted. The value of a grand strategy is as an insurance policy against the future, by providing options to enable governments to deal with any eventualities as they arise. It might be as simple as the construction of a railway, or securing a stockpile of fuel and suitable raw materials; it can be as complex as ensuring the continuance of friendships between nations despite changes in governments. These facts were understood

Barossa after conversion to a radar picket ship. The sheer amount of space required for all the extra personnel and supporting equipment is clearly illustrated here, including the second funnel introduced for the generators to power it all. There is also, clearly visible aft, in the space that used to be dominated by STAAG double 40mm, a Seacat missile launcher, which several of the class received. (*Drachinifel Collection*)

in the 1930s, possibly because of the very recent experiences of the First World War, possibly because, despite the claims of 'peace in our time', many were conscious of the possibility of another war.

The pre-war deployments of the 'Tribals' were about diplomacy. They were well suited to the role, and big enough fulfil it. Warships require a great deal of equipment and weaponry to fight a war, and space to carry out all their functions and activities. In peacetime, warships have ways and means of carrying out functions within a limited space. Reviews, receptions and parades can be conducted on adjacent spaces such as jetties, parks, sports grounds, lawns of government houses, to name but a few. Tribal priests, local leaders and cocktail parties always require more space than initially planned.[359] It might be more food, drinks, or space for dancing, but they always require more and the ability to accommodate it is important. The other side of diplomacy is the projection of power. In the modern world it may be a missile which carries the punch, but

Delight in 1966 in her final 'gunboat' form. The absence of a missile system was a determining factor in the class's later removal from service. (*Maritime Quest*)

the impression of power is as significant. The 'Tribals' were ideally suited for this. They had eight guns which, while not massive, were plenty big enough to impress. Their layout meant they had space, their appearance was striking and they carried a crew which was smartly dressed, well organised, well drilled, well led, but also, when necessary, able to think independently. In peacetime these attributes are impressive, to friend and foe alike. In time of war, they can save ships through fine handling, for example with *Cossack* in the fjord alongside *Altmark*; through damage control on *Eskimo* or *Nubian*, or quick thinking onboard *Sikh*. Pre-war, they took part in a great many exercises, equipping themselves well for these future eventualities. These exercises enabled the Navy to establish whether the ships would be capable of carrying out independent deployments; whether the class, built as much to be small cruisers in terms of mission profile as they were destroyers, would actually be able to perform in the many ways that were

anticipated. They must have been satisfied because the war had not long begun before the 'Tribals' were called on to perform sundry duties.

At War

During the war 'Tribals' were deployed everywhere. It is no surprise that *Nubian* earned so many battle honours. Where there was a fight, the Navy sent 'Tribal' class destroyers because they could rely upon them either to act independently or as part of a task group. They could also be counted on to fight aircraft, ships or submarines. They could be upgraded as technology developed and threats evolved. As their reputation grew they contributed an extra psychological boost within the forces to which they were assigned. This began in Norway and Narvik cemented it; the rescue by *Cossack* of the *Altmark* prisoners taken by the *Graf Spee* certainly began the myth. And it increased with every action, be it racing across the Atlantic to intercept the *Bismarck*, being the key link at Matapan, singlehandedly facing off against a battleship, sinking cruisers at Cape Bon, fighting at Île de Batz or forging a path during Operation Irregular.

Diamond in 1952, highlighting in her original form the advantages of her layout and the reasoning for parts of the class's design, for example the shaping of the superstructure's angled corners which were designed in such a way as to allow 'B' turret the maximum field of fire. She was only scrapped in November 1981 after being a dockside training ship for ten years and serving queen and country for nearly three decades.(*Maritime Quest*)

Nubian is, thanks to her wartime service, the best example of a 'Tribal' class destroyer as a tool of grand strategy. 'Tribals' offered the capability to fill cruiser shortages, the destroyer gap, the amphibious command

ship gap, and the smaller frigate/sloop/corvette gap; their capabilities were as such that they would often find themselves turned to fill many roles. Where the fighting was heaviest she would be found; she was always a significant asset, and whether this was because through procuring to fill gaps the Navy managed to acquire an excellent design which was so often called upon, or whether it was because there were those gaps and there were no other ships to call upon, it is difficult to be sure. It was probably a bit of both.

Like any class, the 'Tribals' were not perfect. As 'super-destroyers' they were arguably not as good as their Japanese or Italian equivalents. However, as they were built under the 'destroyer leader'/'super-destroyer' allowance of the naval arms treaties, they were not built exclusively for that role. The Navy built them for the role for which they were needed, as light cruisers and

This photo of *Diana* alongside *Eagle* is testimony to the enduring link of the large destroyers with the carriers. The large destroyers served as some of the most potent defenders of the carriers, but for the destroyers, when operating as pickets, it was the carriers' aircraft which were the cavalry. They could be called upon should something the destroyers could not themselves contend with come into view. (*Michael Rainsforth, Maritime Quest*)

Duchess with her canvas awnings spread. Awnings offered protection to crew working on torpedo and Squid launchers, or just an opportunity for the off-duty watches to enjoy life. (*Drachinifel Collection*)

fighting destroyers, and as such they performed well. Their design was flexible and adaptable and, most importantly, strong. In the cases of *Eskimo* and *Nubian* the loss of large sections of their hulls was counterbalanced by the damage control efforts. However, such efforts would have been futile if the rest of the hull had not been strong and able to take the strain of the damage imparted upon it.

The flexibility and generalist nature of 'Tribals' was so undoubtedly a positive. Today, the slogan is more along the lines of 'doing more with less'; but as the two World Wars illustrated, no matter how great the technological advantage, more was always better. For example, individually most variants of the American Sherman were outclassed by almost every late-war German tank, yet more often than not they were deployed in larger numbers and as a consequence were either able to overwhelm, destroy or outmanoeuvre their foe. By contrast, today's debates are almost always more focused on tactics than strategy, and when considering the design of warships, it is anti-submarine, air-defence, and naval gunfire support missions which are discussed; the ships are built for very specific roles. This is fine when there are sufficient numbers to generate a balanced task group. The 'Tribals' were built at a time when the Navy fielded more than fifteen times the force it does today, yet still they were procured as generalists, with a focused capability yes, but still generalists.

During the war, when building for the Royal Cana-dian Navy, some 'Tribals', as mentioned earlier, had to be completed with 4in rather than 4.7in guns. Essential to the war effort was putting hulls in the water, and the rest could be sorted out later. The key reason for this was that in the early years of the war the 'Tribals' were critical for making up for numbers of destroyers and cruisers, a force much greater in size than that possessed today but still not great enough for all the missions required of it. The continued utility of the 'Tribals' for the Royal Navy, even after greater numbers of destroyers and newer cruisers came into service, was obvious because fighting what was in reality a four-ocean (plus Mediterranean) conflict meant the Navy could never have enough ships. This was the conflict that erupted at the end of the 1930s, a truly global conflict. It is the worst-case scenario even today, a conflict which can only be waged through alliances, not necessarily of equals, but of equally committed.

This is the reality of grand strategy, of which 'Tribals', together with many other classes and their ships' companies, the hundreds of thousands of soldiers and thousands of aircraft, were all a part. While Britain might not have equalled all the contributions of some others by numbers, by the time the conflict was ending, the value of her contribution was great enough to ensure that a powerful voice was retained at the table. But the grand strategy, however, was not the whole reason for the 'Tribals'' greatness and their retention. As has been said many times, their design enabled them to be upgraded, which meant they could adapt as the tools, if not the nature, of the conflict evolved. Perhaps most significantly, the 'Tribals' were good ships which had built up an enviable reputation that ensured a strong esprit de corps. Fleet commanders could rely upon

Corunna in her final form with radar, the Type 965's AKE-2 aerial proudly aloft. A Seacat launcher is at the ready aft. The ship straddled the eras, with an early missile system aft and the slowly maturing radar in the middle that linked the two, as well as the guns of an earlier epoch. (*Drachinifel Collection*)

them not only to be prepared for the seemingly impossible task, but to relish it. In any war the impossible and the unexpected have to be expected, and in a global war this reality is just made bigger and infinitely more likely.

Admiral John Eaton

Philip Vian is the name most often cited as an example of the 'Tribal' class officer, but there is another, John Eaton, who despite being less well known, is as deserving of the connection. During his service in the Second World War he commanded three 'Tribals'. His first was *Mohawk*, from October 1939 to April 1941, followed by *Somali* from March 1942 to July 1942, and finally *Eskimo* from November 1942 to August 1943.[360] During these twenty-two months in charge he fought at Matapan with *Mohawk*, took part in Artic Convoys PQ15 and PQ17, as well as Operation Pedestal with *Somali* and *Eskimo*. He commanded the destroyer screen for Force H as part of Operation Torch, led them again in Operation Retribution and was doing so a third time when his ship was damaged during Operation Husky. This was the middle of his long career in the Navy, a career which during its early phases offered opportunities to gain the experience that enabled him to achieve his commands, and which in its post-war phase would both build upon and utilise the experience of command he had acquired in the 'Tribal' destroyers.

'Tribals' were not Eaton's first commands. Following his experiences as a young officer during the First World War, in 1935 he achieved his first command of the war-built 'W' class destroyer, *Westminster*, after nineteen years' service. By modern standards this would not have been considered an auspicious posting because *Westminster* was, at that time, a reserve ship. Despite this, in 1936 was given command of the 1930-built 'B' class destroyer *Boreas*, which he commanded until 1939. This was an important command because *Boreas* was a regular part of the British commitment to the Spanish blockade which was part of the response to the Spanish Civil War by the international community. This was no easy task, and required a commander to exercise diplomacy with understanding while enforcing rules with power. There was a constant struggle between dealing with the combatants (the two sides were in many ways easier to manage than their unofficial sponsors the Soviet Union, Germany and Italy), managing the crew and maintaining moral in what was, in many ways, a trail blazing operation.[361] Peace keeping, even in a sort of blockade and convoy role, was not something which had really been done before and certainly not something there was an extensive literature or institutional memory to fall back on for advice. It was the crews, officers and commanders on the spot who had had to make the decisions as best they could, making it up as they went along. Eaton successfully managed these conflicting demands and at the beginning of the Second World War assumed command of *Mohawk*, the second, and last officer to hold that responsibility.[362]

As mentioned earlier, *Mohawk*'s first commander, Commander Jolly, had died after bringing his ship back to shore despite suffering terrible woundsduring the first German air raid on the United Kingdom during the war. The German aircraft had managed to get in close because reports of RAF aircraft in the area had constrained the destroyers to hold their fire. They were actually inside the Firth of Forth when the attack happened. As previously related, Jolly suffered devastating wounds but remained conscious and in command of his ship for eighty minutes, and brought her safely back to shore. He died in hospital in South Queensbury five hours later. This was the character of the officer whose shoes Eaton had to fill.

From his own words in reports and newspapers articles we know Eaton was no great orator, nor given to speeches, and no diaries exist that anyone knows of. We have little knowledge about his style of command, or how he went about successfully assuming command after Jolly's death. However, what is certain is that in the case of a crew which regarded themselves as an elite, as any 'Tribal' destroyer crew did, a commander's mere reliance upon the authority of the uniform would not have maintained that esprit de corps which was just as important to the class's success as their design.[363] The ship's subsequent service record is a testimony to Eaton's success as a commander, and there are some clues which offer an insight into how he achieved that success.

Mohawk had been damaged, although not as severely as *Eskimo* at Narvik, and, crucially, had lost many of

her executive crew.[364] This put extra pressure on her new commander, not only in finding and integrating new officers into the wider crew, but also in carrying out extra duties normally performed by more junior officers. This could well have been beneficial as it would have allowed him far more opportunity for meeting the crew and going all over his ship than a regular change of command would have facilitated in wartime. Furthermore, Eaton had a reputation for leading from the front, setting an example and encouraging others to live up to it. He was not only good at commanding a team, but at building and maintaining one. These were skills which would prove useful when helping to set up NATO many years later. In 1939 it enabled him to forge a new crew from the remains of the old.

Unsurprisingly, *Mohawk* was not out of action for long. Having been repaired, she had barely left the yard when on 14 December, together with the destroyer *Kelly* – also leaving the yard after repairs – she was despatched to secure two tankers in trouble off the Tyne.[365] Both tankers were found to have been mined, although at first it was presumed they had been torpedoed. While Eaton was able to manoeuvre *Mohawk* alongside to rescue survivors, *Kelly*'s commander was not so blessed and the destroyer was caught by a mine and put out of action. *Mohawk* successfully took her under tow for a short time before a tug turned up and took over for the passage back to the shipyard she had just left.[366] *Mohawk* escorted them back in case of further attack. In a way it was an omen of things to come for *Kelly*, and in May 1940 during the Battle for Norway, when they

The 'Battle' class *Dunkirk* in earlier times during a visit to Malta. This represented almost the zenith of the torpedo-armed destroyer, only to be exceeded by their own slightly larger progeny, the *Daring* class. (*Drachinifel Collection*)

were again assigned together, *Kelly* was torpedoed by the schnellboot *S31*, commanded by Oberleutnant zur See Hermann Opdenhoff. Despite suffering heavy damage, she survived.[367]

For Eaton, his time with *Mohawk* was one of constant action with nineteen months spent at sea in the North Atlantic, the North Sea, Norway and the Mediterranean, which included some rather specialist missions. For example, in May 1940 he took *Mohawk* to shell the Dutch coast to prevent the Germans landing transports on the beaches behind the Dutch Army.[368] Another example was the recovery of British diplomats from The Hague, at the Hook of Holland, while part of the force that covered the rescue and evacuation of the Dutch royal family.[369] These were two of Eaton's earliest missions during his first command of the 'Tribal' class destroyer. As described in Chapter 3, this, unfortunately for *Mohawk*, came to an end in spectacular fashion in the Mediterranean, but it was a sign of the confidence in which he was held that in less than a year Captain Eaton was given a new command.[370]

This new command was *Somali*, which he assumed in time to participate in the escort of Convoy PQ15.[371] For good reason, the Arctic convoys are legendary.

The Royal Australian Navy's HMAS *Vampire* (D11), photographed here in 1969. *Vampire* made such a name for herself over her career that like HMCS *Haida*, she has been preserved and is the remaining living example of this class. (*Lynn Monson, Maritime Quest*)

Fighting the German forces was often secondary to fighting the forces of Mother Nature, which could neither be eluded nor defeated, only endured. For Eaton this was more than just a challenge of his leadership skills. *Somali* was the flotilla leader, and he had to combine the role of captain of his ship with command of the flotilla, Captain (D) as it was known in the naval parlance of the time. In comparison to other convoys, escorting PQ15 was relatively straightforward, although this does not mean it was without incident, and one which involved Eaton personally, as recalled by the Flotilla Signals Officer, John Buckeridge.

The Germans operated long range aircraft which circled the convoy out of the range of our guns, homing the torpedo bombers and U-boats on to the convoy. They were seldom able to make a surprise attack as we kept watch on their frequencies and could estimate within minutes when the attack was due, based on the build-up of their transmissions. This was a godsend as it meant that action stations need not be sounded until just before the whistle went. An interesting moment occurred when I reported to Captain D in his sea cabin that the time had come, and found that something was on fire. The 'something' was me – I was wearing a heavy kapok suit and had leant against his radiator. As the attack came in D was wrapping his flaming signal officer in a blanket.[372]

It was the events before this somewhat unusual and unintended version of shooting the messenger which had

Solebay bristling with guns. All her 40mm Bofors are out and at 45° and she looks not just purposeful, but menacing. (*Drachinifel Collection*)

made PQ15's 'straightforward' passage possible, events which illustrate how important the Battle of Narvik and the losses it had inflicted on the Kriegsmarine's destroyer force had been. These events had occurred around QP11, a return convoy which had left Russia a little before PQ15 left for Russia. This convoy had faced significant surface attacks, attacks which brought about the loss of the 'Town' class cruiser *Edinburgh*, sister ship of *Belfast*, the final blow delivered by a British destroyer to prevent the enemy boarding her.[373] The reason the Germans themselves had failed to deliver this blow was because they had mistaken minesweepers for destroyers, categorising them, in order of threat, 'Tribal', *Jervis*, 'F' or 'H' classes and one American.[374] The Germans felt comfortable attacking a lone cruiser, but a flotilla of destroyers, including 'Tribals', was justification for the withdrawal and the presence of such a group forced a sort of short reset of German surface forces. But the reduction of German surface actions and submarine attacks, which justify the description of PQ15 being termed 'straightforward', did not mean that it was safe. Air attacks, which sank three merchant ships, continued and there were always submarines with which to contend. However, it was weather and 'friendly fire' which accounted for the loss suffered by the escorts.[375] *Eskimo* and *Somali*'s sister ship *Punjabi* collided with the battleship *King George V* and sank.[376]

From that time, under Eaton's command, *Somali*'s operations became harder and included escorting the legendary PQ17, and Operation Pedestal in the Mediterranean. Eaton went from one battle to the next, from one responsibility to the next, and it is quite plausible that Brice's claim in his book *The Tribals* that Eaton was relieved on 30 July 1942 due to a stress-related illness is correct; he had certainly had enough for three lifetimes by this point.[377] What is certainly known is that when *Somali* was sunk by torpedo less than two months later, on 24 September 1942, while escorting PQ18, she was commanded by Lieutenant Commander Maud, who had relieved a Commander Currey (who had taken over after Eaton) just three weeks previously.[378]

It was not that long till Eaton was once again back at sea, in command of another flotilla and another 'Tribal' destroyer, *Eskimo*, suggesting that if his removal had been due to illness, it was quickly and successfully treated.[379] During his time with *Eskimo*, Eaton played an important role in Operation Husky – an operation covered in more detail in *Tartar*'s story.[380] Operation Torch, the invasion of North Africa, is well known, while Operation Retribution gives a far clearer picture both of Eaton and the style of officer encouraged by the Navy in its destroyers of the 1930s, a style which reached its zenith in the 'Tribals'.

Militarily, Operation Retribution was an anticlimax. The Axis naval forces never showed up.[381] From the British perspective, normal rules of war indicated that the Axis forces would evacuate their remaining troops from Tunisia, and when the Allied light forces prevented the merchant ships from getting through, the Italian battle fleet would sally forth to attempt to blast a passage. This is what Britain had done at Dunkirk, St Nazaire and Saint-Malo, and for their forces deployed to Norway and Crete. To the British, not retrieving those soldiers would have been an anathema. Perhaps

Trafalgar, due to time in reserve, missed Suez, and then returned again to reserve in 1947. After 1958 she had periods as an admiral's flagship before rejoining the reserve in 1962. (*Drachinifel Collection*)

it was the difference between a dictatorship and a democracy; total war, as was fought in the two world wars, required total commitment, but in a democracy, where the support of the electorate matters, troops could not be so easily sacrificed. Whatever the case, the big battle never happened, but the operation did. 'I regret that this patrol did not yield more substantial results, but I feel it was of high nuisance value and strongly discouraged enemy yachtsmen.' These lines from Eaton's operation summary highlight the frustration felt by some of the crews and officers involved.[382] Even though the patrol captured several useful prisoners, including the Chief of Staff of a Panzer division, it was not the battle or the prize they yearned for.[383] For an officer like Eaton it was a disappointment. In many ways it was, operationally, a rerun of the Spanish Civil War – a good deal of rushing about, picking up people from small boats, but not much of the sort of action that had been anticipated.[384] It was more a matter of maintaining the patrol and engaging with small craft, rather than Admiral Cunningham's vision for the operation to 'Sink, burn and destroy. Let nothing pass'.[385] While it is certain there was a desire for more action during Operation Retribution, in the subsequent operation in which *Eskimo* and her flotilla were involved, Eaton must have wished for rather less.

Between Operation Retribution and Operation Husky, Eaton's Flotilla was charged with the special mission, discussed in Chapter 5, of escorting the *Arethusa* class light cruiser *Aurora* and her special cargo.[386] *Aurora* was carrying King George VI, who had decided to visit Malta, which had recently been awarded the George Cross.[387] Although Admiral Cunningham had by this point, 19–21 June, declared the Mediterranean safe, it was but a relative safety. To ensure the King's security, nothing but the best could be deployed, and Eaton and his flotilla were the best Cunningham had.[388] The mission went off without a hitch. Leaving Tripoli, the King spent a day touring the island, before returning to Tripoli overnight. Following the King's disembarkation, the force returned to Malta to take part in Operation Husky, the end of Eaton's time in command of 'Tribals'. For the remainder of the war he was given staff appointments co-ordinating destroyers and operational planning until, at the end, when the conflict was over, he was given command of the 'Town' class cruiser *Sheffield* (of hunting the *Bismarck*, the Battle of Barents Sea and the Battle of North Cape fame).

After the War

The end of the Second World War was a huge watershed and turning point for the Royal Navy, but not all the changes that would follow were immediately discernible nor registered that quickly. The Navy was still confronted by the problem that to had the problem that to build a properly capable cruiser, was to build something to compare with the 'Town' class. The trouble was that those ships, in terms of cost, performance, manning and overall capability of weaponry, were top of the line vessels. And this was in the context of six hard years of war and the effect on the fleet. As the Navy started to demobilise from a war footing, and set about carrying out a thorough inspection of ships, assets and projects, it was apparent that there was a mishmash of vessels, some of which would be returned to previous owners or given back under Lend-Lease; many pre-war ships, which had once been the bastions of naval power, were now either no more, virtually shattered hulks or had had so many refits and patches that a lot of work by the DNC and the shipyards would be required to get them back into shape. Thrown into this scenario were a few precious new builds, but they had been ordered in times of war, when the pace was high, resources were tight and space on a ship a luxurious premium. Finally, there was the transition represented by the end of the 'big-gun' era, or the beginning of the end, and the Navy had to establish what a peacetime, carrier-centric navy would look like. What it would need? How it would conduct naval diplomacy?

This last part was especially important with the fracturing world being further complicated by the newly emerging superpower dynamic over and above the existing global and regional power system which governed the world for the previous century or so. Before the Second World War naval diplomacy was simple, a case of showing the flag and building bridges of understanding to help solve crises, as well as to help promote British interests, occasionally both at the same time. When it went slightly wrong, on a domestic level in a minor nation in Africa, Asia or South America, depending upon the status of the nation, a sloop or light cruiser could be sent. It would be gleaming white, the crew would be well drilled, a dinner would be hosted and the diplomats would talk with the important people. If matters were not resolved to the British Government's satisfaction, a heavy cruiser would be sent and the rituals repeated. If this did not succeed, a small force of cruisers, which usually included the station flagship, would arrive. The Admiral or Commodore, depending upon station, would host a bigger party, with even more senior people invited. Governments usually understood the next thing to turn up would be a battleship or battlecruiser, to which they certainly did not have the capability to withstand, or if they did then they would be treading the high wire of potential war.

The purpose was not to overawe with sheer power, in fact the first approaches were carefully calculated not to send something overwhelmingly powerful. The preference was for sloops and light cruisers. It is true they were powerful units for their size, but most nations possessed either enough cumulative force or even individual units capable of defeating them. They were a reminder of the Fleet across the horizon, and provided an opportunity for diplomacy. The next levels above were threats; they were the transition from something which could almost be regarded as de-escalatory, to something which was the equivalent of a heavy gauntlet being dropped; they were the embodiment of might. However, after 1945 the Royal Navy had lost most of its battleships, its cruiser force was weak and it was dif-

HMS *Vigo* was a 1942 Batch 'Battle' class, and spent most of her time with either 3rd DS or as gunnery training ship attached to HMS *Excellent*, a role in which she replaced *Finisterre*. (*Maritime Quest*)

ficult mobilising enough of them to perform the normal 'meet and greet' of naval presence. And the new capital ships, the aircraft carriers, were not really as powerful sitting in another nation's harbour, under their guns and unable to launch their aircraft. They were probably at their most intimidating when out at sea, just using their air groups for displays, but this kind of display could be heavy-handed diplomatically, unless the situation really demanded it. Submarines, the other success of the war, were, for diplomatic tasks, quite unsuited. Submarines are ambush hunters, operating with stealth, and going into port negates this attribute, as would cruising up and down on the surface in sight of land. Post-war navies were faced with an issue, and the Royal Navy with its tradition and institutional memory more so than most. How to project power?

For a navy, if it is impossible to maintain the hierarchy, and building a new version solely for purposes of stronger diplomatic posturing is not a practicable solution, the answer might be to ask why not build an intermediate layer? The ships would need to be larger than the frigates and destroyers which, when not practising for a possible war, were taking on the traditional role of sloops. They should be big enough, but not so big that the existing cruisers could not be justifiably retained and employed, a real fear if they made the ships 'too capable'. And they needed to be capable of diplomacy and for going to war, so the Navy required a 'light' light cruiser. This is where the 'Battle' class lost out. They were too obviously ships of war, being too aggressive in looks and design. They were crammed with weaponry, leaving too little space for diplomatic entertaining, although this might have been forgiven in times of Cold War and the threat of global nuclear conflict when it was expected that such weapons would be used against fleet concentrations. Their lack of space and issues with top weight made upgrades that much more difficult.

Furthermore, of the three classes of general-purpose destroyer which the Navy possessed in this period, the 'Battles' were the ones whose visual impact came from their weapons, largely because of their placement. The amount of weaponry crammed onto the 'Battles' gave them a slightly 'messy' outline, especially aft, accentuating that aggressive look. When coupled with the limited nature of potential diplomatic dining space, their unsuitability becomes apparent. A navy, especially the Royal Navy of the early Cold War global period, required a ship to be visually about being a ship, rather than just its weapons. This was where the *Daring*s and their design proportions come in. Naval diplomacy was not the only concern for the Royal Navy at the time.

The emergence of superpowers, the transition from Empire to Commonwealth, the start of the Cold War and post-war reconstruction efforts were further issues to worry about. In addition, the end of the big-gun era and the start of the missile age, the proliferation and diversification of nuclear weapons, the introduction of a new generaton of jet aircraft and the emergence of 'fast submarines' added yet further pressure. It is a wonder that any navy functioning within the limitations of a budget managed to build anything in this era, because of the constant discussion of around the new threats that would eradicate everything that had come before. The reality was there was no panacea, excluding nuclear oblivion which was an extreme method with which to contemplate winning a war, and it was quickly relegated to be used as a deterrent. This resulted in the clamouring for the specialist ships which were the 'perfect' antidote to this threat or the other.

The classic example of this is the impact of nuclear weapons, and also recently hypersonic weaponry, which tend to lead to the belief that submarines are the solution. This view is based on the argument that the threat to surface ships is now so great that all navies most go completely underwater. But if a navy wants to land more than small special forces units of ground troops, or provide air support, or conduct naval diplomacy, in fact any of the peacetime duties that navies carry out, then submarines are unlikely to be the answer.

The answer the Royal Navy found to the threats posed in the 1930s, was effectively a general-purpose destroyer, a design that was better than average, but not perfect, at dealing with all the extensive range of threats for the time, through the weaponry carried or its manoeuvrability. This approach was almost universally decried as being 'too conservative', largely because it had made concessions to the design of more specialist ships for other threats.

Taking a conservative stance is not without some merit, and the fact is that the general-purpose destroyer, as the issues Henderson had with the Mediterranean Fleet over the 'Tribals' and McGrigor had with Churchill over the *Daring*s, showed that they were being radical in their conservatism. They were covering eventualities in building a ship which could carry out a range of roles moderately successfully either alone or working with a specialist, and could support that vessel while also offering a modicum of protection from other threats. This was a sensible solution. The ships of the three classes studied in this book were force multipliers. This is important. When the lessons of history, particularly recent history, are forgotten, decisions often

Diamond's immediate forbear, commissioned in 1932 (H22). She displaced less than 1,400 tons which was less half that of the 1952 (D35) vessel, which displaced 2,830 tons. It was not only displacement that doubled, so had the complement and nearly every other metric. Most significantly, where H22 was built around her torpedoes, D35 was built around getting the best out of all her weapons to give her the general-purpose fighting profile needed for her new role. (*Drachinifel Collection*)

become progressively less optimal, and the lessons of the 'back pocket cruisers' should be applied to a modern navy, most obviously to the navy which created them in the first place, the Royal Navy.

The Modern Royal Navy

As the Royal Navy approaches its 475th year, based on its creation by Henry VIII's in 1546, it appears those officers arguing for specialisation in order to reduce costs have won their battle but lost the war. The ships have grown in size. Type 45 *Daring* class (8,500 tons at full load) area air defence destroyers and Type 23 'Duke' class (4,900 tons at full load) anti-submarine frigates are the size of Second World War cruisers. The Type 23's successors, the Type 26 'City' class (8,000 tons at full load) anti-submarine frigates and the Type 31 (6,600 tons at full load) general-purpose frigates even more so. However, they have lost the biggest fight. Despite all their willingly made sacrifices, they have failed to preserve either numbers of ships or manpower in the face of the most relentless enemy the Royal Navy

has ever fought, its own government or rather its own government's wishes to be re-elected. This has been compounded by winning the battle for specialisation. For example, a frigate might have shorter-range air defence missiles to provide a measure of air defence, but it needs the protection of a destroyer in a medium to high threat environment. While both these ships are to be likely to be fitted with, an anti-ship or land attack missile system, there is still the worry that remedying this traditional deficiency will mean a reduction in attack submarine numbers. The Navy as a whole is a strong force, but problems occur when specialist vessels are built to counter a single threat. If that threat lessens, then the need for such ships also lessens. But the pace of ship building means that reacting to an uptick in threat might have to be measured in decades. What is at present available to the Navy it is unlikely to change unless the context and criteria of funding change.

When the Type 45s were being built the world appeared relatively peaceful, wars were talked of as a 'choice' and so a reduction from twelve to six seemed a prudent financial decision. In addition, there were other things like the National Health Service, education and roads, all equally and immediately just as worthy of spending on as defence. Making the case for an air defence destroyer when there is nothing to defend against is difficult; the lack of an obvious enemy or threat, and membership of the world's most powerful military alliance provided the security. Perhaps that is the relative advantage which the Navy of the 1930s, 1940s and

Diana was the last *Daring* to commission, and in October 1955 she paid a reciprocal visit to the Soviet Union along with the *Colossus* class light fleet carrier *Triumph*, the *Abdiel* class fast minelayer *Apollo*, and two 'Ch' class destroyers, *Chieftain* and *Chevron*. (*Drachinifel Collection*)

1950s made the most of when compared to the modern navy – evident enemies. However, they also made the case for general-purpose destroyers. In the case of the 'Tribals' and the *Daring*s they were ships which could with ease, as we have reiterated, carry out presence duties and provide a decent level of land attack, as well as air defence and anti-submarine capability. However, it cannot be denied that their capabilities made them bigger and more expensive units than their more specialist counterparts. This is worth bearing in mind when considering all the plans that have been made for a 'frigate factory', the idea that it is cheaper and more efficient for the nation if a constant flow of orders is kept up. Specialist vessels don't suit this approach, as designs have to change to fit a particular need; a general-purpose design, would have been a practicable solution, not just the practical one. This all though matters for nought at the current time.

Currently, in terms of production, it is the Type 31 class which is important. They will be general-purpose vessels, but already they are being spoken of as if such a designation makes them second tier, makes them perhaps more easily discarded or forgotten. Particularly

strange is that these ships will be forward based, they will be the presence ships, those most often seen around the world wherever the Navy visits. The Type 26 and Type 45 will perform the majority of the duties of the task forces, and act as the reinforcements sent to supplement these forward deployed ships when the situation demands. No doubt the favour will be returned should a task force have to go to war.

Under such circumstances it can be argued that the Type 26 and Type 45 are inheritors of the sub-strand started with the 'Battle' class: a general-purpose orientated design rather than necessarily a 'general-purpose' design, although also used as a fighting class. The Type 31s are the inheritors of the full tradition as displayed in the 'Tribal' and *Daring* classes. They must be armed commensurate with their role, but more importantly must be outfitted as befits their diplomatic and engagement roles. In the modern world this means that when fitting out galleys, wardrooms and messes, for example, provision is made to support the large community required to run the ship. It means that effort and emphasis needs to go into the electronic systems, to allow the gathering of as much information as possible wherever they travel. Information about their surroundings, especially in its raw form, is critical for officers on a vessel required to act independently, whether in peace or in times of war. They are often called upon to make decisions which have ramifications far above their rank and beyond their locality. And this brings about perhaps

Above: *Duchess,* after the Royal Australian Navy lost one of their *Daring* class destroyers, HMAS *Voyager,* in 1964. The Royal Navy settled on the offer of the then HMS *Duchess* as she was already in the Far East and in need of refit. The Australian government accepted the offer and so began thirteen years of service, which included many operations with her sisters of both navies as the Indonesian Confrontation, the Vietnam War and other issues in the Far East were addressed. (*Drachinifel Collection*)

Below: *Dunkirk* had been commissioned in 1946 and spent two years with the 4th DF in the Mediterranean. In 1949 she was paid off and would not be returned to service till 1958 when again she would voyage to the Mediterranean where she remained, barring Cod Wars and South American excursions, until 1963 when she retired from service. She was the last unconverted 1943 Batch 'Battle' in service. (*Drachinifel Collection*)

Trafalgar pictured here with two other 'Battle' class vessels, probably *Dunkirk* and *Jutland*, her sisters in the 7th DS whose purpose was to try to shore up Britain's position in the Mediterranean by conspicuous presence and action. (*Drachinifel Collection*)

the most difficult requirement needed to help them accomplish their role.

The crew, like the 'Tribal' and *Daring* crews, have to believe they are special, an 'elite', which we have discussed earlier. They will be representing a navy which no longer has the squadrons of battleships and cruisers, the fleets of aircraft carriers which their forebears had when they went to the front. This is a navy which depends far more upon international cooperation. Such cooperation is built upon relations and impressions, and there is seldom a chance for a second first impression. The Type 31s will, by virtue of their station and their role, be the first impression, and the idea they might be second tier or less is so potentially corrosive. They are going to be an essential constituent of the capabilities of that fleet and for the nation. A navy is not about one ship or even one class, it is the sum of all its parts. A good navy is more than the sum of all its parts – made so by the crews that make it work, by the culture and tradition, which are its foundations, and by the nation which it represents. They will be frigates, but they will

need to carry themselves with the presence of cruisers of the 1920s and 1930s. Using that definition these ships, especially those which are forward based, in Bahrain or elsewhere, will be the 'back pocket cruisers' of their generation.

The smaller the navy the more important are flexible assets, for example, an aircraft carrier which can have its air group adapted at need. Amphibious ships are similarly flexible, and can be quite different in their capabilities. For escorts, flexibility is not a virtue of their core design. It is something which has to be built in, not only physically, but also culturally within the crew, and if the modern Royal Navy succeeds in inculcating this culture within the Type 31s, they will achieve a result that not only continues a legacy, but which will provide for flexible capability to underpin national security, in both presence and reach, for decades to come. Thus far the signs are good. The selection of the large Arrowhead 140 design, with its open architecture and space to develop within the existing builds which are planned currently, let alone potential further builds, is a very good sign. Signs though alone will not be enough; it will be time, commitment, support and the personnel of the Navy and Britain's political leaders which will decide what becomes of it.

Just as important as the escorts will be the core of the force around which they are built. While 'River' class Offshore Patrol Vessels (OPVs) and future Mine Countermeasures Vessels (MCMVs) will be the sloop stand-ins, together with the Type 31s taking on the light cruiser/intermediary role and Type 45 *Daring* class destroyers along with Type 26s 'City' class frigates fulfilling the gauntlet function, the future of British naval diplomacy would seem well placed. However, its success and capacity to deliver will depend upon the numbers procured and the quality of the core, or capital ships, around which they are built. What first comes to mind are the *Queen Elizabeth* class aircraft carriers, *Queen Elizabeth* and *Prince of Wales*. Relatively large and capable, they have been the subject of much debate for not being of Catapult Assisted Take Off/Barrier Assisted Recover (CATOBAR) design, being instead of the Vertical/Short Take Off and Landing (VSTOL) design with a ski ramp to assist with take-off. CATOBAR allows for the use of a wider range of heavier, more capable aircraft, but the Navy will get only two of these ships. Two flight decks are not enough to guarantee constant availability for a medium or global power. To guarantee that the strategic deterrent is permanently at sea requires four submarines. When taking into account maintenance, deployment and accident, to guarantee continual availability requires at least three vessels of any type, which is expensive. However, there is an obvious solution in which VSTOL is not only a strategic advantage for Britain to pursue, it is the critical enabler.

This is the opportunity to replace, in time, the existing Landing Platform Docks (LPDs), *Albion* and *Bulwark*, with two to three Landing Platform Helicopter/Docks (LHDs) that are also fitted with ski jumps for full VSTOL operational capability. If the case could be made for these vessels, to replace the already departed *Ocean*, the Landing Platform Helicopter (LPH) sold to Brazil, Britain would be truly capable. Having three ski ramp-enhanced LHDs and two strike carriers, Britain would have three amphibious operations (AMW) major/strike and air defence (S/AAD) minor and two S/AAD major/AMW minor ships around which to build task force.

This would mean that Britain would have five flight decks which could operate the same mix of aircraft and three major docks from which to draw to service its national and global reach. Under such circumstances, it is hard to think that a major task force would ever be assembled without both a strike/air defence designated flight deck and an amphibious flight deck. As important as the flight decks are, the large docks are key for enabling the deployment of heavier equipment, like main battle tanks; but also because, potentially, those same docks would be able to support medium-sized Unmanned Surface Vehicles (USVs), which themselves could be a critical part of the task forces' operation and conception.

Therefore, while it would always be conceded that CATOBAR and the aircraft that come with it produce the better technical solution, the case can be made that

Vigo's claim to fame is as the first winner of the Bulawayo Cup. This was awarded to the Royal Navy or Royal Fleet Auxiliary ship which, in the opinion of the Committee, was felt to be the most efficient in fleet replenishment at sea on the Mediterranean station. It was only awarded ten times, and only twice won by a warship, both times 'Battle' class vessels, *Vigo* and *Aisne* in 1955. (*Drachinifel Collection*)

Diamond in an obviously relaxed state, with guns turned inwards and numbers of crew spread all around the ship. Days like this were what helped to build the bonds of a crew; they allowed sailors to get to know their fellows outside of their divisions. It was days like this which helped forge the friendships that the Navy's destroyer force relied on. *(Drachinifel Collection)*

for Britain, VSTOL and the interoperability of all those decks would produce the most capable strategic and tactical solution. To produce the same level of security capability would require four CATOBAR aircraft carriers and four LHDs – eight ships, when for five Britain can achieve a flexible, but still potent, capability enabling it to reassure allies and defend its interests against even the most dangerous of potential opponents.

Britain, as she currently stands, would be classified as a medium global power. As a nation she is not in the superpower realm, a status which is allocated really to one global and two regional alliances with nuclear arsenals, but only one truly global power when it comes to logistical capability and their conventional arsenal. And Britain benefits from global reach thanks to the hard work of the Royal Fleet Auxiliary, the RAF Transport Command and Royal Logistics Corps. Unfortunately, there is not enough depth to that capability, but it could well be deepened and developed by sufficiently capable LHDs as outlined above. This is all far

away from the history on which this book is concentrated, but it demonstrates how lessons and experience in history can provide useful signposting for how we may approach the problems of today.

Conclusion – the 'Back Pocket Cruisers'

The stories that have been examined in this book offer a small window into the contribution the 'Tribal' class made to their country. The 'Tribal' class ships were designed as general-purpose destroyers, and we have seen the way they went about doing it. They sacrificed a torpedo set for an extra gun mount and included more destroyer guns to achieve rapid fire instead of going 'complete light cruiser' with 6in guns, and all this was packed into a 'destroyer leader' hull, giving the class the speed and manoeuvrability that was necessary to maximise their capabilities. In doing this the Admiralty had chosen to build a general-purpose destroyer, rather than a light cruiser. As such they were the 'back pocket' cruisers of the Royal Navy, not cruisers, but something in the 'back pockets' of admirals which could fill the void when needed – and they were used a lot. They were well armed (for their period) in terms of air defence, even before the refits, though they were never really AA destroyers. They had depth charges, but never enough to be a true 'AS' ship. Thus was their general-purpose design, their ability to fill a lot of gaps in the Navy's surface forces (a result of the reduced numbers of those forces), the factor that gave them their worth.

The 'Battle' class were too much of war-influenced design to follow this. They certainly shared the same tenets. They crammed everything into a destroyer hull – the guns, the torpedoes, the strength and the size. Yet the concept did not really work. If it had not been for the class which came after them, it could have been said the general-purpose destroyer faded away. They looked both too aggressive and unbalanced with their main firepower forward and the almost messy mass of medium weapons aft. Despite the justifiable reasons, they would always look like a compromise forced out of the experience of war, especially when single guns appeared amidships to provide cover. This was solved in the *Daring* class which was built for a nation which, although no longer the foremost of the imperial powers, was still a forward, outward-looking nation, a nation which believed in itself and its need and duty to influence events. Unfortunately, first the Suez Crisis, then the long-term effects of recovery from the Second World War, the dawn of the Cold War, combined with decisions that were penny-wise and pound-foolish,

such as the forced consolidation of industry, all were to sap Britain of much of her self-belief, a belief which would only begin to return after the *Daring*s were retired (which might be thought a waste as they would actually have been useful if operational) and after the successful deployment in the 1982 Falklands War. It is very hard to evaluate the use of ships as presence ships when it is arguable that the nation does not seem to wish to be present at all. However, that was all after 1953.

During 1930s, after the 'Tribal' class, the Admiralty built the *Laforey* or 'L' class, a more traditional destroyer design to fill the role established by the 'Tribals'. This was done because the Admiralty preferred cruisers to try to fill the 'cruiser gap'. As the war progressed, however, the 'Tribal' class's value was proved while, more importantly, the cruiser construction never reached the levels required by the Admiralty. They returned to the principles of the design which had led to the 'Tribal' class, then the 'Battles' and later the *Daring*s, which were arguably the next generation of general-purpose destroyers, without the treaty limitations to contend with. This *Daring* class drew from the lesson of the 'Tribals', with their emphasis on fighting capability provided by guns rather than torpedoes, but adjusted for the context and nuance of their time. The 'Tribal' class emphasis on cruiser-style capabilities in a destroyer hull also appeared with the 'County' class destroyers, when

Duchess in company with her sisters during what was probably the 1953 Coronation Review. 1953 was in many ways the Navy's peak of capability and flexibility. Ever since the flexibility of numbers has been sacrificed on the altar of increased capability. (*Drachinifel Collection*)

One name has appeared several time in this work, but this is the first picture of HMS *Nubian,* saved because in the end for all the discussion of the concept of the 'fighting destroyer'/'back pocket cruisers' being about diplomacy, presence and winning the peace, at their base point they are a concept of a warship and no ship in all these classes, not even her valiant sister the mighty HMS *Eskimo* are more of a warship, than *Nubian*, the stalwart warrior of the Second World War. (*Drachinifel Collection*)

the Royal Navy was again facing a cruiser shortage, or rather no cruisers. Instead, they built large, well-armed and spacious destroyers, albeit in a more circumspect manner, with less obvious space for diplomatic functions than either the 'Tribals' or the *Daring*s. However, even with this reservation the 'County' class proved, as had the 'Tribals' and 'Battles', to be easy to upgrade thanks to their space. The major advantage of the 'Counties' was that they were designed to fulfil command roles for which the 'Tribals' had been used, and deftly stepped into the gaps left by the disappearing cruiser force. Design, however, is just one aspect of the legacy of the 'Tribals', 'Battles' and *Daring*s.

It was not only the design of the 'Tribals' that has lived on as a legacy within the Navy, but also the *espritde corps*, the fighting aggression and pride of the 'Tribal' crews, which has been retained in the modern Navy. Mixed with the traditions and personalities of the cruiser crews it has provided a twenty-first-century version of it – the 'can do' attitude which is the mantra of

the modern Navy. The legacy reaches right back to their pre-war service and actions, and it was also a product of the classes that came after it, the 'Battles' and the *Daring*s.

The Royal Navy won many successes in the Second World War, and the capital ships and carriers gained the glory, the cruisers being awarded much of what was left, but much of what they achieved was with the help and sacrifice of remarkable smaller ships, foremost amongst them being the 'Tribal' class destroyers. It was these 'back pocket cruisers', the first general-purpose destroyers to serve with the Royal Navy, and the forebears of the vessels plying their duties on the world's oceans today, that made such a difference. That difference is exemplified by the service of the sisters *Cossack, Eskimo, Sikh* and *Nubian*. These were the ships which fought the war, day in and day out, and they could do this because their design enabled them to adapt to every circumstance, a lesson which should not be forgotten by contemporary governments or naval architects.

It was these ships and their capabilities that the Navy was most desperately seeking to emulate later in the war, a task the Admiralty set the DNC. Goodall responded first with the 'Battle' class and then, post-war, dealing with the challenges of the changing world by bringing into service updated version of the concept for the 1950s, the *Daring* class. It was not easy to justify sometimes; general-purpose is never an easy case to make, as there is always another design which is better dealing with some specific threat. General-purpose is about aggregate and whole-force capabilities. In a world which prized the sophistication of technology, which prided itself achieving perfection and problem solving, the nuance and context required for making the case for a general-purpose vessel, especially one not built on the traditional scale for it, to wit the full cruiser, it was certainly not easy. Luckily, for the Royal Navy, they did make it, successfully.

This book started with the story of *Mashona*, and it seems appropriate to finish it with another story, that of *Matabele*, a ship that has, by comparison, hardly been mentioned. She survived the early years of the war until January 1942 when, along with *Somali*, she joined the escort of Arctic Convoy PQ8. The convoy had almost reached safety, when the merchant ship SS *Harmatris* was torpedoed by a U-boat, Kapitanleutnant Hack-

lander's *U-454*.[389] The *Harmatris* was taken in tow by *Speedwell*, a *Halcyon* class minesweeper, and as the rest of the convoy steamed ahead to gain the safety of harbour, the two 'Tribal' class vessels were left to escort the tow.[390] They were the vessels judged most capable of delivering the *Harmatris* and, most importantly, her cargo to their destination. They were the general-purpose destroyers which stood a chance of protecting their charges against all threats, and indeed this was a mission in which they would succeed, though as it turned out not without loss. During the night *Matabele* was sunk by torpedo in another attack by *U-454*. There was no warning and all but two of her crew were lost in the icy waters of the Artctic.[391] It was another grim loss, another 'Tribal' sacrifice. But it was not in vain for *Harmatris*, with her cargo, made it to Murmansk.

NOTES

Chapter 1

1 Kennedy, 1942, pp. 91–4
2 Brice, 1971, p. 166
3 Ibid; Kennedy, 1942, pp. 91–4
4 Kennedy, 1942, pp. 91–4
5 Brice, 1971, p. 166; Kennedy, 1942, pp. 91–4
6 Twenty-seven of the class were built in total, HMCS *Micmac*, HMCS *Nootka*, HMCS *Cayuga*, HMCS *Athabaskan* (II) and HMAS *Bataan* were all completed after the war was over.
7 Brice, 1971, p. 11; the 'Tribal' class were not the only class to suffer so, as Lt-Cdr Hugh Hodgkinson states in his work *Before the Tide Turned; The Mediterranean Experiences of a British Destroyer Officer in 1941* (1944, pp. 239-40), 'The little *Hotspur* still fights. She is almost the last of the old Second Flotilla. Five went into Narvik. The *Hardy* and *Hunter* were lost, and the VC won. The *Hotspur* came out terribly damaged, but got home to be repaired. The rest of the flotilla were operating in the South Atlantic in those days, but once again they all joined up in the Med. In 1940 [*sic*]. For two years they took part in almost every action in that sea, and gradually their numbers lessened. It would be hard to count the honours they gained. The *Hyperion* and *Hostile* were the next two to go, and the *Herward* went in our Heraklion evacuation. Then the *Hasty* was lost in a night operation, and finally the *Havock*, who was always our particular friend, became a total loss. So remain the *Hero* and *Hotspur* to carry on the old name.'
8 A good example of this is *Ashanti* which between 22 May 1942 and 13 August, took part in two Arctic Convoys, PQ16 and PQ17, and Operation Pedestal, the critical resupply of Malta (Brice, 1971, pp. 49–55; Smith, 2002, pp. 112, 148 & 152–5; Woodman, 2007, pp. 146–61); in less than twelve weeks, this one destroyer took part in actions which spread from the Arctic circle to the Mediterranean, and she was not unusual in this (Burt, 1985, pp. 41–2)
9 TNA - ADM 1/9355, 1933; TNA - ADM 116/3734, 1936-1938
10 Morris, 1987, p. 174, & TNA - ADM 1/9427, 1937
11 Ibid
12 Ibid
13 TNA - ADM 1/8828, 1934-1935
14 *Signatories of the 1930 London Treaty for the Limitation and Reduction of Naval Armament*, 2003
15 *Signatories of the 1930 London Treaty for the Limitation and Reduction of Naval Armament*, 2003
16 Kennedy, 1942, p. 46. Furthermore, it is interesting to note that Plevy (*Destroyer Actions, September 1939–June 1940*, 2008, p. 11) describes this meeting of Kennedy & *Tartar* no less elegantly, but slightly differently: '…a little way downstream I glimpsed her for the first time – as sleek and elegant and powerful-looking ship as I have yet seen. From the bow there rose in successively higher tiers A gun, B gun, the convex armoured wheelhouse and – the high point of the ship – the open bridge, some forty feet above the waterline. At the back of the bridge was the foremast with its aerials, aft of that the raked funnel, and in the waist of the ship the torpedo-tubes. Up again to the pom-pom and X gun and the down to Y gun, the quarterdeck and the stack of depth charges. The whole effect was one of symmetry and grace.'

17 TNA - ADM 1/9355, 1933; Friedman, 2010, p. 186
18 TNA - ADM 1/9384, 1933-1936
19 TNA - ADM 1/8828, 1934-1935
20 Ibid.
21 TNA - ADM 1/9384, 1933-1936; TNA - ADM 1/8828, 1934-1935; Friedman, 2010, p. 186
22 TNA – ADM 1/8828, 1934-1935
23 Ibid
24 Ibid
25 Ibid
26 Ibid
27 TNA - ADM 116/3734, 1936-1938
28 Temple Patterson, A. (1973), *Tyrwhitt of the Harwich Force*; Friedman, 2010, p. 186; a good example of this 'interchangeability' with cruisers is discussion in TNA - ADM 116/3734 (1936-1938), where it was proposed that the 1st 'Tribal' class Destroyer Flotilla would make up the balance of the 3rd CS.
29 TNA - ADM 1/9355, 1933; TNA - ADM 1/9355, 1933; Hill-Norton & Decker, 1982, p. 60.
30 TNA - ADM 116/3617, 1931-1933
31 For an in-depth examination of First World War destroyer tactics and the operational difficulties they faced please read - Brooks, John. 'British Destroyers at Jutland: Torpedo Tactics in Theory and Action'. *British Journal for Military History*, v. 3, n. 3, Jun. 2017. Available at: http://bjmh.org.uk/index.php/bjmh/article/view/167. Date accessed: 03 Jun. 2017.
32 TNA - ADM 1/9384, 1933-1936; TNA - ADM 1/9355, 1933
33 Field, 2004, pp. 242–3: 'Tribals' were always key in the Mediterranean, for example four would take part in Operation Pedestal, *Somali, Eskimo, Tartar* and Ashanti; (Smith, 2002, pp. 253–5).
34 TNA - T 161/243 (25613). (1924-5). Navy Estimates 1925-26; Preliminary discussions as to total; TNA - T 161/243 (25613a). (1924-5). Papers relating to: Japan & USA Navies, Singapore Naval Base, Vote 10, Vote 9, Fleet Air Arm, Guns & Ammunition, Vote A; TNA - T 161/243 (25613b). (1924-5). Papers relating to USA Navy Estimates} in comparison with Navy Estimates 1925/26; TNA - T 161/243 (25613c). (1924-5). Disarmament in connection with Navy Estimates 1925/26; TNA - T 161/243 (25613d). (1924-5). Papers relating to Cabinet Memoranda of Decisions in connection with Navy Estimates 1925/26; TNA - T 161/243 (25613e). (1924-5). Papers relating to Ministerial Correspondence in connection with Navy Estimates 1925/6; TNA - T 161/243 (25613f). (1924/25). Papers relating to New Construction & British Naval Strength in connection with Navy Estimates 1925/26
35 Brice, 1971, pp. 252–5; TNA - ADM 1/15323. (1943). Tribal Class Destroyers: Cost of Building in the United Kingdom
36 Batchelor & Chant, 2008, pp. 174–5; Friedman, 2010, p. 186. TNA - ADM 1/9355. (1933, August 10). Cruiser Design: Requesting views of Commanders-in-Chief, Home and Mediterranean Fleets; Stern, 2008, p. 94; TNA - ADM 1/9384. (1933-1936). Required for R.A.(D)'s Flagships: Proposed investigation of new design for - Preliminary Staff Requirements; TNA - ADM 1/8828. (1934–35). New Construction Programme for Cruisers 1936;

Hansard HC Deb. vol. 345 cols. 433–4, 15 March 1939
37 Brice, 1971, p. 254
38 The largest destroyers ordered by the RN until the war-built 'L' or *Laforey* class destroyers entered service; Plevy, 2008, p. 254; TNA - ADM 187/1. (1939). Pink List, September 1939; Smith, 2010, pp. 13–48); Brice, 1971, p. 255: Jordan, 2011, p. 304
39 TNA - ADM 1/10160, 1939
40 TNA - ADM 1/10160, 1939
41 Hill-Norton & Decker, 1982, pp. 111–2
42 Friedman, 2010, pp. 390 & 402
43 TNA - ADM 227/277, 1940
44 TNA - ADM 1/10160, 1939
45 Whitley, 2000, pp. 114-7
46 TNA - ADM 1/12287, 1942; TNA - ADM 136/19, 1935–40
47 TNA - ADM 1/8828, 1934–35
48 TNA - ADM 1/9384, 1933–36; TNA - ADM 186/350, 1938. Handbook for the Admiralty Fire Control Clock, Mark 1; Brice, 1971, p. 15
49 TNA - ADM 1/8672/227 (1924), Light-Cruisers Emergency Construction Programme; TNA - ADM 203/90 (1929), Strategical Exercise MZ - Altantic and Mediterranean Fleets 1929; TNA - ADM 1/9355, 1933. TNA - ADM 1/8828, 1934–35; TNA - ADM 1/9384 (1933–36); TNA - ADM 116/3734, 1936–38
50 TNA - ADM 186/296. 1930. Handbook For High Angle Control System Marks I and I★. Book II - Plates
51 TNA - ADM 186/278, 1927. Pamphlet on the Drill Procedure and Upkeep of the Admiralty Fire Control Table, Mark II ('Kent' Class and later Cruisers); TNA - ADM 186/296, 1930; TNA - ADM 186/350, 1938; TNA - ADM 1/12516, 1943; TNA - ADM 220/1668, 1944; TNA - ADM 212/51, 1921–27. A.R.L. Domestic File: AA Predictor and AA Fire Control Equipment (A.R.L. Predictors); TNA - ADM 186/345, 1925, January, April, July, October. Vernon's Quarterly Letter to the Fleet (No. 23, 24, 25, 26.); TNA - ADM 220/211, 1940-1946). General Fire Control Papers - R.D.F; TNA - ADM 212/72, 1934. A.R.L. Domestic File (un-numbered); E.T. Hanson (A.R.L. Predictor and other Fire Control Problems)
52 TNA - ADM 186/350, 1938
53 Ibid
54 *Transactions of the Institution of Naval Architects*, 1939, p. 349
55 Royal Aero Club, *The Development of the Fleet Air Arm*, 1934, p. 113
56 Barrett, 2015 (online publication)
57 Tyne & Wear Archives - DS VA 6/36/17 (1936–39)
58 Ibid
59 Ibid
60 Ibid
61 Brice, 1971, p. 19
62 TNA - ADM 116/3871 (1939), highlights this delicate and complicated situation; however, Brice, 1971, p. 20, D'Este, 1990, Greene & Massignani, 1998, and Smith, 2011, all agree and go into wide detail of the affects this had on RN and to an extent wider British Government thinking. Although it wasn't just the RN, the wider British defence establishment worried about the Mediteranean, as shown by the 1928 Air Ministry Report, Air Threat in the Mediterranean (TNA - AIR 2/1457).
63 Brice, 1971, p. 11; TNA - ADM 116/3734, 1936–38
64 TNA - ADM 136/19, 1935–40
65 Brice, 1971, p. 20. A fairly common patrol to be issued with at this time, although considering its requirements, and their capabilities, the 'Tribal' class must have seemed a perfect fit (TNA - ADM 116/3679, 1937–38; Lyon, 1970, pp. 36–7)
66 TNA - ADM 116/3873, 1937–39

67 Brice, 1971, p. 20
68 Ibid
69 Ibid, p. 21
70 TNA - ADM 116/3873, 1937-39; TNA - ADM 1/9942, 1939
71 Brice, 1971, p. 105; Plevy, 2008, pp. 81–95; Carton De Wiart, 1950, p. 165; Dannreuther, 2006, p. 116; TNA - ADM 202/352, 1941; TNA - ADM 1/9942, 1939
72 Brice, 1971, p. 105
73 Ibid
74 Ibid, p. 11; TNA - ADM 116/3734, 1936–38
75 Ibid, p. 40
76 Ibid, p. 252
77 TNA - ADM 1/10160, 1939; TNA - CO 323/1694/8, 1939
78 TNA - ADM 1/10160, 1939; TNA - CO 323/1694/8, 1939
79 Brice, 1971, p. 40; The National Commission on Culture, 2007; TNA - ADM 1/10160, 1939; TNA - CO 323/1694/8, 1939
80 Ibid
81 TNA - ADM 1/10160, 1939
82 Brice, 1971, p. 41
83 Ibid
84 Manning, 1979, p. 100
85 Konstam, 2013, p. 38; Winton, 1986, p. 152; Brice, 1971, pp. 40–65; Smith, 2002, pp. 152–5; TNA - ADM 1/15784, 1944
86 TNA - CO 323/1694/8, 1939
87 TNA - ADM 116/3818, 1939
88 Ibid
89 Ibid
90 Ibid
91 Ibid
92 Ibid
93 Ibid
94 Brice, 1971, p. 42; TNA - ADM 116/3818, 1939
95 Ibid

Chapter 2

96 TNA - ADM 116/3734, 1936–38: very similar to the four roles outlined for a fleet cruiser '1. Reconnaissance in which the ultimate aim is visual touch with the Enemy Battlefleet. For this to be effective, equal total cruiser strength with that of the enemy is required. 2. The support of the Flotillas in the van. 3. Screening the Fleet night and day. 4. Detached Operations.' TNA - ADM 1/9355, 1933
97 TNA - ADM 1/9355, 1933; TNA - ADM 1/8828, 1934–35
98 Brice, 1971, p. 228
99 Ibid, p. 44
100 TNA - ADM 116/3893, 1937–39
101 Brice, 1971, p. 23; TNA - ADM 187/2, 1939
102 TNA - ADM 358/73, 1940; Creswell, 1967, p. 75; Carton De Wiart, 1950, p. 165; Vian, 1960, pp. 23–73; Kennedy, 1974, p. 144
103 Brice, 1971, p. 108; Vian, 1960, p. 50
104 TNA - ADM 196/52/83, 1946
105 Ibid
106 Ibid
107 TNA - ADM 187/1, 1939; TNA - ADM 187/2, 1939; TNA - ADM 187/3, 1939; TNA - ADM 187/4, 1939; TNA - ADM 187/5, 1940, Pink List, January 1940; TNA - ADM 187/6, 1940, Pink List, February to March 1940; TNA - ADM 187/7, 1940; Vian, 1960, pp. 23–73; Kennedy, 1974, pp. 151–88
108 TNA - ADM 196/52/83, 1946
109 Brice, 1971, p. 23
110 TNA - ADM 187/2, 1939; TNA - ADM 187/3, 1939; TNA - ADM 187/4, 1939

111 Brice, 1971, p. 24; Vian, 1960, p. 23
112 TNA - ADM 358/3300, 1939; Brice, 1971, pp.179–80
113 Ibid
114 Brice, 1971, p. 24; Vian, 1960, p. 23
115 Ibid
116 Ibid
117 Ibid
118 Ibid
119 Ibid
120 Ibid
121 Ibid
122 TNA - ADM 187/2, 1939; TNA - ADM 187/3, 1939; TNA - ADM 187/7, 1940; TNA - ADM 199/473, 1940; Vian, 1960, p. 23)
123 Brice, 1971, p. 24; Vian, 1960, p. 23
124 Ibid
125 TNA - ADM 187/1, 1939; TNA - ADM 187/2, 1939; TNA - ADM 187/3, 1939; TNA - ADM 187/4, 1939; TNA - ADM 187/5, 1940; TNA - ADM 187/6, 1940; TNA - ADM 187/7, 1940; Vian, 1960, pp. 23–73; Kennedy, 1974, pp. 15188
126 Vian, 1960, p. 7
127 Ibid, pp. 12–13
128 Ibid, pp. 13–14
129 Vian, 1960, p. 14
130 Ibid
131 Ibid
132 Ibid
133 Ibid
134 Ibid
135 TNA - ADM 199/281, 1940
136 Ibid
137 Ibid
138 Haarr, 2013, pp. 352–89; TNA - FO 952/2, 1940, Report on the *Altmark* incident and local correspondence; TNA - ADM 223/27, 1940, *Altmark* Action Feb 1940; TNA - ADM 199/280, 1940, War History: Interception and Boarding of German Auxilary *Altmark*, 16.2.1940; Vian, 1960, pp. 24–31; TNA - ADM 199/281, 1940, German auxiliary *Altmark*: interception and boarding
139 Ibid
140 Haarr, 2013, pp. 366–73; Plevy, 2008, p. 90; TNA - ADM 223/27, 1940; TNA - FO 952/2, 1940; TNA - ADM 199/280, 1940; Vian, 1960, pp. 26–7; TNA - ADM 199/281, 1940
141 Lyon, 1970, p. 32; Vian, 1960, p. 27; TNA - ADM 199/281, 1940
142 Haarr, 2013, pp. 374–6; Rodger, 2004, pp. LXII–LXV; Rodger, 1997, pp. XXI–XXVI
143 TNA - ADM 223/27, 1940; TNA - ADM 199/281, 1940
144 Plevy, 2008, pp. 122–3; TNA - ADM 223/27, 1940; Vian, 1960, p. 29; TNA - ADM 199/281, 1940
145 Lyon, 1970, p. 32; TNA - ADM 223/27, 1940; Carton De Wiart, 1950, p. 165; Vian, 1960, p. 30; TNA - ADM 199/281, 1940
146 Clarke, 2017, *Tribal Class Destroyers Part 1: Some Battles of HMS Sikh*
147 TNA - ADM 1/12287, 1942; Brice, 1971, pp. 128–9; TNA - ADM 187/7, 1940
148 Brice, 1971, p. 128; Vian, 1960, p. 37
149 Ibid
150 Vian, 1960, p. 37
151 Friedman, 2010, pp. 156–62
152 TNA - ADM 1/12287, 1942
153 Vian, 1960, p. 37
154 TNA - ADM 1/12287, 1942
155 Ibid
156 Vian, 1960, p. 38
157 Ibid
158 Haarr, 2013, pp. 3–33; Cope, 2015, pp. 137–92
159 TNA - ADM 199/473, 1940: See Chapter 5 for details of the VC
160 Cope, 2015, pp. 137–92; TNA - ADM 199/473, 1940; Hodgkinson, 1944, p. 239
161 TNA - ADM 199/473, 1940; TNA - ADM 187/1, 1939
162 TNA - ADM 199/473, 1940; Plevy, 2008, p. 134
163 TNA - ADM 199/473, 1940
164 Ibid; Plevy, 2008, p. 136
165 Ibid
166 Ibid
167 TNA - ADM 199/473, 1940; Plevy, 2008, p. 138
168 Ibid
169 Ibid
170 Ibid
171 Ibid
172 TNA - ADM 199/473, 1940
173 Ibid; Plevy, 2008, p. 139
174 Ibid; Plevy, 2008, pp. 140–1
175 Brice, 1971, p. 116
176 Clarke, 2017, *Tribal Class Destroyers Part 3: HMS Ashanti, a Soft Power Entrepreneur*
177 Brice, 1971, p. 116
178 TNA - ADM 199/473, 1940
179 Brice, 1971, p. 90; TNA - ADM 199/473, 1940
180 TNA - ADM 199/473, 1940
181 Brice, 1971, p. 91; TNA - ADM 199/473, 1940
182 Ibid
183 TNA - ADM 199/473, 1940
184 Brice, 1971, p. 92; TNA - ADM 199/473, 1940
185 Ibid
186 Ibid
187 TNA - ADM 1/15795, 1944; TNA - ADM 1/15791, 1944; TNA - ADM 267/21, 1944
188 Brice, 1971, p. 123; TNA - ADM 199/473, 1940; TNA - ADM 234/509, 1941; TNA - ADM 267/21, 1944; TNA - ADM 1/15791, 1944; TNA - ADM 1/15795, 1944
189 Brice, 1971, pp. 116–26
190 Plevy, 2008, pp. 149–70; Brice, 1971, pp. 24–7; Carton De Wiart, 1950, pp. 163–75; Vian, 1960, pp. 32–50
191 Ibid
192 Ibid
193 Carton De Wiart, 1950, p. 174
194 Ibid; Vian, 1960 pp. 47–50
195 Vian, 1960, p. 48
196 TNA - ADM 187/7, 1940; TNA - ADM 187/8, 1940; TNA - ADM 187/9, 1940; TNA - ADM 199/810, 1941

Chapter 3

197 TNA - ADM 203/90, 1929; TNA - ADM 186/145, 1929; TNA - ADM 186/158, 1937
198 Simmons, 2011, p. 110 & 133; Cunningham, 1951, p. 329
199 TNA - CAB 121/447, 1941; TNA - DEFE 2/140, 1941; TNA - PREM 3/328/7, 1941; TNA - ADM 1/20611, 1947; Brice, 1971, pp. 94–5
200 Ibid
201 Ibid
202 Ibid

203 Ibid
204 Ibid
205 Ibid
206 Ibid
207 Ibid
208 Ibid
209 Ibid
210 Ibid
211 TNA - ADM 116/3734, 1936-1938
212 Vian, 1960, p. 56; Kennedy, 1974, inside book cover & pp. 142–3
213 Vian, 1960, p. 56
214 Ibid
215 Vian, 1960, p. 57; TNA - ADM 234/509, 1941, The Sinking of the *Bismarck*, 27 May, 1941 - Official Dispatches
216 Vian, 1960, p. 57
217 Kennedy, 1974, p. 177; TNA - ADM 234/509, 1941
218 Ibid
219 TNA - ADM 234/509, 1941
220 Kennedy, 1942, pp. 85–9; Dannreuther, 2006, p. 95
221 TNA - ADM 367/137, 1941, Hood & Bismarck - Capital Ships vs Tirpitz; TNA - ADM 234/509, 1941; TNA - ADM 234/510, 1941, The Sinking of the Bismarck, 27th May, 1941 - Plans
222 TNA - ADM 367/137, 1941, Hood & Bismarck - Capital Ships vs Tirpitz; TNA - ADM 234/509, 1941; TNA - ADM 234/510, 1941, The Sinking of the Bismarck, 27th May, 1941 - Plans
223 TNA - ADM 234/509, 1941; Kennedy, Sub-Lieutenant; a personal record of the war at sea, 1942, pp. 85–9
224 TNA - ADM 234/509, 1941
225 TNA - ADM 234/509, 1941; Kennedy, 1974, pp. 217–19
226 Ibid
227 TNA - ADM 1/8828, 1934–35; TNA - ADM 1/12325, 1942. HNMS *Isaac Sweers* often accompanied the 'Tribals' on operations; in fact it was she which played a crucial role (in spite of a submarine being in the vicinity, stayed stopped for over an hour) in picking up the *Laforey* class destroyer HMS *Ghurkha*'s company, when the latter was torpedoed; whilst escorting a convoy from Alexandria, along with two other ships from the battle of Cape Bon team, HMS *Legion* & the 'Tribal' *Maori*; TNA - ADM 1/12287, 1942
228 TNA - ADM 1/12325, 1942
229 Ibid
230 Ibid
231 Ibid
232 Some historians argue that it was the aggressiveness of the RN's destroyer force which was the decisive factor in forcing the European Axis powers to adopt a defensive mind-set; Smith, 2010, p. 156; TNA - ADM 1/8828, 1934-1935
233 TNA - ADM 178/280, 1942. Although even in death *Maori* proved useful, as the diesel generator she had aboard 'proved its worth and enabled the supply of light and power in the fore part of the ship to be maintained after the loss of steam.' As a consequence of this experience diesel generators were more widely fitted, to provide support in such extreme circumstances.
234 *Sikh* does, like *Tartar*, have a book written about her, but unlike Kennedy's *Sub-Lieutenant* (1941), Davies's *Lower Deck* (1946) does not call her *Sikh* but *Skye*.
235 Smith, 2010, p. 156
236 TNA - ADM 199/681, 1942; Smith, 2010, pp. 147–56; Brice, 1971, pp. 221–2; Britannia Naval Histories of World War II, 2013, pp. 104-15
237 TNA - ADM 199/681, 1942; Smith, 2010, pp. 147–56; Brice, 1971, pp. 221–2
238 TNA - ADM 199/681, 1942; Smith, 2010, pp. 147–56; Brice, 1971, pp. 221-2
239 TNA - ADM 199/681, 1942; Smith, 2010, p. 149; Brice, 1971, pp. 221–2
240 TNA - ADM 199/681, 1942; Smith, 2010, p. 149; Brice, 1971, pp. 221–2; Britannia Naval Histories of World War II, 2013, p. 110
241 Britannia Naval Histories of World War II, 2013, p. 110
242 TNA - ADM 199/681, 1942; Smith, 2010, p. 149; Brice, 1971, pp. 221–2
243 TNA - ADM 199/1110, 1942; Britannia Naval Histories of World War II, 2013, pp. 129–39
244 TNA - ADM 199/1110, 1942; Britannia Naval Histories of World War II, 2013, pp. 134–5; Brice, 1971, p. 97
245 Brice, 1971, p. 97
246 TNA - ADM 199/1110, 1942; Britannia Naval Histories of World War II, 2013, pp. 134-5; Brice, 1971, p. 97
247 TNA - ADM 199/1110, 1942; Britannia Naval Histories of World War II, 2013, pp. 134–5; Brice, 1971, p. 97
248 Ibid
250 Ibid
251 Ibid
252 Ibid
253 Ibid
254 TNA - ADM 1/12325, 1942; Creswell, 1967, p. 105; TNA - ADM 1/12326, 1942; TNA - ADM 1/12771, 1942
255 TNA - ADM 1/12326, 1942; TNA - ADM 1/12771, 1942
256 Ibid
257 Ibid
258 Ibid
259 Ibid

Chapter 4

260 Boniface, 2007, p. 1
261 TNA - ADM 1/9416, 1937
262 Whitby, 1993, p. 5; Hodges, 1971, pp. 20–1
263 Lambert, 2019, pp. 176–7
264 Johns, 1934, p. 11
265 A calculation which had led to the focus on the 6in gun over the 8in by the RN. The Mk IV mount combined with its two Mk V 4.5in guns was a powerful weapon system. The RN needed it in service and it would go on to become ubiquitous with the RN, serving in the Falklands War thirty-plus years later, only having begun to be replaced as the 'go-to' weapon in new builds in 1972 by the Mk 8 4.5in gun, which is the standard weapon of the RN to the present day. This was despite it not living up to its promised potential at the time, as the automatic loader was complex and prone to issues which would lead to the gunnery crew manually carrying out tasks, rather than letting the machinery cycle through as had been planned.
266 *Transactions of the Royal Institution of Naval Architects* (1983), p. 113
267 Thursfield, 1936, pp. 12–13

Chapter 5

268 Roskill, 1976, p. 262
269 Brice, 1971, p. 57
270 Ibid, p. 58
271 Ibid, p. 118
272 Ibid, p. 207
273 Ibid, p. 208
274 Ibid, p. 209
275 Ibid, p. 210

276 Ibid

277 Ibid

278 TNA - WO 204/7522, *Experiences Operation Husky* by Major J. M. Lind, 1943

279 TNA - WO 204/7522, 1943

280 Ibid

281 Ibid

282 Ibid; Brice, 1971, p. 120

283 TNA - WO 204/7522, 1943

284 Ibid

285 Ibid

286 Clapp & Southby-Tailyour, 1997, pp. 27–74

287 TNA - WO 204/7522, 1943

288 Brice, 1971, p. 238

289 TNA - ADM 199/861, War History Case 7775 (Operation Avalanche), 1945

290 Clarke, 2017, *Tribal Class Destroyers Part 1: Some Battles of HMS Sikh,*

291 TNA - ADM 199/861, 1943

292 TNA - ADM 199/861, 1945

293 TNA - ADM 199/861, 1945; Clapp & Southby-Tailyour, 1997, pp. 27–74

294 TNA - WO 204/7522, 1943

295 TNA - ADM 199/861, 1945

296 Brice, 1971, p. 208

297 Ibid, p. 209

298 Ibid

299 Jones, 1979, pp. 74–5

300 Brice, 1971, p. 60–1

301 Whitby, 1993, p. 5

302 TNA - ADM 1/15784, 1944

303 Ibid

304 Whitby, 1993, pp. 10 & 20, quoting from Jones, 'A Matter of Length and Breadth,' in *The Naval Review*, XXXVIII, May 1950, p. 139

305 Brice, 1971, p. 69

306 TNA - ADM 1/15784, 1944; Brice, 1971, p. 122

307 Ibid; Whitby, 1993, pp. 14-19

308 TNA - ADM 199/810, 1941

309 During which time *Nubian* reached the milestone of steaming 300,000 miles since her first commission (TNA - ADM 199/810, 1941), the distance from the earth to the moon and a little over a quarter of the way back.

310 TNA - ADM 199/810, 1941

311 Ibid

312 Ibid

313 Clarke, 2017, *Tribal Class Destroyers Part 2: The Leadership of HMS Afridi*

314 TNA - ADM 187/7, 1940; TNA - ADM 187/8, 1940; TNA - ADM 187/9, 1940; TNA - ADM 199/810, 1941

315 Lambert, 2008, pp. 399-401

316 Simmons, 2011, pp. 109–10; Clarke, 2017, *Tribal Class Destroyers Part 1: Some Battles of HMS Sikh.*

317 This can be considered both a practical and expedient use of suitable ships, but also a legacy of Jutland, where the German High Seas Fleet had performed such a manoeuvre to escape.

318 Lambert, 2008, pp. 399–401; Simmons, 2011, pp. 129–34; Clarke, 2016, *What can be learned from the Fairey Swordfish?*

319 (Simmons, 2011, p. 129; TNA - ADM 186/72, 1925)

320 So short and sharp that Cunningham compared it to murder and only one Italian vessel, the destroyer *Alfieri* was felt to have offered resistance Simmons, 2011, pp. 130–1; TNA - ADM

321 Simmons, 2011, p. 133

322 This is the only way that it can be explained how a 15,000-strong force managed to defeat a 40,000-strong force.

323 There were Italian landings on 26 May, but these were after the British fleet was concentrating on evacuation. They were also not even part of the original operational plan. Simmons, 2011, pp. 155–60; Lambert, 2008, pp. 401–5; Brice, 1971, pp. 203–6

324 Lambert, 2008, p. 404

325 www.armouredcarriers.com, 2017

326 Brice, 1971, p. 205; TNA - ADM 199/810, 1941

327 Ibid; Clarke, 2017, *Tribal Class Destroyers Part 7 (I); HMS Eskimo, often bowless but never bowed*

328 Brice, 1971, p. 205; TNA - ADM 199/810, 1941

329 Evans, 2010

330 TNA - ADM 199/810, 1941

331 Brice, 1971, p. 206

332 Ibid

333 Ibid, p. 210

334 Clarke, 2017, *Tribal Class Destroyers Part 7 (II); HMS Eskimo – legend forged in steel made real by the leaders forged within*

335 Brice, 1971, p. 212

336 Clarke, 2014, *Sverdlov Class Cruisers, and the Royal Navy's Response*

337 Brice, 1971, pp. 140–8

338 Brice, 1971, p. 213

Chapter 6

339 Whitley, 1996, pp. 68-9

340 TNA - ADM 1/30452, 1945; TNA - WO 203/4780, 1945

341 Ibid

342 Ibid

343 Ibid

344 Ibid

345 Ibid

346 Ibid

347 Ibid

348 Ibid

349 Boniface, 2007, p. 122

350 Ibid, p. 150

351 Manning, 1961, p. 116. Similar comments are repeated in the later version of the work (1979) and in McCart, 2008, p. X

352 McCart, 2008, p. X

353 TNA - PREM 11/498, 1953

354 Ibid

355 Ibid

356 Ibid

357 Boniface, 2007, pp. 70–1

358 TNA - PREM 11/498, 1953

Chapter 7

359 Clarke, 2017, *Tribal Class Destroyers Part 3: HMS Ashanti, a Soft Power Entrepreneur*

360 Brice, 1971, pp. 126, 190 & 234

361 In terms of previous experience there was perhaps the much shorter Abyssinian crisis, and before that it was the counter-slavery patrols off the West Coast of Africa; so the RN really did not have a lot of experience to draw on in terms of how to manage the force and act in the role when conducting what was in effect a *de facto* blockade against a nation that Britain was not at war with. As such it was a steep learning curve that required a lot from ships and their ratings, but perhaps even more so from the officers in command, who were burdened with trying to implement what was written as a very black and white policy in an extremely grey situation.

362 Brice, 1971, p. 190
363 Clarke, 2017, *Tribal Class Destroyers Part 1: Some Battles of HMS Sikh*
364 Brice, 1971, p. 180
365 Ibid
366 Ibid
367 Ibid, p. 181
368 Ibid
369 Ibid
370 Ibid, pp. 190 & 234
371 Arctic convoys have a simple naming system. In the first series PQ were to Russia, QP away from Russia; in the second it was JW and RA. However, that did not mean that PQ15 was therefore the 15th convoy to Russia of the war; in fact it was the 16th, thanks to there being both a PQ7A & a PQ7B, the combining of PQ9 & PQ10 and the running of Operation Dervish.
372 Kent, 2004, p. 136
373 McCart, 2012, pp. 262–70; *A Naval Staff History*, 2007, pp. 246; Friedman, 2010, pp. 178–85 ; TNA - ADM 1/9360, 1933; TNA - ADM 1/9390, 1936

374 *A Naval Staff History*, 2007, p. 25
375 Brice, 1971, p. 233
376 Ibid
377 Ibid, p. 234
378 Ibid
379 November 1942; Brice, 1971, p. 126
380 Clarke, 2017, *Tribal Class Destroyers Part 4; HMS Tartar, the Survivor*
381 Roskill, 2011, pp. 301–46; Brice, 1971, pp. 118–19; Eisenhower, 2011, pp. 47–8; Tomblin, 2004, pp. 119–21
382 Brice, 1971, p. 119
383 Ibid
384 Clarke, 2017, *Tribal Class Destroyers Part 7 (II); HMS Eskimo – legend forged in steel made real by the leaders forged within*
385 Brice, 1971, p. 118
386 Ibid, p. 119
387 Ibid
388 Eisenhower, 2011, pp. 47–8; Roskill, 2011, pp. 301–46; Brice, 1971, p. 119
389 Wadsworth, 2009, pp. 71–9, Brice, 1971, pp. 168–70, Evans, 2010, pp. 88–9, and Woodman, 2007), pp. 56–9
390 Woodman, 2007, pp. 56–9
391 Pearson, 2007, p. 22

BIBLIOGRAPHY

Churchill Archives, Churchill College Cambridge

Churchill Archives - Roskill: 7/163. (1964). Exercises, Fleet, and Tactical Training (including Sail Training) R.N. and U.S.N. *Rosk: 7/163*. Cambridge: Churchill Archives, Churchill College (Cambridge).

Churchill Archives - Roskill: 7/187. (1968). Naval Policy, General. The 'Ten Year Rule'. *Rosk: 7/187*. Cambridge: Churchill Archives, Churchill College (Cambridge).

Churchill Archives - Roskill: 7/203. (1965). U.S. Navy, Strength, Building and Expenditure 1929-39. *Rosk: 7/203*. Cambridge: Churchill Archives, Churchill College (Cambridge).

Churchill Archives - Roskill: 7/209. (1938, October). War Manual, 1938 Edition Typescript. *Rosk: 7/209*. Cambridge: Churchill Archives, Churchill College (Cambridge).

Churchill Archives - Roskill: 8/9. (1970). Article 'Imperial Defence 1910-1950' for The Round Table Jubilee Number. *Rosk: 8/9*. Cambridge: Churchill Archives, Churchill College (Cambridge).

Tyne & Wear Archives, Newcastle

Tyne & Wear Archives – DS. VA 6/36/17 (1936-9): Service Trials. Newcastle.

Tyne & Wear Archives - DS.HL/4/21/88 (1944-5): Yard no. 681 and 682, 1944 programme battle class destroyers, new design. Newcastle.

The United Kingdom National Archives, Kew

TNA - ADM 1/10160. (1939). HMS "Ashanti" - Report of Proceeedings, dated 12/5/39, Visit to Sierra Leone and Gold Coast; Presentation to ship of Gold Ashanti Shield and Silver Ship's Bell. Admiralty 1/10160. London: United Kingdom National Archives (Kew).

TNA - ADM 1/10351. (1939-40). Bombing Attack at sea on ships of the Humber Force on 9/10/39. Admiralty 1/10351. London: United Kingdom National Archives (Kew).

TNA - ADM 1/11030. (1941). Naval Operations and Naval Air Work 1939-1941; Lessons Learnt, notes for information of naval flying personal at training establishments issued by R.A.N.A.S. Admiralty 1/11030. London: United Kingdom National Archives (Kew).

TNA - ADM 1/11846. (1941-2). Loss of HMS Cossack. 23-10-1941. Admiralty 1/11846. London: United Kingdom National Archives (Kew).

TNA - ADM 1/11847. (1941, October 23rd - 25th). The Loss and Attempted Salvage of HMS Cossack. Admiralty 1/11847. London: United Kingdom National Archives (Kew).

TNA - ADM 1/12252. (1941, December 22-7). HMS Arethusa - Raid on Lofoten Islands (Operation Anklet); 2 Awards. London: United Kingdom National Archives (Kew).

TNA - ADM 1/12287. (1942, January 17). Loss of HMS Gurkha. Admiralty 1/12287. London: United Kingdom National Archives (Kew).

TNA - ADM 1/12325. (1942, March 8). HMS "Sikh", "Maori", "Legion" and HNLMS "Isaac Sweers"; Sinking of two Italian cruisers off Cape Bon 13th of December 1941. Admiralty 1/12325. London: United Kingdom National Archives (Kew).

TNA - ADM 1/12326. (1942). Operation "Agreement", Landing Behind Enemy Lines near Tobruk, September 1942. Admiralty 1/12326. London: United Kingdom National Archives (Kew).

TNA - ADM 1/12516. (1943). Organisation of Fire Control Research and Development. Admiralty 1/12516. London: United Kingdom Nationl Archives (Kew).

TNA - ADM 1/12647. (1943). Translated Captured Japanese Documents - Torpedo Methods. London: United Kingdom National Archives (Kew).

TNA - ADM 1/12771. (1942). Operation Agreement - Reports of Proceedings, 12-18th September 1942. Admiralty 1/2771. London: United Kingdom National Archives (Kew).

TNA - ADM 1/15323. (1943). Tribal Class Destroyers Cost of Building in the United Kingdom. Admiralty 1/15323. London: United Kingdom National Archives (Kew).

TNA - ADM 1/15784. (1944). 10th Destroyer Flotilla, Action fought with 4 enemy destroyers off Ile de Bas on 9th June, 1944. Admiralty 1/15784. London: United Kingdom National Archives (Kew).

TNA - ADM 1/15791. (1944, June 25). Sinking of U-Boat 971, by HMS Eskimo & HMS Haida. Admiralty 1/15791. London: United Kingdom National Archives (Kew).

TNA - ADM 1/15795. (1944, June 28). Report of Action against Enemy light craft on night of 27th/28th of June, 1944, by HMS Eskimo in company with HMSC Huron. Admiralty 1/15795. London: United Kingdom National Archives (Kew).

TNA - ADM 1/16264. (1943-4). Destroyers: New Classes under Construction "Battle" and "C" Classes - Formation of Flotillas/Flotilla Leaders/HMS Oudenarde. ADM 1/16264. London: United Kingdom National Archives (Kew).

TNA - ADM 1/17590. (1937-45). A/S.W. 972 - Anti-Submarine Exercises - Analysis of Attacks. Admiralty 1/17590. London: United Kingdom National Archives (Kew).

TNA - ADM 1/17856. (1945-55). Battle Class Destroyers: Subsequently Daring Class 1944 Programme. ADM 1/17856. London: United Kingdom National Archives (Kew).

TNA - ADM 1/19739. (1946-9). Battle Class Destroyers - Performance of... Reports from H.M. Ships Barfleur, Trafalgar, Camperdown, Hogue and Armada. ADM 1/19739. London: United Kingdom National Archives (Kew).

TNA - ADM 1/20611. (1947). Combined Operations Raid on German Occupied Lofoten Islands, 4/3/41 - Operation 'Claymore' - Publications of Commander in Chief Home Fleet's despatches as Supplement to London Gazette 23/6/48. Admiralty 1/20611. London: United Kingdom National Archives (Kew).

TNA - ADM 1/23133. (1952). Request For Details of Ship's Badge and Motto - HMS Nubian. Admiralty 1/23133. London: United Kingdom National Archives (Kew).

TNA - ADM 1/27569. (1959, December 15). Staff Requirements for Modernisation of Daring Class Destroyers (2nd D.S). ADM 1/27569. London: United Kingdom National Archives (Kew).

TNA - ADM 1/30452. (1945). Operation "Irregular" - HMS Eskimo & HMS Tartar. Admiralty 1/30452. London: United Kingdom National Archives (Kew).

TNA - ADM 1/8570/287. (1919). British Imperial Naval Bases in the Pacific. General Policy. Admiralty 1/8570/287. London: United Kingdom National Archives (Kew).

TNA - ADM 1/8672/227. (1924). Light-Cruisers Emergency Construnction Progrmme. Admiralty 1/8672/227. London: United Kingdom National Archives (Kew).

TNA - ADM 1/8759/207. (1932). Informal visits of U.S. Ships to British ports on the China & East Indies Stations. Admiralty 1/8759/207. London: United Kingdom National Archives (Kew).

TNA - ADM 1/8828. (1934-5). New Construction Programme for Cruisers 1936. Admiralty 1/8828. London: United Kingdom National Archives (Kew).

TNA - ADM 1/9355. (1933, August 10th). Cruiser Design: Requesting views of Commanders-in-Chief, Home and Mediterranean Fleets. Admiralty 1/9355. London: United Kingdom National Archives (Kew).

TNA - ADM 1/9360. (1933, October). 6" Cruisers with Triple Turrets: Modified Sketch Design. ADM 1/9360. London: United Kingdom National Archives (Kew).

TNA - ADM 1/9384. (1933-6). Required for R.A.(D)'s Flagships: Proposed investigation of new design for - Preliminary Staff Requirements. Admiralty 1/9384. London: United Kingdom National Archives (Kew).

TNA - ADM 1/9390. (1936, January). Southampton Class Cruisers, 1933, 1934 and 1935 Programmes. Revised Legend. ADM 1/9390. London: United Kingdom National Archives (Kew).

TNA - ADM 1/9416. (1937, October 20). "L" Class Leader and Destroyer 1937 Programme. Sketch Design. Admiralty 1/9416. London: United Kingdom National Archives (Kew).

TNA - ADM 1/9427. (1937). Cruiser Policy - Response to Mr Churchill. London: United Kingdom National Archives (Kew).

TNA - ADM 1/9942. (1939). Anti-Submarine Exercises - Mediterranean Station Report from Half-Year ending 31-3-1939. Admiralty 1/9942. London: United Kingdom National Archives (Kew).

TNA - ADM 116/2509. (1926-8). China Station Proceedings. Admiralty 116/2509, I. London: United Kingdom National Archives (Kew).

TNA - ADM 116/2510. (1927-8). China Station Proceedings. Admiralty 116/2510, II. London: United Kingdom, National Archives (Kew).

TNA - ADM 116/2547. (1926-8). China Station - Reports. Admiralty 116/2547. London: United Kingdom National Archives (Kew).

TNA - ADM 116/3617. (1931-3). Disarmament Conference of the League of Nations: Armament for aircraft carriers, reductions in size and numbers of 6" cruisers and below. Admiralty 116/3617. London: United Kingdom National Archives (Kew).

TNA - ADM 116/3679. (1937-8). Spanish Civil War; Proceedings of H.M. Ships in Spanish Waters. Admiralty 116/3679. London: United Kingdom National Archives (Kew).

TNA - ADM 116/3734. (1936-8). Tribal Class and I Class Destroyers - Disposition of on Completion with Regard to Organisation of the Fleet and Destroyer Flotillas. Admiralty 116/3734. London: United Kingdom National Archives (Kew).

TNA - ADM 116/3818. (1939). Reports of salvage and life saving services by Rear Admiral (Submarines) and others. Admiralty 116/3818. London: United Kingdom National Archives(Kew).

TNA - ADM 116/3871. (1939). Air Instructions to the Mediterranean Fleet 1934-1939. Admiralty 116/3871. London: United Kingdom National Archives (Kew).

TNA - ADM 116/3872. (1933-8). Fleet Exercises: China Station 1933, Mediterranean Fleet 1935 & 1937, Submarine Exercises 1933-36, Home Fleet Exercise 1937 & 1938. Admiralty 116/3872. London: United Kingdom National Archives (Kew).

TNA - ADM 116/3873. (1937-9). Combined Fleet Exercises . Admiralty 116/3873. London: United Kingdom National Archives (Kew).

TNA - ADM 116/3893. (1937-9). Spanish Civil War: attacks on HM Ships Royal Oak, Blanche, Brilliant, Shakespear, Intrepid and Imperial. Admiralty 116/3893. London: United Kingdom National Archives (Kew).

TNA - ADM 116/4109. (1940). Battle of the River Plate: reports from Admiral Commanding and from HM Ships Ajax, Achilles and Exeter. Admiralty 116/4109. London: United Kingdom National Archives (Kew).

TNA - ADM 116/4320. (1941). Battle of the River Plate: British views on German pocket battleship Admiral Graf Spee in Montevideo harbour; visits to South America by HMS Ajax and HMS Achilles. ADM 116/4320. London: United Kingdom National Archives (Kew).

TNA - ADM 116/4381. (1941, December). Combined Allied Raid on Lofoten Islands, Norway - 25/12/1941 (Operation "Anklet"). London: United Kingdom National Archives (Kew).

TNA - ADM 116/4470. (1940). Battle of the River Plate: messages and Foreign Office telegrams. ADM 116/4470. London: United Kingdom National Archives (Kew).

TNA - ADM 116/5150. (1942-3). Future Shipbuilding Committee. Volume 1. London: United Kingdom National Archives (Kew).

TNA - ADM 116/5151. (1942-3). Future Building Committee. Vol 2. London: United Kingdom National Archives (Kew).

TNA - ADM 136/19. (1935-40). Ship's Log, H.M. Ship Afridi (1938). Admiralty 136/19. London: United Kingdom National Archives (Kew).

TNA - ADM 137/1777. (1923). Mediterranean Operation Orders 1922/3 (Case 1191). Admiralty 137/1777. London: United Kingdom National Archives (Kew).

TNA - ADM 178/280. (1942, March 30). Loss of HMS Maori: Board of Inquiry. Admiralty 178/280. London: United Kingdom National Archives (Kew).

TNA - ADM 182/44. (1926). Admiralty Fleet Orders. Admiralty 182/44. London: United Kingdom National Archives (Kew).

TNA - ADM 186/145. (1929). Exercises & Operations 1929 (C.B. 1769/29). Admiralty 186/145, I. London: United Kingdom National Archives (Kew).

TNA - ADM 186/158. (1937). Exercises and Operations. Vols I and II. London: United Kingdom National Archives (Kew).

TNA - ADM 186/278. (1927). Pamphlet on the Drill Procedure and Upkeep of the Admiralty Fire Control Table, Mark II ("Kent" Class and later Cruisers). Admiralty 186/278. London: United Kingdom National Archives (Kew).

TNA - ADM 186/296. (1930). Handbook For High Angle Control System Marks I and I*. Book II - Plates. Admiralty 186/296. London: United Kingdom National Archives (Kew).

TNA - ADM 186/345. (1925, January, April, July, October). Vernon's Quarterly Letter to the Fleet (No. 23, 24, 25, 26.). Admiralty 186/345. London: United Kingdom National Archives (Kew).

TNA - ADM 186/350. (1938). Handbook for the Admiralty Fire Control Clock, Mark 1. Admiralty 186/350. London: United Kingdom National Archives (Kew).

TNA - ADM 186/66. (1925). Naval War Manual. Admiralty 186/66. London: United Kingdom National Archives (Kew).

TNA - ADM 186/72. (1925). Battle Instructions. Admiralty 186/72. London: United Kingdom National Archives (Kew).

TNA - ADM 186/78. (1929). War Games Rules. Admiralty 186/78. London: United Kingdom National Archives (Kew).

TNA - ADM 186/80. (1929). Naval Tactical Notes. Admiralty 186/80, I. London: United Kingdom National Archives (Kew).

TNA - ADM 187/1. (1939). Pink List, September 1939. Admiralty 187/1. London: United Kingdom National Archives (Kew).

TNA - ADM 187/2. (1939). Pink List, October 1939. Admiralty 187/2. London: United Kingdom National Archives (Kew).

TNA - ADM 187/3. (1939). Pink List, November 1939. Admiralty 187/3. London: United Kingdom National Archives (Kew).

TNA - ADM 187/4. (1939). Pink List, December 1939. Admiralty 187/4. London: United Kingdom National Archives (Kew).

TNA - ADM 187/5. (1940). Pink List, January 1940. Admiralty 187/5. London: United Kingdom National Archives (Kew).

TNA - ADM 187/6. (1940). Pink List, February to March 1940. Admiralty 187/6. London: United Kingdom National Archives (Kew).

TNA - ADM 187/7. (1940). Pink List, April to May 1940. Admiralty 187/7. London: United Kingdom National Archives (Kew).

TNA - ADM 187/8. (1940). Pink List, June to July 1940. Admiralty 187/8. London: United Kingdom National Archives (Kew).

TNA - ADM 187/9. (1940). Pink List, August to September 1940. Admiralty 187/9. London: United Kingdom National Archives (Kew).

TNA - ADM 196/52/83. (1946). Name Creswell, George Hector Date of Birth: 17 June 1889 Rank: Rear Admiral. Admiralty 196/52/83. London: United Kingdom National Archives (Kew).

TNA - ADM 199/1110. (1942). War History. Admiralty 199/1110. London: United Kingdom National Archives (Kew).

TNA - ADM 199/280. (1940). German auxiliary ALTMARK: interception and boarding. Admiralty 199/280. London: United Kingdom National Archives (Kew).

TNA - ADM 199/280. (1940). War History: Interception and

Boarding of German Auxilary 'Altmark', 16.2.1940. Admiralty 199/280. London: United Kingdom National Archives (Kew).

TNA - ADM 199/281. (1940). German auxiliary ALTMARK: interception and boarding. Admiralty 199/281. London: United Kingdom National Archives (Kew).

TNA - ADM 199/473. (1940). Norway - Combined Operations (Naval): First and Second Battles of Narvik, 10th and 13th of April 1940. Admiralty 199/473. London: United Kingdom National Archives (Kew).

TNA - ADM 199/681. (1942). War History; Battle of Sirte. Admiralty 199/681. London: United Kingdom National Archives (Kew).

TNA - ADM 199/810. (1941). Naval operations in the Mediterranean. Admiralty 199/810. London: United Kingdom National Archives (Kew).

TNA - ADM 202/351. (1941). Force 115 Operation Anklet: Outline Plan & Maintenance Project. London: United Kingdom National Archives (Kew).

TNA - ADM 202/352. (1941, December 6). Operations Anklet and Bracelet - Brigade Force 115, War Diary - Nov 20th - Dec 6th 1941. London: United Kingdom National Archives (Kew).

TNA - ADM 203/84. (1924, December). Admiral Richmond's report on the Combined Exercise conducted at Salsette Island (Bombay) Combined Exercise. Admiralty 203/84. London: United Kingdom National Archives (Kew).

TNA - ADM 203/90. (1929). Strategical Exercise MZ - Atlantic and Mediterranean Fleets 1929. Admiralty 203/90. London: United Kingdom National Archives (Kew).

TNA - ADM 204/281. (1939). Interference from Boiler Room Fans with Communication Between Signal Deck and Upper Bridge of H.M.S. "Southampton". London: United Kingdom National Archives (Kew).

TNA - ADM 212/51. (1921-7). A.R.L. Domestic File: AA Predictor and AA Fire Control Equipment (A.R.L. Predictors). Admiralty 212/51. London: United Kingdom National Archives (Kew).

TNA - ADM 212/72. (1934). A.R.L. Domestic File (un-numbered); E.T. Hanson (A.R.L. Predictor and other Fire Control Problems). Admiralty 212/72. London: United Kingdom National Archives (Kew).

TNA - ADM 217/634. (1944). HMS Tartar - Report of Proceeedings, 14th/15th November, 1944. Admiralty 217/634. London: United Kingdom National Archives (Kew).

TNA - ADM 220/1668. (1944, November). Report: On the Visit to the United States in August and Septmber 1944 - Admiralty Signal Establishment. Admiralty 220/1668. London: United Kingdom National Archives (Kew).

TNA - ADM 220/211. (1940-60). General Fire Control Papers - R.D.F. Admiralty 220/211. London: United Kingdom National Archives (Kew).

TNA - ADM 223/27. (1940). Altmark Action Feb 1940. Admiralty 223/27. London: United Kingdom National Archives (Kew).

TNA - ADM 223/565. (1942). Operation Agreement - Landing at Tobruk. London: United Kingdom National Archives (Kew).

TNA - ADM 223/714. (1959, September 02). Translation of the 1949 Russian Book "Some Results of the Cruiser Operations of the German Fleet" by L. M. Eremeev - translated and distributed by RN Intelligence. ADM 223/714. London: United Kingdom National Archives (Kew).

TNA - ADM 227/277. (1940). Tribal Class Destroyers HP Turbine Impulse Blading. Admiralty 227/277. London: United Kingdom National Archives (Kew).

TNA - ADM 234/509. (1941). The Sinking of the Bismarck, 27th May, 1941 - Official Dispatches. Admiralty 234/509. London: United Kingdom National Archives (Kew).

TNA - ADM 234/510. (1941). The Sinking of the Bismarck, 27th May, 1941 - Plans. Admiralty 234/510. London: United Kingdom National Archives (Kew).

TNA - ADM 239/428. (1952). A.B.C.D. Book 'Daring' Class. ADM 239/428. London: United Kingdom National Archives (Kew).

TNA - ADM 267/21. (1944, July 12). HMS Eskimo Bomb Damage. 12-7-43. Admiralty 267/21. London: United Kingdom National Archives (Kew).

TNA - ADM 275/17. (1938). Dock Book. Volume I. London: United Kingdom National Archives (Kew).

TNA - ADM 275/18. (1938). Dock Book. Volume II - Plates. London: United Kingdom National Archives (Kew).

TNA - ADM 358/2992. (1940, May). Afridi - Casualty List . Admiralty 358/2992. London: United Kingdom National Archives (Kew).

TNA - ADM 358/3055. (1942, June 15). HMS Bedouin - Destroyer Sunk. Admiralty 358/3055. London: United Kingdom National Archives (Kew).

TNA - ADM 358/3179. (1940-1941). HMS Cossack Casualties. Admiralty 358/3179. London: United Kingdom National Archives (Kew).

TNA - ADM 358/3300. (1939). Firth of Forth: 16 October 1939; air raid; HMS Mohawk, HMS Edinburgh, HMS Southampton and HMS Iron Duke damaged by enemy action. Admiralty 358/3300. London: United Kingdom National Archives (Kew).

TNA - ADM 358/73. (1940, May). HMS Afridi - Sunk 3rd May 1940. Officer Casualty. R Mellor. Admiralty 358/73. London: United Kingdom National Archives (Kew).

TNA - ADM 367/137. (1941). Hood & Bismarck - Capital Ships vs Tirpitz. Admiralty 367/137. London: United Kingdom National Archives(Kew).

TNA - AIR 2/1457. (1928). Air Threat in the Mediterranean. Air Ministry 2/1457. London: Public Records Office: United Kingdom, National Archives (Kew).

TNA - AIR 5/877. (1919). Some Letters to "The Times" by Admiral of the Fleet, Lord Fisher, regarding Aviation as seen in 1919. Air Ministry 5/877. London: United Kingdom National Archives (Kew).

TNA - CAB 121/445. (1941). Operation "Anklet". London: United Kingdom National Archives (Kew).

TNA - CAB 121/447. (1941). Operation Claymore. Cabinet Office 121/447. London: United Kingdom National Archives (Kew).

TNA - CO 323/1694/8. (1939). H.M. Ships; a) Empire Names for - b) Presentations from Colonies, HMS "Ashanti". Colonial Office 323/1694/8. London: United Kingdom National Archives (Kew).

TNA - DEFE 2/140. (1941). SECRET 56 C.O.J.Q. Records: Operation Claymore - Narrative & Appendicies. Ministry of Defence 2/140. London: United Kingdom National Archives (Kew).

TNA - DEFE 2/66. (1941). Operations Aconite / Ambassador / Anklet / Alacrity. London: United Kingdom National Archives (Kew).

TNA - DEFE 2/74. (1941). Operation Anklet - Photographs. London: United Kingdom National Archives (Kew).

TNA - FO 371/106559. (1953). Soviet ships off the Shetlands; visit of Soviet cruiser Sverdlov to Spithead for the Coronation. Code NS file 1211. Foreign Office 371/106559. London: United Kingdom National Archives (Kew).

TNA - FO 952/2. (1940). Report on the ALTMARK incident and local correspondence. Foreign Office 952/2. London: United Kingdom National Archives (Kew).

TNA - HS 2/198. (1941). SOE Group C: Operation ANKLET (formerly Operation WALLAH and Operation ASCOT): second LOFOTEN raid including evacuation of town of Reine to UK. London: United Kingdom National Archives (Kew).

TNA - PREM 11/498. (1953, May-June). Deployment of Daring Class to Far East for Korea - Questions by Prime Minister Winston Churchill. PREM 11/498. London: United Kingdom National Archives (Kew).

TNA - PREM 3/328/7. (1941). 1941 Norway (Claymore Operation). Premier 3/328/7. London: United Kingdom National Archives (Kew).

TNA - PREM 3/47. (1942, January). Prime Minister's Office: Operational Correspondence and Papers - Operation Anklet (Norway). London: United Kingdom National Archives (Kew).

TNA - T 161/243 (25613). (1924-5). Navy Estimates 1925-26; Preliminary discussions as to total. Treasury 161/243 (25613). London: United Kingdom National Archives (Kew).

TNA - T 161/243 (25613a). (1924-5). Papers relating to: Japan & USA Navies, Singapore Naval Base, Vote 10, Vote 9, Fleet Air Arm, Guns & Ammunition, Vote A. Treasury 161/243 (25613a). London: United Kingdom National Archives (Kew).

TNA - T 161/243 (25613b). (1924-5). Papers relating to USA Navy Estimates in comparision with Navy Estimates 1925/26. Treasury 161/243 (25613B). London: United Kingdom National Archvies (Kew).

TNA - T 161/243 (25613c). (1924-5). Disarmament in connection with Navy Estimates 1925/26. Treasury 161/243 (25613c). London: United Kingdom National Archives (Kew).

TNA - T 161/243 (25613d). (1924-5). Papers relating to Cabinet Memoranda of Decisions in connection with Navy Estimates 1925/26. Treasury 161/243 (25613d). London: United Kingdom National Archives (Kew).

TNA - T 161/243 (25613e). (1924-5). Papers relating to Ministerial Correspondence in connection with Navy Estimates 1925/6. Treasury 161/243 (25613e). London: United Kingdom National Archives (Kew).

TNA - T 161/243 (25613f). (1924-5). Papers relating to New Construction & British Naval Strength in connection with Navy Estimates 1925/26. Treasury 161/243 (25613f). London: United Kingdom National Archives (Kew).

TNA - WO 106/1988. (1941-2). Operation "Anklet". London: United Kingdom National Archives (Kew).

TNA - WO 106/2246. (1942). Operation Agreement & Bigamy. London: United Kingdom National Archives (Kew).

TNA - WO 107/98. (1941, November-December). Anklet - Operations against Lofoten Islands. London: United Kingdom National Archives (Kew).

TNA - WO 201/745. (1942, September/October). Notes on Individual Raids. London: United Kingdom National Archives (Kew).

TNA - WO 203/4780. (1945). Operation "Irregular", 1945 June-July. War Office 203/4780. London: United Kingdom National Archives (Kew).

TNA - WO 204/7522. (1943). Experiences Operation Husky by Major J.M.Lind. War Office 204/7522. London: United Kingdom National Archives (Kew).

Published Works

A Naval Staff History. (2007). *The Royal Navy and the Arctic Convoys*. Routledge: Abingdon.

Ashmore, E. (1997). *The Battle and the Breeze; The Naval Reminiscences of Admiral of the Fleet Sir Edward Ashmore*. (E. Grove, Ed.)

Stroud: Sutton Publishing Limited.

Bacon, R., & Mc Murtie, F. E. (1941). *Modern Naval Strategy* (2nd ed.). London: Frederick Muller.

Batchelor, J., & Chant, C. (2008). *The Complete Encyclopedia of Warships*. London: Publishing Solutions Ltd.

Boniface, P. (2007). *Battle Class Destroyers*. London: Maritime Books.

Brice, M. H. (1971). *The Tribals, Biography of a Destroyer Class*. Shepperton: Ian Allan.

Britannia Naval Histories of World War II. (2013). *Between Hostile Shores; Mediterranean Convoy Battles 1941-42*. Plymouth: Plymouth University Press.

Brooks, J. (2017, June). British Destroyers at Jutland: Torpedo Tactics in Theory and Action. *British Journal for Military History, 3*(3), 30-52.

Brown, D. K. (2010). *The Grand Fleet: Warship Design and Development 1906-1922*. London: Seaforth Publishing.

Brown, E. (1980). *Wings of the Navy*. London: Jane's Publishing Company.

Brown, E. (2007). *Wings on My Sleeve*. London: Phoenix.

Brown, E. (2010). *Wings of the Luftwaffe; Flying the captured German aircraft of World War II*. Manchester: Crecy Publishing Limited.

Brown, L. (1999). *Technical and Military Imperatives: A Radar History of World War 2*. London: Routledge.

Burt, R. A. (1985). *Warships Illustrated No 4; British Destroyers in World War Two*. London: Arms and Armour Press Limited.

Cable, J. (1981). *Gunboat Diplomacy 1919-1979, Political Applications of Limited Naval Force*. London: Macmillan, Studies in International Security.

Carlyon, L. A. (2003). *Gallipoli*. Australia, Great Britain: Pan Macmillan Australia, Doubleday, Bantam.

Carton De Wiart, A. (1950). *Happy Odyssey*. Oxford: Jonathan Cape.

Cope, R. (2015). *Attack at Dawn; Reliving the First Battle of Narvik in World War Two*. London: Clink Street.

Corbett, J. S. (1911). *Some Principles of Maritime Strategy*. Uckfield: The Naval & Military Press Ltd.

Corbett, J. S., & Edwards, H. J. (Eds.). (1914). *The Cambridge Naval and Military Series*. London: Cambridge University Press.

Cresswell, J. (1936). *Naval Warfare*. London: Sampson Low, Marston & CO., LTD.

Creswell, J. (1967). *Sea Warfare 1939-1945*. London: Cambridge University Press.

Cunningham, A. B. (1951). *A Sailor's Odyssey; the Autobiography of Admiral of the Fleet Viscount Cunningham of Hyndhope K.T. G.C.B. O.M. D.S.O.* London: Hutchinson & Co. (Publishers) Ltd.

Dannreuther, R. (2006). *Sommerville's Force H; The Royal Navy's Gibraltar-based Fleet, June 1940 to March 1942*. London: Aurum Press Ltd.

Davies, J. (1946). *Lower Deck*. London: Macmillan & Co. Ltd.

D'Este, C. (1990). *World War II in the Mediterranean 1942-1945*. Chapel Hill, North Carolina: Algonquin Books.

Evans, A. S. (2010). *Destroyer Down; An Account of HM Destroyer Losses 1939-1945*. Barnsley: Pen & Sword Maritime.

Felker, C. C. (2007). *Testing American Sea Power: U.S. Navy Strategic Exercises, 1923-1940*. College Station, Texas: Texas A&M University Press.

Ferris, J. (1997). The last decade of British maritime supremacy, 1919-1929. In K. Neilson, & G. Kennedy (Eds.), *Far Flung Lines; Studies in Imperial Defence in Honour of Donald Mackenzie Schurman* (pp. 124-70). Abingdon: Routledge.

Field, A. (2004). *Royal Navy Strategy in the Far East 1919-1939; planning for war against Japan*. London: Frank Cass.

First Lord of the Admiralty. (1939). *FLEETS: The British Commonwealth of Nations and Foreign Countries*. London: His Majesty's Stationery Office.

Friedman, N. (1983). *U.S. Aircraft Carriers*. Annapolis, Maryland: Naval Institute Press.

Friedman, N. (1988). *British Carrier Aviation*. Annapolis, Maryland: Naval Institute Press.

Friedman, N. (2006). *British Destroyers & Frigates; The Second World War and After*. Barnsley: Seaforth Publishing.

Friedman, N. (2010). *British Cruisers; Two World Wars and After*. London: Seaforth Publishing.

Friedman, N. (2016). *Fighters over the Fleet; Naval Air Defence from Biplanes to the Cold War*. Barnsley: Seaforth Publishing.

Goodall, S. V. (1939). H.M.S. Ark Royal. In G. V. Boys (Ed.), *Transactions of the Royal Institution of Naval Architects 1939* (pp. 1-19). London: Institution of Naval Architects.

Gorshkov, S. G. (1980). *The Sea Power of the State*. Oxford: Pergamon Press.

Greene, J., & Massignani, A. (1998). *The Naval War in the Mediterranean 1940-1943*. London: Chatham Publishing.

Haarr, G. H. (2010). *The Battle for Norway, April - June 1940*.

Barnsely: Seaforth Publishing.

Haarr, G. H. (2013). *The Gathering Storm*. Barnsley: Seaforth Publishing.

Hastings, M. (2010). *The Korean War*. London: Pan Books.

Hill-Norton, P., & Decker, J. (1982). *Sea Power*. London: Faber and Faber Ltd.

Hodges, P. (1971). *Battle Class Destroyers*. London: Almark Publishing Company.

Hodgkinson, H. (1944). *Before the Tide Turned; The Mediterranean Experiences of a British Destroyer Officer in 1941*. London: George G. Harrap & Co. Ltd.

Howse, D. (1993). *Radar at Sea; The Royal Navy in World War 2*. London: Palgrave Macmillan.

Hunt, B. D. (1982). *Sailor-scholar: Admiral Sir Herbert Richmond, 1871-1946*. Waterloo (Canada): Wilfred Laurier University Press.

Jane's. (2001). *Fighting Ships of World War II*. London: Random House Group.

Johns, A. W. (1934). Aircraft Carriers. In R. W. Dana (Ed.), *Transactions of the Royal Institution of Naval Architects* (pp. 1-19). London: Royal Institution of Naval Architects.

Jones, B. (1979). *And So To Battle*. Battle (East Sussex): B.Jones (Self Published by Author).

Jordan, J. (2011). *Warships after Washington; the development of the five major fleets 1922-1930*. Barnsley: Seaforth Publishing.

Kemp, P. (2000). *Convoy! Drama in Arctic Waters*. London: Cassell & Co.

Kennedy, L. (1942). *Sub-Lieutenant; a personal record of the war at sea*. London: B. T. Batsford Ltd.

Kennedy, L. (1974). *Pursuit; The Sinking of the Bismarck*. London: Collins.

Kennedy, L. (1989). *On My Way To The Club; An Autobiography*. London: Collins.

Kent, B. H. (2004). *Signal!: A History of Signalling in the Royal Navy* (2nd ed.). East Meon: Hyden House Ltd.

Konstam, A. (2013). *The Battle of North Cape; the death ride of the Scharnhorst, 1943*. Barnsley: Pen & Sword Maritime.

Lambert, A. (2008). *Admirals*. London: Faber and Faber.

Lambert, H. J. (2019). *British Naval Weapons of World War Two, The John Lambert Collection - Volume I: Destroyer Weapons*. (N. Friedman, Ed.) Barnsley: Seaforth Publishing.

Lavery, B. (2006). *River-class Frigates and the Battle of the Atlantic*.

London: National Maritime Museum Greenwich.

Lord Chatfield. (1942). *The Navy and Defence; The Autobiography of Admiral of the Fleet Lord Chatfield*. London: William Heinemann ltd.

Lyon, D. (1970, December). 2: HMS Cossack / Tribal Class Destroyer. *Profile Warship Series*.

Lyon, D. (1978). The British Tribals 1935. (R. Gardiner, Ed.) *Warship Special 2, Super Destroyers*, pp. 48-61.

Madgwick, E. (2003). *Tribal Captain*. Helston: Blue Island Books.

Malkasian, C. (2001). *The Korean War 1950-1953*. Oxford: Osprey Publishing Ltd.

Manning, T. D. (1961). *The British Destroyer*. London: Putnam.

Manning, T. D. (1979). *The British Destroyer*. London: Godfrey Cave Associates Ltd.

McCart, N. (2008). *Daring Class Destroyers*. Liskeard: Maritime Books.

McCart, N. (2012). *Town Class Cruisers*. Liskeard: Maritime Books.

Morris, Douglas. (1987). *Cruisers of the Royal and Commonwealth Navies*. Liskeard: Maritime Books.

Neilson, K., & Kennedy, G. (Eds.). (2009). *Far Flung Lines; Studies in Imperial Defence in the Honour of Donald Mackenzie Schurman*. Abingdon: Routledge.

Obituary: Admiral Sir Reginald G. H. Henderson. (1939). In G. V. Boys (Ed.), *Transactions of the Royal Institution of Naval Architects 1939* (pp. 348-9). London: Institution of Naval Architects.

Pearce, F. (1990). *Sea War, Great Naval Battles of World War II*. London: Robert Hale Limited.

Pearson, M. (2007). *Red Sky in the Morning; The Battle of the Barents Sea 1942*. Barnsley: Pen & Sword Maritime.

Plevy, H. (2008). *Destroyer Actions, September 1939 - June 1940*. Port Stroud: The History Press Ltd.

Richmond, H. W. (1914). Naval Officers Point of View. In J. S. Corbette, & H. S. Edwards (Eds.), *The Cambridge; Naval and Military Series* (pp. 39-54). London: Cambridge University Press.

Richmond, H. W. (1934). *National Policy and Naval Strength*. London, New York, Toronto: Longmans, Green and Co.

Rodger, N. (2004). *The Command of the Ocean*. London: Penguin Books.

Rodger, N. (2004). *The Safeguard of the Sea; A Naval History of Britain, 660-1649*. London: Penguin Books.

Rose, L. A. (2007). *Power at Sea; The Breaking Storm, 1919-1945*.

Missouri: University of Missouri.

Roskill Library - Admiral Sir R.P. Ernle-Erle-Drax. (1943, March). *The Art of War; Twentieth Century Version*. Cambridge: Churchill Archives, Churchill College (Cambridge).

Roskill, S. (1968). *Naval Policy Between the Wars: The Period of Anglo-American Antagonism 1919-29*. London: Collins.

Roskill, S. (1976). *Naval Policy Between the Wars: The Period of Reluctant Rearmament 1929-39*. London: Collins.

Rottman, G. L. (2006). *Inch'on 1950; the last great amphibious assault*. Oxford: Osprey Publishing Ltd.

Royal Aero Club. (1934, February 1). The Development of the Fleet Air Arm; A lecture, abridged, delivered by Wing Commander W.R.D. Acland, D.F.C., A.F.C., before the Royal United Service Institution on January 24, 1934. *Flight; the Aircraft Engineer and Airships*, p. 113.

Simmons, M. (2011). *The Battle of Mattapan 1941; The Trafalgar of the Mediterranean*. Stroud: Spellmount.

Smith, P. C. (2002). *Pedestal, The Convoy that saved Malta*. Manchester: William Kimber, Crecy Publishing Limited.

Smith, P. C. (2010). *Fighting Flotilla; RN Laforey Class Destroyer in World War II*. Barnsley: Pen & Sword Maritime.

Smith, P. C. (2011). *Critical Conflict, The Royal Navy's Mediterranean Campaign in 1940*. Barnsley: Pen & Sword Maritime.

Stephen, M. (1999). *Sea Battles in close-up: World War 2*. (E. Grove, Ed.) London: Ian Allan Ltd.

Stern, R. C. (2008). *Destroyer Battles, Epics of Naval Close Combat*. Barnsley: Seaforth Publishing.

Stille, M. (2005). *Imperial Japanese Navy Aircraft Carriers 1921-45*. Oxford: Osprey Publishing.

Stille, M. (2014). *The Imperial Japanese Navy in the Pacific War*. Oxford: Osprey.

Temple Patterson, A. (1973). *Tyrwhitt of the Harwich Force*. London: Military Book Society.

Thursfield, H. G. (1936). Modern Trends in Warship Design. In G. V. Boys (Ed.), *Transactions of the Institution of Naval Architects 1936* (pp. 1-20). London: Institution of Naval Architects.

Till, G. (1977). Airpower and the Battleship. In B. Ranft (Ed.), *Technical Change and British Naval Policy 1880-1939* (pp. 108-122). London: Hodder and Stoughton.

Till, G. (1979). *Air Power and the Royal Navy, 1914-1945 a historical survey*. London: Jane's Publishing Company.

Till, G. (2002). Retrenchment Rethinking Revival 1919-1939. In J. R. Hill (Ed.), *The Oxford Illustrated History of the Royal Navy* (pp. 319-47). Oxford: Oxford University Press.

Till, G. (Ed.). (2006). *The Development of British Naval Thinking*. Abingdon: Routledge.

Tomblin, B. B. (2004). *With Utmost Spirit: Allied Naval Operations in the Mediterranean, 1942-1945*. Lexington: The University Press of Kentucky.

Transactions of the Royal Institution of Naval Architects. (1983). *Selected Papers of British Warship Design in World War II*. London: Conway Maritime Press Ltd.

Vian, P. (1960). *Action This Day*. London: Frederick Muller Limited.

Wadsworth, M. (2009). *Arctic Convoy PQ8; The Story of Capt Robert Brundle and the SS Harmatris*. Barnsley: Pen & Sword Maritime.

Whitby, M. J. (1993). Masters of the Channel Night: The 10th Destroyer Flotilla's Victory off Ile De Batz, 9 June 1944. *Canadian Military History, 2*(1), 4-18.

Whitley, M. J. (1996). *Cruisers of World War Two, an International Encyclopaedia*. London: Cassell & Co.

Whitley, M. J. (2000). *Destroyers of World War Two, an international encyclopedia*. London: Cassell & Co.

Williamson, G. (2010). *U-boat Tactics in World War II*. Oxford: Osprey Publishing Ltd.

Winton, J. (1986). *Carrier Glorious; the life and death of an aircraft carrier*. London: Leo Cooper.

Woodman, R. (2007). *Arctic Convoys 1941-1945*. Barnsley: Pen & Sword Maritime.

Wragg, D. (2011). *The Pacific Naval War 1941-1945*. Barnsley: Pen & Sword Maritime.

Zimmerman, D. (2010). *Britain's Shield: Radar and the Defeat of the Luftwaffe*. Chalford: Amberly.

Published Works (Online)

Barrett, K. (2015). *Voyage to Barbados on HMS Tartar*. Retrieved June 03, 2018, from Cambridge Digital Library: http://cudl.lib.cam.ac.uk/view/ES-LON-00002

DiGiulian, T. (2009, May 10). *The British High Angle Control System (HACS)*. Retrieved June 22, 2010, from NavWeaps: http://www.navweaps.com/index_tech/tech-066.htm

Eisenhower, D. D. (2011, July 20). *Report of the Commander-in-Chief Allied Forces to the Combined Chiefs of Staff on Operations in Northwest Africa*. (P. Clancey, Ed.) Retrieved September 12, 2017, from HYPERWAR: A Hypertext history of thhe Second World War: http://www.ibiblio.org/hyperwar/USA/rep/TORCH/DDE-Torch.html#retribution

Gustin, E. (2011). *British ASV radars*. Retrieved 08 2011, 18, from uboat.net: http://www.uboat.net/allies/technical/uk_radars.htm

Liddell Hart Centre for Military Archives. (2010). *Survey of the Papers of Senior UK Defence Personnel, 1900-1975: Richmond, Sir Herbert William (1871-1946), Admiral*. (King's College London) Retrieved November 24, 2010, from King's College London, Liddell Hart Centre for Military Archives: http://www.kcl.ac.uk/lhcma/locreg/RICHMOND.shtml

Liddell Hart Centre for Military Archives. (2012). *Survey of the Papers of Senior UK Defence Personnel, 1900-1975; Sir Reginald Guy Hannam Henderson*. Retrieved March 04, 2012, from King's College London, University of London: http://www.kcl.ac.uk/lhcma/locreg/HENDERSON4.shtml

Liddell Hart Centre for Military Archives. (2012). *Survey of the Papers of Senior UK Defence Personnel, 1900-1975; Sir Reginald Yorke Tyrwhitt, Admiral of the Fleet (1870-1951)*. Retrieved March 14, 2012, from King's College London, Liddell Hart Centre for Military Archives: http://www.kcl.ac.uk/lhcma/locreg/TYR-WHITT.shtml

Robinson Jr, C. A. (2007, June). Radar Counters Camouflage. (*SIGNAL* Magazine: the Armed Forces Communications and Electronics Association) Retrieved October 11, 2010, from Signal Online: http://www.afcea.org/signal/articles/templates/Signal_Article_Template.asp?articleid=1323&zoneid=209

Roskill , S. W. (2011, July 20). *WAR AT SEA 1939-1945, Volume II The Period of Balance*. (R. Pitz, Ed.) Retrieved September 12, 2017, from HYPERWAR: A Hypertext history of thhe Second World War: http://www.ibiblio.org/hyperwar/UN/UK/UK-RN-II/UK-RN-II-19.html

Siedel, J. (2017, December 12). *Operation MAQ3; the Stuka Bombing of HMS Formidable*. Retrieved February 11, 2018, from Armoured Aircraft Carriers in World War II: http://www.armouredcarriers.com/operation-maq3-may-26-1941/

Siedel, J. (2018, June 30). *Britain's 'Midway'; Operation C: The Battle for Ceylon, April-May 1942*. Retrieved December 08, 2018, from Armoured Aircraft Carriers in World War II: http://www.armouredcarriers.com/battle-for-ceylon-hms-indomitable-formidable/

Signatories of the 1930 London Treaty for the Limitation and Reduction of Naval Armament. (2003, October 11). (T. Lanzendorfer, Ed.) Retrieved June 25, 2016, from The Pacific War: The U.S. Navy: http://www.microworks.net/pacific/road_to_war/london_treaty.htm

Signatories of the Washington Naval Limitation Treaty. (2005, December 20). *Washington Naval Limitation Treaty*. Retrieved June 11, 2006, from navweaps.com: http://www.navweaps.com/index_inro/INRO_Washington_Naval_Limitation_Treaty_1922.htm

The Honourable Company of Master Mariners. (2016). *History of the Ship*. Retrieved January 17, 2016, from The Honourable Company of Master Mariners: http://www.hcmm.org.uk/hqs-wellington/history/

The National Commission on Culture. (2007, August 3). *Otumfuo Nana Sir Agyeman Prempeh II; He restored the Ashanti confederacy*. Retrieved January 21, 2016, from The National Commission on Culture : http://www.ghanaculture.gov.gh/index1.php?linkid=65&archiveid=921&page=1&adate=03/08/2007

Tucker, S., & Matysek-Vood, L. (1996). *The European powers in the First World War: an encyclopedia*. United States: Routledge. Retrieved March 03, 2012, from http://books.google.co.uk/books?id=EHI3PCjDtsUC&pg=PA198&lpg=PA198&dq=Admiral+RGH+Henderson&source=bl&ots=YOJY-Ca_xq&sig=NDxSdkd4iaqyB5K8l5ODDV_bTTA&hl=en&sa=X&ei=4s5ST7iJNcKg0QXYv8GsDg&ved=0CE0Q6AEwCA#v=onepage&q=Admiral%20RGH%20Henderson&f=false

Author's Own Works

Clarke, A. (2008). The Illustrious, the Ark and the Unicorn; Admiral Henderson; how important were the changes that he instituted in Royal Navy carriers and naval aviation to gaining control of the Mediterranean? *Bachelor's 15 Credit Dissertation*. Twickenham: St Mary's University College.

Clarke, A. (2014, May 12). *Sverdlov Class Cruisers, and the Royal Navy's Response*. Retrieved February 22, 2015, from British Naval History: http://www.britishnavalhistory.com/sverdlov_class_rn_response/

Clarke, A. (2016, September 26). *What can be learned from the Fairey Swordfish?* Retrieved February 2018, 2018, from Global Maritime History: https://globalmaritimehistory.com/can-learned-fairey-swordfish-2/

Clarke, A. (2017, March 11). *Tribal Class Destroyers Part 1: Some Battles of HMS Sikh*. Retrieved September 28, 2018, from Global Maritime History: https://globalmaritimehistory.com/tribals-class-destroyers-pt-1-battles-hms-sikh/

Clarke, A. (2017, April 17). *Tribal Class Destroyers Part 2: The Leadership of HMS Afridi*. Retrieved September 28, 2018, from Global Maritime History: https://globalmaritimehistory.com/tribal-class-destroyers-part-2-leadership-hms-afridi/

Clarke, A. (2017, July 17). *Tribal Class Destroyers Part 3: HMS Ashanti, a Soft Power Entrepreneur*. Retrieved September 28, 2018, from Global Maritime History: https://globalmaritimehistory.com/tribal-class-destroyers-3-hms-ashanti-soft-power-entrepreneur/

Clarke, A. (2017, September 7). *Tribal Class Destroyers Part 4; HMS Tartar, the Survivor*. Retrieved September 28, 2018, from Global Maritime History: https://globalmaritimehistory.com/tribal-class-destroyers-4-hms-tartar-the-survivor/

Clarke, A. (2017, September 11). *Tribal Class Destroyers Part 5; the hard War of HMS Somali*. Retrieved September 28, 2018, from Global Maritime History: https://globalmaritimehistory.com/tribal-class-destroyers-5-the-hard-war-of-hms-somali/

Clarke, A. (2017, November 13). *Tribal Class Destroyers Part 6; HMS Gurkha, living up to History.* Retrieved September 28, 2018, from Global Maritime History: https://globalmaritimehistory.com/tribal-class-destroyers-part-6-hms-gurkha-living-up-to-history/

Clarke, A. (2017, December 11). *Tribal Class Destroyers Part 7 (I); HMS Eskimo, often bowless but never bowed.* Retrieved September 28, 2018, from Global Maritime History: https://globalmaritimehistory.com/tribal-class-destroyers-part-7-hms-eskimo-often-bowless-never-bowed/

Clarke, A. (2017, December 25). *Tribal Class Destroyers Part 7 (II); HMS Eskimo – legend forged in steel made real by the leaders forged within.* Retrieved September 28, 2018, from Global Maritime History: https://globalmaritimehistory.com/tribal-class-destroyers-part-7-ii-hms-eskimo-legend-forged-in-steel-made-real-by-the-leaders-forged-within/

Clarke, A. (2018, January 8). *Tribal Class Destroyers Part 7 (III); HMS Eskimo – legend forged in steel made real by the leaders forged within.* Retrieved September 28, 2018, from Global Maritime History: https://globalmaritimehistory.com/tribal-class-destroyers-part-7-iii-hms-eskimo-legend-forged-steel-made-real-leaders-forged-within/

Clarke, A. (2018, January 22). *Tribal Class Destroyers Part 7 (IV); HMS Eskimo – Legacy of Leadership and Legend.* Retrieved September 28, 2018, from Global Maritime History: https://globalmaritimehistory.com/tribal-class-destroyers-part-7-iv-hms-eskimo-legacy-leadership-legend/

Clarke, A. (2018, February 19). *Tribal Class Destroyers Part 8 (I); HMS Nubian, an almost unmatchable record.* Retrieved September 28, 2018, from Global Maritime History: https://globalmaritimehistory.com/tribal-class-destroyers-part-8i-hms-nubian-almost-unmatchable-record/

Clarke, A. (2018, Mar 5). *Tribal Class Destroyers Part 8 (II); HMS Nubian, Tool of Grand Strategy.* Retrieved September 28, 2018, from Global Maritime History: https://globalmaritimehistory.com/tribal-class-destroyers-8-hms-nubian/

Clarke, A. (2018ii, November 2). *The Royal Navy and the Far East in the 1930s: Promoting Stability and Preserving the Peace on a Budget.* (R. Mahoney, Ed.) Retrieved November 17, 2018, from The Second World War Research Group: https://www.swwresearch.com/single-post/2018/11/02/The-Royal-Navy-and-the-Far-East-in-the-1930s-Promoting-Stability-and-Preserving-the-Peace-on-a-Budget

INDEX

All ships are British Royal Navy unless otherwise indicated.
Page numbers in *italics* indicate illustrations.

Abbreviations:

Adm. = Admiral; Cdr = Commander; Cpt = Captain; HMAS = His Majesty's Australian Ship; HMCS = His Majesty's Canadian Ship; Fr = France; Ger = Germany; It = Italy; Neths = Netherlands; Nor = Norway; Pol = Poland; R/A = Rear Admiral; RFA = Royal Fleet Auxiliary; V/A = Vice Admiral